Joan of Arc and the
God of the Bible
~THE WITCH THAT WASN'T~
God's Game Changers-Volume One

Chris Snidow

Joan of Arc and the God of the Bible
~THE WITCH THAT WASN'T~
God's Game Changers-Volume 1
© Snidow 2015

All rights reserved. No part of this book may be used or reproduced by any means, graphic, electronic, or mechanical, including photocopying, recording, taping or by any information storage retrieval system without the written permission of the author or publisher except in the case of brief quotations embodied in critical articles and reviews.

Bible quotations come from the NIV translation, unless otherwise noted.

Cover painting by Gaston Bussière.

Email: **cowrind@sbcglobal.net**
Tel: **214-327-4579**
For **Biblical Sound Pictures** and **Joan of Arc Pilgrimages** to France, go to:

www.pilgrimwitnesses.com

What are people saying about Joan of Arc and the God of the Bible THE WITCH THAT WASN'T?

"...it's so reader-friendly ...a work of Bible scholarship that reveals Joan's life as relevant today as it was hundreds of years ago." **Kathryn Harrison, New York Times bestselling author and a frequent reviewer.**

"This book is a fascinating read! I have thoroughly enjoyed learning more about Joan of Arc and now see how she has been a neglected figure among Protestants especially. Her life as revealed in this book is an inspiration and she is a true hero of the faith. What a fascinating figure!" **S. Michael Craven, President of the Center for Christ & Culture, www.battlefortruth.org**

"Wow. Very impressive!" **The Rev. Josh Acton, Episcopal priest, Dallas, TX**

"A great success! This is not your typical Joan of Arc book, one full of scholastic, boring pretentiousness. Rather it is an easy read...and carries you along like a good detective story. The parallels between Joan and the prophets are great! The author thus makes accessible to everyone the story of Joan of Arc, her personal development, and her feelings. This serious book has a sense of humor to it also, and so spurs the reader on to read it to the very end." **Father Claude Girault, Rector of the Cathédrale Sainte Croix, Orléans, France**

"Excellent work; nothing like it! Very interesting; FIVE stars (out of five). *Having been an admirer of Joan of Arc for many years, this book interested me. I have seen no others like it. Excellent study of Joan in relationship to the Bible. He makes a very strong case for her being sent by God, using frequent Bible quotations to make his points. Easy to read and keeps your attention. Well researched, and written. If you are interested in either Joan or God, then I HIGHLY recommend this book."* **ReviewScout.co.uk, an English book review organization.**

"I found this book very inspired, luminous, readable and enjoyed it very much...it makes you want to read it to the very end...and it speaks to the young people of today." **Father Mengin, Former Recteur of the Saint Joan of Arc Basilique of Domrémy, France**

"Joan of Arc and the God of the Bible is to my mind a literary masterpiece as the author does a splendid job of weaving the remarkable life of Saint Joan of Arc and holy Scripture together in such a manner as to reveal the true character of Saint Joan of Arc and proves the direct intervention of Almighty God in her life and mission. In remarkable clarity he also convicts all who condemned her. The book is an excellent guide for anyone seeking for a deeper spiritual meaning to life or especially for those who are seeking for the first time...." **Denis Goyet, Confraternity of Saint Joan of Arc**

"This book is excellent!... (It) is the most well documented case of some divine intervention from a supreme power, paranormal activity or whatever someone can dream up to explain it." **Brian Morgan, Park Falls, Wisconsin, USA**

"Highly recommended! Chris Snidow's book, <u>Joan of Arc and The God of the Bible</u> is fascinating! Irrespective of whether the reader is Catholic, Protestant, or agnostic, I believe that their understanding of Joan of Arc will be greatly affected by this book, if not entirely changed...her personal testimonies, well documented throughout the text, coupled with the author's unique insights, shed light on one of the most mysterious and intriguing characters in European history..." **5 stars (out of five) from Amazon.com reviews. Terence Moeller, author of <u>Dramas of Kalalau</u>**

"I read this book in one sitting. I couldn't put it down ... This book is a wonderful success." **Jacques Lecat, lawyer, le Touquet, France**

"Chris Snidow has created a wonderful book that explains Saint Joan's life in reference to Jesus and the Bible... I highly recommend this book as one that everyone should read who is serious about learning the truth about Joan's true motivation. There are many biographies that cover the life of Joan of Arc but Chris' approach is unique in that he focuses on explaining HOW Joan of Arc was able to do what she did...it is well written and flows easily along in the 16 chapters...in the final analysis, this book is as much about God as it is about Joan of Arc, which is exactly how it should be ...." **5 stars (out of 5) from Amazon.com reviews. Ben D. Kennedy, author of <u>Maid of Heaven</u>**

"I was impressed and intrigued with his unique perspective as he carefully explained the many similarities between Joan and the Prophets of the Bible...his writing style is easy to read, very interesting, and

informative. I highly recommend this book…" **Virginia Frohlick, President of the Joan of Arc Center, Albuquerque, New Mexico, www.stjoan-center.com**

"I found this book very well organized and researched…the style is quite a relief from the scholarly approach used by so many books on Joan…" **Bill Harper, Dallas, TX USA**

"I was strongly impressed by Chris Snidow's new book enlightening the life and lessons of Saint Joan of Arc. I knew little about her prior to reading this book. Snidow captures the startling genesis of her journey, the remarkable impact on her country, and the strength that can only come from a love and reliance upon the Lord. There are many Biblical references which he expertly weaves together in tracing the path of Joan's life and the qualities she shared with Moses, Abraham, Paul, and Jesus. The research is deep and compelling…Snidow draws us in with his illuminating and lively writing style. The Angels named her correctly…she was a daughter of God. Kudos to Chris Snidow for his terrific book about a fascinating subject!" **Zach Miller, Dallas**

Very Inspiring Book *"… I highly recommend "Joan of Arc and the God of the Bible," to anyone who wants to experience her life and faith fully… I have underlined many parts of the book and will refer to them often as I continue my study of her life. For anyone interested in Joan of Arc, this book is a must and I feel it deserves all five stars!"* **David H. Fisher, Jr., Topeka, Kansas**

"I chose to read this book because virtually all of my adult life I have heard of Joan of Arc but had only a very superficial knowledge of her, and I wanted to learn some details about her story. The book served that purpose, and I would have been satisfied if it had done no more. But there was a rich surprise in that the author inserts at various points as he is telling her story a series of meditations on several very fundamental and interesting questions concerning the Christian faith… Very much worth reading, and I recommend it." **Warren Greene M.D., TX**

St. Joan of Arc From A Unique Perspective *"Chris Snidow's book is a treasure! Highly recommended for anyone interested in St. Joan of Arc, Christian bible studies, or French history. Very well researched (the footnotes alone are worth the price of* *the book!), clearly organized and presented, and written in plain English (as opposed to academic jargon.)...presents St. Joan of Arc in a new and refreshing light ...I have read many, many books and articles on St. Joan of Arc. I have seen the movies and documentaries. I have traveled in France to visit the places where St. Joan of Arc lived and prayed and fought. I do not consider myself an expert, by any stretch of the imagination, but I know a thing or two. I put Chris's book right up at the top of the list of recommended readings on St. Joan of Arc. For those truly interested in St. Joan of Arc as a spiritually-inspiring historical figure... this is the book for you."* **Bill Singleton, Massachusetts**

Compelling perspective of Joan- *"I thoroughly enjoyed reading this insightful, passionate and at times, humorous book. Chris seems to inch you into Joan's life and circumstances, combine it with Scripture and have you finish feeling like you knew her personally. Whether one is familiar with the Bible or not, it makes no difference in understanding her life, the depth of her faith and her struggles. You may even finish it and feel like you understand the Bible a little better. I love how he phrases the questions in such a familiar fashion- like you or I would- simple and to the point. He then proceeds to dig deeply into searching for the answers. I highly recommend this book."* **Lynne Hardesty, Dallas, TX**

Inspirational and Highly Recommended- *"...If you're looking for an inspirational, well researched, easy-to-read connection between actual historical events and Biblical spirituality, look no further!! Snidow eloquently relates the epic nature of Joan's mission on earth to God and the Bible in easy-to-understand terms. While Joan's time was short-just 19 years-she carved out a history truly inspired by Divinity. From both historical and spiritual perspectives, you would be hard pressed to find a book more relevant both yesterday and today!"* **Bunn Fawcett, AR**

THE WITCH THAT WASN'T

Joan of Arc and the God of the Bible
~THE WITCH THAT WASN'T~
God's Game Changers-Volume 1

Preface by Marie-Veronique Clin ix

Introduction 11

Chapter 1 - Joan of Arc, "Daughter of God" 15

Chapter 2 - The Sign 24

Chapter 3 - A Call to Serve 43

Chapter 4 - Her Time Had Come 50

Chapter 5 - God's Time 53

Chapter 6 - A Lifelong Pilgrimage 59

Chapter 7 - Remarkable Obedience 73

Chapter 8 - Enduring Persecution 81

Chapter 9 - God's Help Ever-Present 95

Chapter 10 - A Warrior of God 115

Chapter 11 - Prophecy and Miracles 145

Chapter 12 - "If you love me..." 171

Chapter 13 - The Ultimate Game Changer 174

Chapter 14 - Joan's France 193

Chapter 15 - All Aboard 198

Chapter 16 - The Witch That Wasn't 201

About the Author 208

Bibliography 209

PREFACE

Chris Snidow gives us a very well documented work. Not only is it an in-depth study of Joan of Arc, but also one on both the New and Old Testaments.

He had already won us over with the powerful yet, paradoxically gentle, melodies of his music. Listening to this 'powerful gentleness' found in his music enables us to just close our eyes, and so capture some of the life of Joan of Arc. Now in this book, the comparisons used from Mr. Snidow's well-chosen and documented texts command their own attention. They stand out by themselves, leading us to one central point: Joan of Arc followed the pattern of the Old Testament prophets, as well as the teachings of Jesus Christ. With each day of her short life (two years of public life, including one year of prison and an unjust trial) she shows us the way to daily reliving the passion of Jesus.

Joan of Arc, or Joan the Maid as she called herself, actually went through five trials, including three during her own short life. The first one was at Toul, a town close to her native village (Domrémy), and the seat of her local diocese, which Domrémy so depended on. This first confrontation with church authorities was instigated by a young man who had asked for her hand in marriage. However, she was quickly released from this trial process, as she had never accepted the engagement in the first place. Next, she was brought to Poitiers to be examined by the leading scholars of the Church; that is, those who remained loyal to the crown of France. There again Joan demonstrated her persuasive powers and proved herself to them. They found nothing in her that was in any way against the doctrine of the Catholic Church, and as the Kingdom's situation was so desperate, the church authorities stated that they "could avail themselves of her help". Her third trial was held in Rouen in enemy territory, and made up of men of the Church who had sold themselves to the English authorities. This "beautiful trial" was presided over by Bishop Pierre Cauchon, and ended at the stake on May 30, 1431! Then after her death, Joan's case was examined once again (Trial of Rehabilitation-1456). One hundred and sixteen witnesses were interrogated, finally leading to the judge's conclusion that Joan was innocent before man and God. And lastly, Joan was canonized in 1920.

Chris Snidow brings to life Joan of Arc's story in an unprecedented and original way. I must say that I've never seen before the comparisons he draws between Joan and Jesus Christ. Although the connections between the two have been mentioned in the past by historians, they have never been explored in such depth. Always basing his words on recognized and accepted facts, he is able to interpret Joan's actions while still making contemporary comparisons.

Joan, like Jesus, recognized the importance of the Old Testament prophecies. Could we say that Moses was perhaps a forerunner of Joan? For like the Old Testament prophets who announced the liberation of their country, Joan too was completely consecrated and dedicated to her God.

For Joan, paradise is where Jesus is. As He said, *"I tell you the truth, today you will be with me in paradise."* Luke 23:43

Chris Snidow is well placed to reveal to us Joan's true mysticism. Having worked some 30 years as a psychiatric Registered Nurse in several psychiatric hospitals and settings, he is well trained to perceive the difference between the pathological and the normal. For Joan, there was never any doubt:

"God first served."

Marie-Véronique Clin
June, 2006
Co-author with Régine Pernoud of *Joan of Arc-Her Story,* and several other books based on Joan of Arc and the Middle Ages.

INTRODUCTION

There's no story like Joan of Arc. I remember the first time I read the true facts of her life. It sounded more like a fairy tale than a fairy tale. There are prophecies, knights and legends. Angels, peasants and Heaven. Castles and Kings, witches and Queens, and teen-age Joan as the heroine. There's even a Fairy Tree[1]. The only difference is that Joan's story is true. Perhaps we could call it a God tale. In any case, it gave me a strong hunger to know more, especially regarding the spiritual aspects of her case. I diligently searched for some kind of a scriptural look at her life and, much to my surprise, couldn't find one. Although there are many biographies, historical studies, works of fiction, and a few that take aim at the spiritual aspects, none focused on a Biblical examination. And so, in this age of increasing competing religions and 'gods', I gratefully offer here my own modest contribution to this spiritual arena. May it be a blessing to you.

There are many striking similarities between Joan of Arc and the prophet/saints of the Bible. The same can be said about Joan and Jesus Christ. Of course, I am not the first who has noticed this. But the differences between Joan and Jesus are also great. In drawing some comparisons between the two, it should be clear that in no way am I encouraging any form of worship of Joan of Arc, or any other saintly person. Scripture is clear on this. Jesus said, *"It is written: Worship the Lord your God and serve him only."* Luke 4: 8 (See also Exodus 20:3, Deut. 6: 5; Deut. 6: 13)

Joan, for her part, always dissuaded people from bowing down to or worshipping her in any way. As Marguerite la Touroulde tells us, *"I remember that several women came to my house while Joan was staying there, and brought chaplets and other objects of piety that she might touch them which made her laugh and say to me, 'Touch them yourself, they will be as good from your touch as from mine.'"*[2] Joan of Arc was a worshipper/servant of the God of the Bible. She was a saint, a prophet, and a 'holy warrior'. Like all true prophet/saints, she always pointed to God as the source of all she did and was.

Jesus, on the other hand, was not only the epitome of a prophet/saint, but also the only son of the Living God. For Christians all over the world, He is both our Lord and Savior. As it says in the Nicene Creed: *"...God from God, Light from Light, true God from true God."* He accepted worship as something that was entirely appropriate. *"Then the man said, 'Lord, I believe', and he worshipped him. Jesus said, 'For judgment I have come into this world, so that the blind will see and those who see will become blind.'"* John 9: 38 Or again: *"Thomas said to him, 'My Lord and my God!' Then Jesus told him, 'Because you have seen me, you have believed; blessed are those who have not seen and yet have believed.'"* John 20: 28

The goal of using all these comparisons in this book is simply to show that Joan does indeed follow the same pattern seen with the prophet/saints of the Bible, including at times Jesus Himself. Through her own well documented words, actions, and life, Joan of Arc makes a powerful witness for the Triune God of the Bible. And according to the Bible, there is no other God.[3] She provides a strong example of why we should turn to Him alone to be saved.

With a subject as large as this, it would be impossible to give a complete history and/or understanding of either of the principal characters of this book (i.e. Joan of Arc and the God of the Bible). Although I have addressed both extensively in these pages, for those of you who are not as knowledgeable as you would like to be, here are two recommendations:

1) I believe the best beginning book on Joan of Arc is Joan of Arc-Her Story, by Marie-Veronique Clin and Regine Pernoud. Ms. Pernoud, until her death in 1998, was the leading historian, scholar and author in France on Joan of Arc and the Middle Ages. Ms. Clin had both worked with her and been her friend. They collaborated on this excellent, accurate, and historical account of Joan's life. Thoroughly researched, well documented and written, with appendixes and brief bios of all the principal players, this choice was not a difficult one. At this time Ms. Clin is Director of the Museum of Medical History in Paris.

2) Regarding further information on the God of the Bible, the obvious first choice would be God's own book, The Bible. An accurate and readable translation is recommended, and I believe the NIV or ESV translation fits the bill. The NIV is used throughout this book, except where otherwise noted.

This book first appeared in 2006 under the title Joan of Arc and the God of the Bible. A French version followed in 2009. In 2013 I completed a revised and expanded edition which provided numerous additional quotes, examples, references and information. Now in this 2015 edition, The Witch That Wasn't, there are again a number of improvements, including additional information, footnotes, quotes etc., as well as the never-ending attempt to make the final manuscript as readable as possible. It has been an ongoing labor of love and reward.

I wish to thank all those who have been of great assistance to me, and without whom this project would never have been completed. My love and special thanks especially go to my wonderful wife, Catherine.

This book is dedicated to the God of the Bible, and Sainte Jeanne d'Arc. To Jeanne, because she remains an example in many ways. And to the God of the Bible, to whom we owe our very existence. May His name be praised forever.

Chris Snidow
April, 2015

[1] "Not far from Domrémy there is a tree that they call 'The Ladies' Tree-others call it The Fairy Tree; nearby, there is a spring where people sick of the fever come to drink, as I have heard, and to seek water to restore their health. I have seen them myself come thus; but I do not know if they were healed. I have heard that the sick, once cured, come to this tree to walk about it. It is a beautiful tree, a beech, from which come the 'beau may.' It belongs to the Seigneur Pierre de Bourlemont, Knight. I have sometimes been to play with the young girls, to make garlands for Our Lady of Domrémy. Often I have heard the old folk- they are not of my lineage- say that the fairies haunt this tree. I have also heard one of my Godmothers, named Jeanne, wife of the Marie Aubrery of Domrémy, say that she has seen fairies there; whether this is true, I do not know. As for me, I never saw them that I know of. If I saw them anywhere else, I do not know. I have seen the young girls putting garlands on the branches of this tree, and I myself have sometimes put them there with my companions; sometimes we took these garlands away, sometimes we left them. Ever since I knew that it was necessary for me to come into France, I have given myself up as little as possible to these games and distractions. Since I have grown up, I do not remember to have danced there. I may have danced there formerly, with the other children. I have sung there more than danced. There is also a wood called the Oakwood, which can be seen from my father's door; it is not more than half-a-league away. I do not know, and have never heard if the fairies appear there; but my brother told me that it is said in the neighborhood that 'Jeannette received her mission at the Fairies' Tree. It is not the case; and I told him the contrary. When I came before the King, several people asked me if there were not in my country a woods, called the Oak-wood, because there were prophecies which said that from the neighborhood of this woods would come a maid who should do marvelous things. I put no faith in that." Joan of Arc, Trial of Condemnation, Saturday, Feb. 24, 1430. http://stjoan-center.com/Trials/sec03.html, accessed Feb. 2014. Great attempts were made at Joan's trial to connect her with some superstitious practices supposed to have been performed around this 'Fairy Tree', but the sincerity of her answers baffled her judges. She had sung and danced there with the other children, and had woven wreaths for Our Lady's statue, but since she was twelve years old she had held aloof from such diversions. When others were asked about it during the Trial of Nullification, their answers were duly taken down

under oath, including Joan's godfather: *'I heard tell often that women and the enchantresses who are called fairies used to go dance there beneath that tree, but, according to what they say, ever since the Gospel of St. John was read in these parts, they do not go there anymore. In our time, on the Sunday when at the Introit of the mass Laetare Jerusalem is sung, the young girls and young men of Domrémy go out to that tree and often they eat there and when they come back they go to the fountain at Rains and while walking about and singing they drink the water of that fountain and play roundabout and pick flowers.'* Joan's godmother Beatrice added, *'It's a very beautiful tree.'* Another witness, Gerardin of Epinal, said, *'That tree in the spring is as beautiful as lilies and its branches are spread very wide; its leaves and its branches touch the ground.'* There is no hint of devil worship, sorcery or any kind of interaction with 'fairies' in any of their testimony." Regine Pernoud and Marie-Véronique Clin. *Joan of Arc-Her Story*, St Martin's Griffin, New York, New York, 1998. http://stjoan-center.com/Trials/sec03.html, accessed Jan-Feb 2014.

[2] Marguerite la Touroulde, Trial of the Rehabilatation: Régine Pernoud, <u>Joan of Arc-By Herself and Her Witnesses</u>, Scarborough House, Lanham, MD, 1982, p. 65

[3] *"Before me no god was formed, nor will there be one after me I, even I, am the LORD, and apart from me there is no savior."* Isaiah 43: 10-11; *"This is what the LORD says—Israel's King and Redeemer, the LORD Almighty: I am the first and I am the last; apart from me there is no God."* Isaiah 44: 6 (Other examples include Isaiah 45: 12-14; 45: 21 and 46: 9)

Chapter 1
Joan of Arc, "Daughter of God"

"...and when I have made my prayer to God, I hear a voice that says to me? 'Daughter of God, go, go, go! I shall be with you to help you. Go!' and when I hear that voice I feel a great joy!" Joan of Arc [1]

Joan of Arc was some young French girl with short hair who was burned at the stake. I know this because I remember seeing it in our Sunday morning newspaper comic strips. I was ten years old that summer. Although I don't remember much about it, I do recall this short-haired teenager dressed in medieval armor, running around from battle to battle, and always winning. And seems like there was something about witchcraft? Well, I don't remember all the details on that. Or maybe I just missed a couple of episodes. Anyway, summer soon faded into fall, and I moved on to more important things. Such as the World Series, roller skating, model airplanes, and the least interesting of all: going back to school. It wasn't long before I was tossed into the world of Tom Sawyer and Huckleberry Finn. Like most American kids, Mark Twain held my attention and made me laugh, all while transporting me back to an earlier time. I later discovered that Tom and Huck weren't the only things Twain wrote about. He also wrote about Joan of Arc. Now this was a surprise to me. And all the more so, when I saw what he had to say about her. Here's an example:

"Joan of Arc, a mere child in years, ignorant, unlettered, a poor village girl unknown and without influence, found a great nation lying in chains, helpless and hopeless under an alien domination, its treasury bankrupt, its soldiers disheartened and dispersed, all spirit torpid, all courage dead in the hearts of the people through long years of foreign and domestic outrage and oppression, their King cowed, resigned to his fate, and preparing to fly the country; and she laid her hand upon this nation, this corpse, and it rose and followed her. She led it from victory to victory, she turned back the tide of the Hundred Years' War, she fatally crippled the English power, and died with the earned title of DELIVER OF FRANCE, which she bears to this day... She was perhaps the only entirely unselfish person whose name has a place in profane history. No vestige or suggestion of self-seeking can be found in any word or deed of hers." [2]

Apparently there was more to her story than I'd thought as a ten-year-old. Then, many years later, I stumbled on a book by the great

French medieval historian Regine Pernoud, recounting the true story of Jeanne d'Arc. I have since learned, much to my surprise, that she appears to be the most attested figure in history up to the 16th century. This is due to several factors. First of all, we have the record of her 1431 Trial of Condemnation (recorded verbatim and under oath), which led to her being burned at the stake. We also have what is called the Trial of Nullification (also known as the Trial of Rehabilitation) where some twenty five years after her death, her name was cleared and she was found not guilty of all previous charges from the 1431 trial. At that trial, one hundred and sixteen people from all phases of her life were interviewed under oath, and their answers were also taken down verbatim. And then, there is a massive amount of eyewitness accounts and historical sources including letters, city journals, poetry, and others. As Sir Arthur Conan Doyle states, *"...next to the Christ, the highest spiritual being of whom we have any exact record upon this earth is the girl Jeanne."*[3]

Just who was this peasant girl, and what did she do? The goal of this book is not to make an exhaustive study of her life from all the historical sources available. That has already been done many times by numerous capable historians, scholars and authors. No, the focus of this book is on how she was able to do what she did, and what or who was the source of her power. For this, some basic information is in order. So let's begin with a thumbnail sketch of the life of Joan of Arc.

She was born in 1412, in an eastern area of France called Lorraine. She was devoted to prayer, and made it the center point of her life. As a child working in the fields, the sound of church bells would often send her to her knees in prayer.[4] Her childhood friends often teased her for her "excessive piety".[5] In their court depositions, the residents of her native village (*Domrémy*) often describe her as very simple and "much like all the others." [6] She was unfailingly kind to the simple and the poor, even those of the enemy. She went from escorting her family's cows to pasture, to escorting the dauphin (France's rightful heir to the throne) through enemy territory to be anointed and crowned in Reims (*Rheims*), as her "voice from God"[7] told her she must do. Her fondest dream was to be again the simple peasant girl she had been before being called by God; home in her small village, anonymous, surrounded by family and friends. Her reality however, was leading the King's armies into battle, with France's veteran generals as her subordinates.

How did a seventeen-year-old illiterate French peasant girl become the youngest Commander-in-Chief, male or female, in all recorded history?[8] After all, as you might imagine, woman's rights were not exactly in the forefront during the 15th century.

During her Trial of Condemnation, she testified that God sent His messengers to guide her, beginning when she was about thirteen years old.[9] At first they mostly encouraged her to be a good child and to go often to church.[10] However, they soon began to reveal a much greater mission. She had been chosen to liberate France from the English, and escort the dauphin to Reims, where he was to take his rightful place on the throne.[11] At this time (1429), half of France was already under English occupation. The key city to France's survival was Orleans. It had been under siege for seven months, and was not expected to hold out much longer. It was widely believed that France would soon become just another part of the English kingdom.[12] It was at this pivotal moment in history that Jeanne d'Arc came on the scene. She was directed by her messengers to go and see Robert Baudricourt, the 'captain' of Vaucouleurs (a neighboring town of Domrémy).[13] She was to convince him that God had chosen her for this mission, and that he must send her to the Dauphin, Charles VII.[14] Finally, Baudricourt was convinced, and so sent her with escort to meet Charles at Chinon.[15]

When at last she met the dauphin at Chinon, she convinced him as well. How? Hear her words at their first meeting, from eyewitness Raoul de Gaucourt: *"I bring you news from God, that our Lord will give you back your kingdom, bringing you to be crowned at Reims, and driving out your enemies. In this I am God's messenger. Do set me bravely to work, and I will raise the siege of Orleans."*[16]

The official historian of Charles' court was Jean Chartier. He states: *"Then Joan, having come before the king, made the curtsies and reverences that customarily are made to a king as though she had been nourished at the court and, her greeting having been delivered, said in addressing the king, 'God give you life gentle King', even though she did not know him and had never seen him, and there were many pompous lords there more opulently dressed than was the king. Wherefore he replied to Joan: 'What if I am not the king, Joan?' Pointing to one of the lords he said: 'There is the king.' To which she answered, 'In God's name, gentle Prince, it is you and none other."*[17]

And from her soon to be personal priest, Friar Jean Pasquerel: *"When the king saw her, he asked Joan her name and she answered: 'Gentle dauphin, I am Joan the maid, and the King of Heaven commands that through me you be anointed*[18] *and crowned in the city of Reims as a lieutenant of the King of Heaven, who is King of France.' And after further questions asked by the king, Joan said to him anew, 'I say to you, on behalf of the Lord, that you are the true heir of France, and a king's son, and He has sent me to you to lead you to Reims, so that you can receive your coronation and consecration, if you wish it.' This being understood, the king said to his courtiers that Joan had told him a certain secret that no one knew or could know except God; and that is why he had great confidence in her."*[19]

Joan had asked to see him alone for a few minutes, and this was granted. When they returned, witnesses stated that the Dauphin was "radiant".[20] He said that not only had she *"...told him a certain secret that no one knew or could know except God"*, but also that she had given him a sign from God. Joan mentioned this sign in her trial: *"...the King received a sign concerning what I had done before he would believe in me."*[21] Although history paints the Charles of 1429 as indecisive, afraid and weak-willed, it does not paint him as stupid. After receiving this sign, he immediately provided quarters for her in the castle. Neither Joan nor Charles would ever reveal what this sign was, nor what she told him. These secrets went with them both to their graves.

She was subsequently sent Poitiers to be examined by church authorities.[22] Today this would be similar to going to the Vatican to be examined by their top clerics. *"Finally, after long examinations* (three weeks) *by the clergy of several faculties, they all deliberated and concluded that the King could legitimately receive her, and allow her to take a company of soldiers to the siege of Orleans, because they had found nothing in her that was not of the Catholic faith and entirely consistent with reason."*[23]

It was also found that *"...she had responded with as much wisdom as if she had been a member of the clergy. They therefore marveled at her responses, and they believed that this was by Divine inspiration, considering her life and conduct...it was concluded by the clergy, that there was no evil in her, nor anything contrary to the Catholic faith...and...in her has been found nothing evil; only good, humility, virginity, devotion, honesty, and simplicity."*[24]

Joan mentioned this examination during her trial: *"For three weeks I was examined by learned men in Chinon and Poitiers....And the scholars were of this opinion: that they could see nothing but good in my undertaking."*[25]

On getting this word, Charles did indeed turn his military forces over to her. She then set out to liberate Orleans, and within ten days of her arrival, this was accomplished. Victory after victory followed, as she quickly cleared the way for Charles to be escorted through enemy territory to Reims for his anointing and coronation.[26] This is what her messengers had instructed her to do.[27] The coronation on July 17, 1429 was the high point of her career.

Ten months later she was captured at Compiegne. She was put on "trial", an illegal and obviously partisan affair from beginning to end.

The charges included wearing men's clothes, heresy and witchcraft. After all, it had to be witchcraft. Otherwise, how could anyone beat the mighty English? They had suffered some catastrophic defeats, thanks to this Joan of Arc, and this was both unbelievable and unacceptable to them. It was the Hundred Years War[28], and before her appearance, the English had been consistently beating the French for decades. Here's a list of the major battles:

Battle of Cadsand - 1337 - English victory

Naval Battle of Sluys - 1340 - English victory

Battle of Auberoche - 1345 - English victory

Siege of Calais - 1346 - English victory

Battle of Saint-Pol-de-Leon - 1346 - English victory

Battle of La Roche-Derrien - 1347 - English victory

Battle of Saintes - 1351 - English victory

Battle of Ardres - 1351 - French victory

Battle of Mauron - 1352 - English victory

Battle of Poitiers - 1356 - English victory

Battle of Auray - 1364 - English victory

Battle of Navarrette (Najera) - 1367 - English victory

Battle of Montiel - 1369 - French victory

Battle of Chiset (Chizai) - 1373 - French victory

Siege of Harfleur - 1415 - English victory

Battle of Agincourt - 1415 English victory

Siege of Rouen - July 1418 - January 1419 - English victory

Battle of Bauge - 1421 - French-Scots victory

Battle of Cravant - 1423 - English victory

Battle of Verneuil (Vernuil) - 1423 - English victory

Battle of St. James - 1426 - English victory

Battle of Orleans - May 6-8, 1429 - (Joan of Arc appears on the scene) French victory

Battle of Jargeau - June 11-12, 1429 - French victory (led by Joan of Arc)

Battle of Beaugency - June 16-17, 1429 - French victory (led by Joan)

Battle of Patay - June 18, 1429 - French victory (led by Joan of Arc)

Siege of Compiegne - 1430 - French victory (led by Joan of Arc)

Battle of Gerbevoy - 1435 - French victory

Battle of Formigny - 1450 - French victory

Battle of Castillon - 1453 - French victory

As you see, Joan of Arc's entrance on the world stage is both dramatic, and enduring. Oh, how the mighty had fallen! And to add insult to injury, it wasn't a famous and ferocious warlord that beat them. No. It was by this Jeanne d'Arc. A lowly, illiterate, teenage French peasant girl![29]

The outcome of the trial was never in doubt. She was burned at the stake on May 30, 1431. However, for the English the damage had already been done. Before seven years would pass, they would lose Paris, just as Joan prophesied.[30] And thereafter, they would be booted out of France for good.

Joan of Arc's name was written into the history books, and under more than one category: God's servant, military leader, prophetess, patriot ... Unlike some today, her legacy was something she never seemed to consider. She left quite a large one nonetheless. Here are a few interesting points:

-Although she longed to be back in her small village with family and friends, she found herself the honored and valued guest of royalty.[31]

-Her approach to war was quite unorthodox. She took battled hardened soldiers and commanded them to go to confession and take Holy Communion before going in battle. She sent their prostitutes away and ordered a halt to pillaging, rape, and even obscene language (at least, when she was around).[32] She was also considered to be an expert in the new art of artillery.[33]

-She went to her death asking for forgiveness for those who were about to execute her, as well as for her own sins.[34] The last word of her lips was "Jesus".[35]

-Her claims of speaking to God's messengers were backed up by her many unlikely but quite detailed prophecies that all came to pass (see Chapter 11), as well as her compassion and consistent saintly behavior.

-The same church that had her burned at the stake as a witch and heretic in 1431, had her canonized a Saint some 500 years later (May 16, 1920, by Pope Benedict XV).

Over the centuries there have been many theories on how Joan was able to do the amazing things she did. Among these theories are the following:

a. It was all a fluke.
b. She was schizophrenic.
c. She was just plain crazy.
d. She was very lucky.
e. She was actually a man.
f. She was guided by satanic powers.
g. She was in fact a witch.

…and on and on it goes.

What did Joan say? She denied being a witch.[36] But rather, as you've seen above, she consistently stated that she was sent by God. She claimed that He had directed His messengers to her, and that they counseled her on a frequent basis. Which God was she talking about? The God of the Bible.

Could this be true? That is the subject of this book. The case presented in these pages is simply this: after examining all the records available, the best and most logical explanation behind Joan of Arc's amazing feats and life is found in the God of the Bible working through her, just as she said. One thing is sure: Joan's story, heavily flavored with the supernatural and world changing events, is unique in world history. And history would have been very different without her timely entrance on the world stage.

[1]Joan of Arc-from the testimony of Jean, Count de Dunois, the 'Bastard of Orleans', Trial of Nullification
[2]Mark Twain, Personal Recollections of Joan of Arc by The Sieur Louis de Conte, Ignatius Press, San Francisco, 1989, p. 20
[3]Sir Arthur Conan Doyle (1859-1930) is most noted for his stories about the detective Sherlock Holmes.
[4]Jean Waterin, laborer of Greux, Trial of Nullification, 1456; Simonin Musnier, laborer of Domremy, Trial of Nullification, 1456
[5]Hauviette, wife of Gerard of Syonne, near Neufchateau, Trial of Nullification, 1456
[6]Mengette, wife of Jean Joyart, laborer, Trial of Nullification, 1456; Régine Pernoud and Marie-Véronique Clin, Jeanne d'Arc, Editions Fayard, Mesnil-sur-l'Estree, 2001, p. 159 and 161
[7]Trial of Condemnation, Feb. 22, 1431
[8]As Louis Kossuth (1802-1894) says: *"Consider this unique and imposing distinction. Since the writing of human history began, Joan of Arc is the only person, of either sex, who has ever held supreme command of the military forces of a nation at the age of seventeen."* Mr. Kossuth was Regent-President of Hungary in 1849. He was widely

honored during his lifetime, including in the United Kingdom and the United States, as a freedom fighter and bellwether of democracy in Europe.

[9] Régine Pernoud (translated from the French by Edward Hyams), <u>Joan of Arc, By Herself and Her Witnesses</u>, Scarborough House, Lanham, MD, 1982, p. 30-31

[10] Ibid.

[11] Willard Trask, <u>Joan of Arc-Self Portrait</u>, The Telegraph Press, New York, New York, 1936, p. 28-29

[12] *"...the inhabitants were then in such straits, on account of the English, that they knew not where to turn, except to God...I believed, like all in the town, that, had the Maid not come in God's Name to our help, we should soon have been, both town and people, in the hands of the enemy: we did not believe it possible for the army then in the town to resist the power of the enemy who were in such force against us."* Jean Luillier, Burgher of Orleans, Trial of Nullification

[13] Trial of Condemnation, Feb. 22, 1431

[14] Ibid.

[15] Régine Pernoud and Marie-Véronique Clin, <u>Jeanne d'Arc</u>, Editions Fayard, Mesnil-sur-l'Estree, 2001, p.20

[16] <u>Joan of Arc</u> translated by Willard Trask, <u>Joan of Arc: In Her Own Words</u>, Turtle Point Press, New York, 1965, p.21

[17] Régine Pernoud, <u>Jeanne d'Arc par elle-meme et ses temoins</u>, Edition du Seuil, Paris, 1996, p. 56

[18] The act of anointing comes from the Old Testament. It is for office-bearers, such as the high priest (e.g. Leviticus 8: 12), the king (1 Samuel 16: 13), or the prophet (1 Kings 19: 16). Oil was poured on the head of these individuals as they were set apart for service to God. But it is the Lord alone who pours out His spirit on them, thereby equipping them in the office to which He had called them. Thus, the anointing implied the calling for the task and the endowment of the Holy Spirit to carry it out.

[19] Joan of Arc translated by Willard Trask, <u>Joan of Arc: In Her Own Words</u>, Turtle Point Press, New York, 1965, p. 57

[20] Allen Williamson, Joan of Arc Online Archive 2003. Feb 2004. http://archive.joan-of-arc.org

[2] Willard Trask, <u>Joan of Arc-Self Portrait</u>, The Telegraph Press, New York, New York, 1936, p. 47

[22] Régine Pernoud and Marie-Véronique Clin, <u>Jeanne d'Arc</u>, Editions Fayard, Mesnil-sur-l'Estree, 2001, p.15

[23] Quoted from Jean Barbin, a lawyer for the Parliament. Régine Pernoud and Marie-Véronique Clin, <u>Jeanne d'Arc</u>, Editions Fayard, Mesnil-sur-l'Estree, 2001, p. 50; Joan of Arc translated by Willard Trask, <u>Joan of Arc: In Her Own Words</u>, Turtle Point Press, New York, 1965, p. 61

[24] Régine Pernoud and Marie-Véronique Clin, <u>Jeanne d'Arc</u>, Editions Fayard, Mesnil-sur-l'Estree, 2001, p. 50-52

[25] Willard Trask, <u>Joan of Arc-Self Portrait</u>, The Telegraph Press, New York, New York, 1936, p. 47

[26] The way to Reims was entirely through enemy territory, and all the cities they encountered were loyal to the English. And yet, *"The King and his people came without hindrance to Reims. Nowhere was the King turned back, for the gates of all cities and towns opened themselves to him."* Gobert Thibaut, Squire to the King of France, Trial of Nullification

[27] Régine Pernoud and Marie-Véronique Clin, <u>Jeanne d'Arc</u>, Editions Fayard, Mesnil-sur-l'Estree, 2001, p.23

[28] *"Love is like war: easy to begin but very hard to stop."* H. L. Mencken, (1880-1956). The Hundred Years War was began in 1337, and lasted to 1453.

[29]Their disdain began at the very beginning of her military career. Before her first battle, the Battle of Orleans, she exchanged words with some of the English soldiers who were within shouting distance: *"... One of them, called the Bastard of Granville, assailed her with many insults: 'Do you wish us', he said, 'to surrender to a woman?'"* Louis de Contes, Joan's page at Orleans, Trial of Nullification

[30]Willard Trask, Joan of Arc-Self Portrait, The Telegraph Press, New York, New York, 1936, p. 137; see Chapter 11.

[31]Ibid. p 38

[32]*"As a rule, no one in the army dared swear or blaspheme before her, for fear of being reprimanded (by her)."* Louis de Contes, Trial of Nullification

[33]Article by Stephen Richey: Joan of Arc A Military Appreciation, 2000, p. 9; also see Chapter 10

[34]Francis Gies, Joan of Arc-The Legend and the Reality, Harper and Row publishers, New York, 1981, p. 223; John Holland Smith, Joan of Arc, Sidgwick & Jackson, London, 1973, p.173

[35]Willard Trask, Joan of Arc-Self Portrait, The Telegraph Press, New York, New York, 1936, p.185

[36]*"There was neither sorcery nor any other evil art in anything that I have done."* Joan of Arc, Trial of Condemnation, October 31, 1430

Chapter 2
The Sign

"For he is the living God, and he endures forever…He performs signs and wonders in the heavens and on the earth." Daniel 6: 26-27

Hey Dude and/or Dudess. Like, what's your sign?

Me? I'm a Leo. Cool, huh. Now you know my astrological sign. But that isn't really the sign I want to talk about in this chapter.

I once worked on the psychiatric floor at Parkland Hospital in Dallas. We usually had some seriously ill people with us. I remember going to my 3-11 shift one day and noticing that the day-room was virtually empty. I started looking around for the patients, and found a lot of them gathered together in one of the patient's bathrooms. At that time, although we only had eighteen patients, three of them were very delusional. All three were convinced that they were in fact Jesus Christ. Some of the other patients had been telling them that they couldn't <u>all</u> be Jesus. If the real Jesus were there, then He would be able to prove it. For example, the real Jesus would be able to walk of water. Those convinced that <u>they</u> were Jesus readily agreed with that. So back they went, along with some of the other giggling patients, to fill up the bathtub. That's about the time I walked in. They said they were looking for a sign. A sign to see who the real Jesus was.

Looking for a sign of God's presence is nothing new. As they say, what's new is old, and what's old is new. Throughout history many have claimed to be following the call of God, but had no signs to prove themselves. And their actions and lives proved otherwise. David Koresh and Jim Jones are just two of the more recent examples.

       -In 1978 Reverend Jim Jones, in the name of God, led some 1,000 people to the jungles of South America. There he created his own city, Jonestown. Cut off from all contact from the outside world, his disciples believed that Rev. Jones was who he claimed to be: Jesus-Christ come back to Earth. Jones was consumed with drugs, delusions of grandeur and paranoia. He was convinced that the end of the world would come at any moment. On November 18, 1978 under Jones' 'divine' direction and orders, 913 people killed themselves (or if reluctant, were killed).

       -On April 19, 1993, after a fifty-one day siege with the police, David Koresh and seventy-six of his disciples killed themselves by setting their house on fire. Mr. Koresh had told them he was the second coming of Jesus, and convinced them that the end time had come. Indeed, for them it had.

False prophets have always been around, manipulating and deceiving others for their own gain. How can we distinguish a true prophet of God from a counterfeit? Is there any test we can give to validate their claims? Is there a sign we can look for?

Some look for signs from the "the other side". They might attempt this through astrology, channeling, tarot cards, a Ouija board, a witch, mediums (i.e. someone who communicates with the dead) etc.

Did Joan use any of these means? No.

The Old Testament prophets? No

How about Jesus and his apostles? Again, no. Christians and Jews, having been plagued by a multitude of false prophets throughout their history (just as we are today), are instructed to go to the Bible and prayer for answers. Regarding witches, seers, mediums, astrologers, etc., God is quite specific:

"Let no one be found among you who sacrifices his son or daughter in the fire, who practices divination or sorcery, interprets omens, engages in witchcraft[1]*, or casts spells, or who is a medium or spiritist or who consults the dead. Anyone who does these things is detestable to the LORD..."* Deut. 18:10-12

"Do not turn to mediums or seek out spiritists, for you will be defiled by them. I am the Lord your God." Leviticus 19:31

"When men tell you to consult mediums and spiritists, who whisper and mutter, should not a people inquire of their God? Why consult the dead on behalf of the living?" Isaiah 8:19

Signs teach people about God and His ways, and bring them near to Him. So how can we identify a genuine sign of God? Well, here are some guidelines to start with:

    1) A sign from the God of the Bible would always be pointing in some way to its source, God.

    2) It would be consistent with, and not contradict in any way, previous revelation (i.e. the Bible).

    3) It would be, under normal circumstances, something considered impossible for man to do. In fact many signs, but not all, are displayed in the form of a miracle.

Yes, we're talking about something supernatural here. And as we'll see in detail in Chapter 11, prophecy without error is one strong example. But there are other signs. Here are two examples of **Non-Prophetic Signs** from the Old Testament:

1) God instructed Moses to tell mighty Pharaoh of Egypt to let His people go (see Exodus 3:10). God gave him two signs as proof that he was indeed God-sent (Ex 4: 1-17). For the first sign, He told him to throw his staff down on the ground, *"...and it became a snake...Then the LORD said to him, 'Reach out your hand and take it by the tail'...and it turned back into a staff in his hand. 'This', said the LORD, 'is so that they may believe that the LORD, the God of their fathers...has appeared to you.'"* Unconvinced, Pharaoh's heart remained hard, and he eventually lost his firstborn son and more due to his own stubbornness (see Exodus, chapters 11-12).

2) The people of Israel had *"abandoned the LORD's commands and followed* (the gods of) *the Baals."* The prophet Elijah challenged these *'prophets of Baal'*. They were both to call on their respective god to send down fire to ignite a prepared sacrifice. The prophets of Baal couldn't pull it off. Then Elijah called upon God, and *"the fire of the Lord fell and burned up the sacrifice, the wood, the stones, the soil, and also licked up the water in the trench. When all the people saw this, they fell prostrate and cried, 'The Lord-he is God!'"* 1 Kings 18: 38-39 Unlike Pharaoh's case above, this sign was seen <u>and</u> believed, and the people turned to God.

The New Testament is also full of signs. Jesus used many miracles as a sign. Through these He showed himself as Lord over illness, laws of nature, knowledge, the demonic world, creation, and finally life itself. Here are a few examples:

-healing ten men of leprosy (Luke 17: 11-19)
-healing a man born deaf (John 9)
-healing a deaf and mute man (Mark 7:31-37)
-calming a threatening storm (Mt 8: 23-27; Luke 8: 22-25)
-walking on water (John 6: 16-24)
-prophesizing in detail without error (e.g. Luke 18: 31-34)
-exorcising demons (Mt 8: 28-32; Luke 8: 26-39)
-changing water into wine (John 2: 1-11)
-feeding 5,000 people with only 5 loaves of bread and two fish (Mark 6: 32-44)
-raising the dead (three separate examples-Mark 5: 21-43; Luke 7: 11-17; and John 11: 1-44)
-He saved the most amazing and important one for last: his own resurrection (Mt 28: 1-10; Mark 16; Luke 24: 1-35; John 20).

Less well known perhaps, is that, *"The apostles* (also) *performed many miraculous signs and wonders among the people..."* There are many such examples in the New Testament[2], including these two:

1) *"Crowds gathered... bringing their sick and those tormented by*

evil spirits, and all of them were healed." Acts 5: 12, 15-16

2) *"In Joppa there was a disciple named Tabitha...she became sick and...Peter...was taken upstairs to the room...he got down on his knees and prayed. Turning towards the dead woman, he said, 'Tabitha, get up.' She opened her eyes... He took her by the hand...and presented her to them alive. This became known all over Joppa, and many people believed in the Lord."* Acts 9: 36-42

Signs aren't for entertainment. They aren't given 'on demand', as if for a magic show. Those seeking signs for ulterior motives were usually sadly disappointed. Here's an example: *"The Pharisees and Sadducees came to Jesus and tested him by asking him to show them a sign from heaven. He replied... 'A wicked and adulterous generation looks for a miraculous sign, but none will be given it except the sign of Jonah.'"* Matthew 16: 1-4

Just as Jonah had been in the belly of a whale for three days (Jonah 1-2), so was Jesus to be in the belly of the earth (his tomb) for three days before being resurrected to life (see Mt 12: 38-40).

What about Joan? Did she have any signs? There are three questions we'll take a look at here:

I. Did Joan of Arc believe that God sent her?
II. If so, did she have any signs to back up her claims?
III. If so, are there any parallels with her signs and what we see in the Bible?

I. Did she believe that God sent her? Yes. There can be no doubt about this. She stated so many times. Some examples:

-Said to Charles in March of 1429: *"I bring you news from God, that our Lord will give you back your kingdom, bringing you to be crowned at Reims, and driving out your enemies. In this I am God's messenger."*[3]

-Said to the people of Orleans on April 29, 1429: *"My Lord has sent me to succor this good town of Orleans."*[4]

-Said to her hostess at Bourges in October of 1429: *"I am sent to comfort the poor and the needy."*[5]

-From her Trial of Condemnation on Feb. 24, 1431: *"I come, sent by God, I have no business here* (now). *I pray you, send me back to God from whom I am come."*[6]

-Trial of Condemnation, March 3, 1431:

Religious cleric: *"Do those of your faction truly believe that you are sent from God?"*

Joan of Arc- *"I do not know if they believe it: I leave that to their hearts. But if they do not believe it, even so I am sent from God!"* [7]

II. Did she have any signs to back up her claims? Like the prophets of the Bible, she showed signs in more than just one form. Her sign of prophecy, without apparent error, is a strong witness for Joan being a true prophet of God. Her prophecies are so remarkable that they deserve a more detailed examination, which we'll do in Chapter 11. However two other signs, non-prophetic in nature, will be looked at now. First, the sign of…

Orleans

"All this was much more the work of God than of man…"
Jean, Count de Dunois (1402-1468), the 'Bastard of Orleans' [8], Trial of Nullification

Shortly after meeting Charles for the first time, Joan was sent to Poitiers to be examined by the religious authorities. When asked to show them a sign, she answered, *"In God's name, I did not come to Poitiers to give signs! But take me to Orleans, and I will show you the sign for what I am sent!"* [9] In due course, the religious authorities sent her back to the King with their endorsement. Charles subsequently put her in charge of his military forces, and she was then taken to Orleans. Once there, she did indeed show them *"the sign for what I am sent!"* In order to understand what an extraordinary sign this was we need to put it in the context of the times and situation. The French had been on the losing side of this war for decades. Consequently, their morale and confidence were low. For them, Orleans seemed to be just another 'Mission Impossible'. It was the most important city in France not under English occupation, and was in fact the key city to France's very survival. It had been under siege for seven long months before Joan's arrival, and this was taking a heavy toll on the inhabitants. Food and supplies, both military and civilian, were dwindling. There were eleven tower fortresses surrounding Orleans, and the English occupied them all. But that wasn't all. Another well trained and battle experienced English army was already on the way to help deliver the final blow. It appeared to be just a matter of time before Orleans, and therefore all of France, would soon fall to the English.

But a funny thing happened on the way to England's total conquest of France. Seventeen-year-old Jeanne d'Arc showed up. What no one had been able to do during those prior seven months, Joan did in less than one week: she raised the siege and liberated Orleans.

The Journal of the Siege gives an eyewitness account of Joan's first entrance to Orleans (before the actual battle). There were *"...burgesses and matrons of Orleans bearing great plenty of torches and making such rejoicing as if they had seen God descend in their midst...and there was a marvelous crowd pressing to touch her or the horse upon which she rode...and the burgesses of Orleans...bore her company the whole length of their town and city, manifesting great joy."*[10] For them, she was indeed God-sent. And the sign they were praying for as proof for this, was the unlikely liberation of their city. Although Joan had prophesied this, no one had dared believe it possible before she showed up.[11]

On the other hand, the English certainly did not believe that Joan was God-sent to defeat them. Still… she did defeat them. They later admitted that something supernatural might have taken place. But if so, then supernatural from the 'dark side'.[12] From the devil himself, they claimed. After all, how else could they explain being beaten by this illiterate, teenage peasant girl? Them? The masters of war? The most powerful country in the world? They didn't know that this would be only the beginning of their demise in France. They couldn't belief that she would next win battle after battle against their best, opening the way for Charles VII to go to the holy city of Reims to be anointed and crowned King of France. They couldn't imagine that in the near future, they would lose all of France for good.[13]

The day of Orleans' deliverance finally arrived on May 8, 1429. Although, when talking about the liberation of Orleans, deliverance is perhaps not the best word to describe what happened. After all, most saw the city as already lost …dead. Perhaps the more accurate word would be resurrection. Brought back from the dead. *"Thus, by the help of God and the Maid the city was delivered from the hands of the enemy."*[14] And where Orleans would lead, France would soon follow.

Truly, for those paying attention, Orleans was a sign of great wonder and power.

Now we come to Joan's second **Non-Prophetic Sign**. It is shared by all the prophet/saints of the Bible. Although not as dramatic as some signs, such as the resurrection of Jesus (John 20), or the parting of the Red Sea by Moses (Ex. 14:5-31), it is an important sign nonetheless. Without this sign, any prophet's words or deeds would rightly be called into question. Which sign? Well, let's just say that…

The Sign of a Prophet IS the Prophet
"For as Jonah became a sign to the people of Nineveh, so will the Son of Man be to this generation." Luke 11:30 ESV

How many hard-drinking, 'hell-raising', money-grubbin', lots-of-chicks, party-all-night-long prophets have you met? No matter what a 'prophet' may claim, the way they live their lives testifies to their authenticity. As the expression goes, "Your actions speak so loudly, I can hardly hear a word you're saying."

A true prophet of God will always give all credit, honor and glory to God. Not themselves. This is a common theme in the Bible. A couple of examples: *"If anyone serves, they should do so with the strength God provides, so that in all things God may be praised through Jesus Christ. To him be the glory and the power for ever and ever. Amen."* 1 Peter 4: 11 *"Thou art worthy, O Lord, to receive glory and honor and power; for thou hast created all things..."* Revelation 4: 11

Joan was obviously careful in this respect: *"All the people of Orleans agree that they never saw any signs that Joan attributed any of her achievements to her own glory. They say that she attributed all things to God, and did everything that she could to prevent the people from honoring and glorifying her, and that she liked to be alone and solitary, rather than in men's society, except when it was necessary for the conduct of the war for her to be so. All maintain too that they never saw anything in Joan deserving of reproach, but that everything about her was humility, simplicity, charity, and devotion to God and the church. And they say, furthermore, that it was a great consolation to converse with her."* Jacques l'Esbahy, Trial of Nullification[14] Another example: *"Jeanne lamented much, and was displeased when certain good women came to her, wishing to salute her; it seemed to her like adoration, at which she was angered."* Simon Baucroix, Squire, Trial of Nullification.

The False Prophets of History
"Hence today I believe that I am acting in accordance with the will of the Almighty Creator: by defending myself against the Jews, I am fighting for the work of the Lord."
Adolf Hitler, Mein Kamp [16], Houghton Mifflin, New York: Hutchinson Publ. Ltd., London, 1969, p. 60

History is littered with false prophets, both large and small. Let's go back for a moment to Jim Jones and David Koresh. Both were charismatic and spoke persuasively and with passion. They often quoted, and/or misquoted, the Bible. That is, they carefully manipulated the Scriptures to say what they wanted. Simply by changing a word, phrase, or context here and there, they twisted Scripture to their needs. They claimed to be sent by God. They both went so far as to say that they were the second coming of Jesus (see Mt. 24: 23-26). However their lives testified to a Jesus not found anywhere in the Bible. Distorting Scripture, sexual abuses, alcohol and drug abuse, isolating people from family and friends to better control them, the use of fear for their own selfish motivations... None of this is consistent with the Biblical prophets.

All true prophets of God seem to have some personality traits in common. They are straightforward, even bold in speech. They are not manipulative. There is a goodness of heart. They are simple, humble, and perhaps even a little naïve in our eyes. They have courage, and in their presence there is a feeling of holiness. And, of course, there is a deep trust in God and a desire to do His will. Moses is a good example (see Exodus-Deuteronomy). His dealings with Pharaoh and later his own people reflect this straightforwardness, honesty, goodness of heart, simplicity, lack of manipulation or politic playing and yes, a certain purity. A holiness shines through all his story in the Bible.

To be in the presence of a true prophet would probably make most of us ill at ease, reminding us of our own shortcomings and dishonesties inside. However, we need to be clear here. Prophets are not perfect. Like all of us, they carry their own imperfections and sometimes deep flaws. Yet, there is a certain purity seen in a true prophet's life. Even with his faults and mistakes, his trust in God is deep and faithful to the end. The life of such a prophet cannot be faked for any length of time.

In the New Testament, Jesus shows us what a perfect prophet looks like. One without flaws. After all, He was more than a prophet. He was the son of God. His life was a sign of God on many levels. It reflected a goodness, a holiness, and a purity throughout. Politics was not his game or goal. His speech was bold but compassionate. His words went straight to the heart. Speaking with some of the Jews, Jesus asked them, *"Can any of you prove me guilty of sin?"* John 8: 46 To this challenge, they had no response.

Does Joan's life correspond with this idea of purity? Yes, Joan too displayed a purity that can't be faked. Her life itself was a sign of God's presence. From the time she was thirteen, she gave her virginity to God during the first visit of an angel.[17]

Her messengers often told her to 'speak boldly'. And this she did, whether speaking to her King, her subordinates, her friends, or while on trial for her life. We see no hint of her ever trying to manipulate others. She didn't play politics. She must have made some powerful people feel very uncomfortable. Most people in power are not used to being dealt with in such a direct manner. And finally, her dedication and love for God were seen in all she said and did. *"I firmly believe she was sent from God on account of her good works, and her many virtues."* Father Jean Pasquerel, Trial of Nullification[18]

During the 1456 Trial of Nullification, her childhood friends often spoke of her goodness of heart. Humble and simple, she freely admitted her weaknesses. She saw the irony of such a simple person as herself, suddenly thrust to the forefront of history: *"It pleased God thus to act through a simple maid in order to turn back the King's enemies."*[19]

In Scripture, we see this theme frequently. James tells us that, *"God opposes the proud but gives grace to the humble."* James 4:6

Jesus Himself came from a poor family of Nazareth. He said, *"Everyone who exalts himself will be humbled, and he who humbles himself will be exalted."* Luke 18: 24

Paul explains it this way: *"....God chose the foolish things of the world to shame the wise; God chose the weak things of the world to shame the strong. He chose the lowly things of the world and the despised things---and things that are not---to nullify the things that are, so that no one may boast before him... For the foolishness of God is wiser than man's wisdom, and the weakness of God is stronger than man's strength."* 1Corinthians1: 25, 27-29

III. Are there any similarities with Joan's signs and what we see in the Bible? Let's take a look at some interesting parallels between Joan of Arc and Jesus. We'll see examples of both prophetic and non-prophetic signs. We'll begin with Joan's dramatic entrance into Orleans on April 29, 1429, contrasted with that of Jesus' triumphant entrance into Jerusalem on that first Palm Sunday…

    1. A few days before the battle of Orleans began in earnest, Joan rode slowly into town. The people gathered around, welcoming her with great acclamation and praise. *"...and so she entered Orleans…men-at-arms came to receive her, along with the bourgeois of Orleans, carrying many torches and making such joy as if they had seen God Himself descend among them…they felt already comforted, as though freed of the*

siege by the divine virtue that they were told resided in that simple Maid, whom they regarded with strong affection, men as much as women and little children. And there was a marvelous crowd pressing to touch her or the horse on which she rode..." [20]

A few days before His 'battle' (i.e. trial, torture and crucifixion) began in earnest, Jesus rode slowly into the town of Jerusalem. The people thronged around Him, welcoming Him with great acclamation and praise. *"A very large crowd spread their cloaks on the road, while others cut branches from the trees and spread them on the road. The crowds that went ahead of him and those that followed shouted, 'Hosanna to the Son of David!* [21] *Blessed is he who comes in the name of the Lord! Hosanna in the highest!'"* Mt. 21: 8-9

2. She was accompanied by those closest to her at that time, the leaders of the French army. They had been with her from the beginning of this strange and wonderful march to France's freedom from the English. *"And so she entered Orleans, with the Bastard of Orleans at her left, very richly armed and mounted; afterward came other noble and valiant lords, squires, captains, and men-at-arms..."* [22]

He was accompanied by those closest to Him at that time, *"The whole crowd of disciples."* Luke 19: 37. They had been with Him from the beginning of this strange and wonderful march to mankind's freedom from the bondage of sin.

3. Seeing all she had said and done, most of those accompanying her had become convinced that she was a prophet of God.

Seeing all He had said and done, most of those accompanying Him had become convinced that He was more than a prophet of God. They now believed He was the long-awaited Messiah, God's only Son. (see Mark 8: 27-30)

4. The long English siege of Orleans seemed to have no end. Then out of small town anonymity, Joan of Arc showed up.

Satan's long siege of mankind, i.e. man's bondage to sin and death, seemed to have no end. Then out of small town anonymity, Jesus showed up.

5. Many of the people of Orleans considered Joan to be God's servant sent to save them. France and England had been engaged in war nearly 100 years (the Hundred Years War began in 1336). *"I was in town when Jeanne reached it. She was received with as much rejoicing and acclamation from old and young, of both sexes, as if she had been an*

Angel of God; because we hoped through her to be delivered from our enemies. Which indeed was done later...I believed, like all in the town that, had the Maid not come in God's Name to our help, we should soon have been both town and people, in the hands of the enemy; we did not believe it possible for the army then in the town to resist the power of the enemy who were in such force against us." Jean Luillier, burgher of Orleans, Trial of Nullification

Many of the people of Jerusalem believed that Jesus was the Messiah, God's servant sent to save them. They had been waiting for the Messiah's appearance for hundreds of years. *"When he came near the place where the road goes down the Mount of Olives, the whole crowd of disciples began joyfully to praise God... 'Blessed is the King who comes in the name of the Lord! Peace in heaven and glory in the highest!'"* Luke 19: 37-38

6. Joan knew that God's victory over the English was now close at hand. Once inside the city's wall, she immediately went to God's house, the Cathedral of Orleans. *"When Jeanne first entered Orleans, she went, before all else, to the great Church, to do reverence to God, her Creator."* Jacques l'Esbahy, Trial of Nullification

Jesus knew that God's victory over Satan was now close at hand (see Luke 9: 20-22). Once inside the city walls, he immediately went to God's house, the temple. *"...Jesus entered Jerusalem and went to the temple."* Mark11: 11[23]

7. This dramatic entrance into Orleans was a momentous occasion in her earthly life. God's directed servant, Jeanne d'Arc, was bringing the promise of deliverance and freedom from the English to the people or Orleans. Just nine days later, Sunday May 8, 1429[24], this promise would be realized in full, and provide THE turning point in the Hundred Years War (not to mention the history of France): the 'resurrection' of Orleans. This unlikely liberation of Orleans would rally the people throughout the land. It could be said that for the first time in their history, a true feeling of hope began to spread among the people and unite them in a common cause. In a sense, it was the birth of a united France.

This dramatic entrance into Jerusalem was a momentous occasion in His earthly life. God's directed Son, Messiah Jesus, was bringing the promise of deliverance and freedom from sin and death to all those who would turn to Him. Just seven days later (the first Easter Sunday), this promise would be realized in full, and provide THE turning point in human history: the resurrection of Jesus Christ. This unlikely liberation of mankind would rally the people throughout all time and nations. It could be said that for the first time in mankind's history, a true feeling of hope, through God's only Son, began to spread among the people, and unite them in a common cause. In a sense, it was the birth of the church to come.

8. She had prophesized several times this unlikely end of the siege of Orleans. *"First, she said that the English would be defeated and that the siege which was laid to the town of Orleans would be raised and that the town of Orleans would be liberated of the English...all that I have seen accomplished... I believe that Joan was sent by God..."* Br. Seguin Seguin-Trial of Rehabilitation[25]

He had prophesized several times this unlikely end of man's siege of sin and death. *"I tell you the truth, whoever hears my word and believes him who sent me has eternal life and will not be condemned; he has crossed over from death to life."* John 5: 24

9. She also prophesied that she would not last long. *"I shall last a year, and but little longer. We must think to do good work in that year..."* Said to King Charles in March of 1429. On May 23, 1430, she was captured and taken prisoner at Compiegne.[26]

He had also prophesied that He would not last long. *"Now Jesus was going up to Jerusalem. On the way, he took the twelve aside and said to them, 'We are going up to Jerusalem, and the Son of Man will be delivered over to the chief priests and the teachers of the law. They will condemn him to death and will hand him over to the Gentiles to be mocked and flogged and crucified. On the third day he will be raised to life.'"* Mt. 20: 17-19

10. She feared betrayal from those closest to her. *"I fear nothing but treachery."*[27] Indeed, she would soon find herself abandoned by the King himself. Once the King was anointed and crowned at Reims, he would have no further use of her. And once captured, church authorities for their own reasons of power, ambition, and politics would condemn her illegally.

He said that one from within his closest circle would betray Him. *"...Jesus was troubled in spirit and testified, 'I tell you the truth, one of you is going to betray me.'"* John 13: 21 Indeed, He would soon find himself abandoned by all His disciples (see Mt.26: 56). And once captured, religious authorities for their own reasons of power, ambition, and politics would condemn Him illegally.

11. Her entrance into Orleans, along with the events following it, provided strong signs of God's presence, power and blessings, both then and for centuries to come.

His entrance into Jerusalem, along with the events following it, provided strong signs of God's presence, power and blessings, both then and for centuries to come.

12. Although this wonderful entrance into Orleans would be a highpoint in her life, it would not be long before she would be betrayed, tried, and put to death (about one year late). She would die young (at age 19).

Although this wonderful entrance into Jerusalem would be a highpoint in His earthly life, it would not be long before He would be betrayed, tried and put to death (one week later). He would die young (at age 31-33).

13. But her death would have ramifications far beyond the worst fears of her enemies. (See below.)

But His death would have ramifications far beyond the worst fears of His enemies. (See below.)

14. Her name would be remembered forever.
His name would be remembered forever.

15. The rebirth of France itself would spring from her sacrifice.
The rebirth of Mankind itself would spring from His sacrifice.

The similarities are hard to miss:
-There was a triumphant entry into the nation's key city, full of acclamation and praise.
-With their entrance, they were both hitting a climatic point in their own lives, as well as those of uncounted others.
-Right after their entrance into the city, they both went to God's sanctuary, to praise God and give Him thanks.
-Both Jesus and Joan were acknowledged by many as God's servants, and also as a prophet sent to save them.
-Both knew their time on earth was very limited, and said so.
-Both were initiating a turning point of huge proportions. In Joan's case, the rebirth of France itself. In Jesus' case, the beginning of

His final week on earth, leading to the turning point of all history: the resurrection of Jesus the Messiah.

-Both had issued several prophecies about these events, and all of them would be fulfilled.

-Shortly after their entrance to the city, they would both end up in an illegal and partisan court run by their respective 'religious leaders'.

-They would both be condemned and immediately executed.

-Many would recognize the signs of God's presence, power and blessing in all these events.

-The ramifications of their deaths were, both at that time and today, earth-shattering. **In Joan's case**, her 1429 appearance on the world stage was the turning point of the Hundred Years War. France would rally around her sacrifice and a new united French nation would be born. Although the war would continue for several years, the English would never regain the initiative. They would lose their kingdom in France, never to claim it again. France would become a powerful nation, active in world events. For more than 300 years it would be a powerful advocate and light for Christianity.[28] Today, although still a powerful country, it's limelight on the world stage appears to be fading.[29] From a Christian point of view, the long-term results of the destructive French Revolution continue to become more evident. France has become more secular, and many of the French have turned away from the God of the Bible.[30] Meanwhile, Islam is rapidly filling this spiritual void. Will France become just another Muslim country?[31] Or perhaps God will call a new French leader to rise up and defend His name and legacy. After all, He did this once before in 732A.D. when Charles Martel stopped the Muslim invasion at Poitiers, and so saved Christian European civilization. Let us pray that France will yet turn back to Him before it is too late. Time will tell. In any case, we could speculate that perhaps France has already played one of its most important roles in world history hundreds of years ago, when a humble, obedient, seventeen-year-old was called by God to save France, and did what God asked her to do. Historians are in agreement that without Joan of Arc's timely appearance, Orleans would have fallen. With this key city under English control, there would have been nothing left to prevent the fall of the rest of France to England. But with France thus saved, the survival of another powerful country not yet even born was assured. Did God have plans for America? Without France's help during the American Revolutionary War (1775-1783), many historians believe that America would have lost its war for independence from England.[32] And without America, the course of World War II would have most likely tilted towards a German/Japanese victory. Indeed, without the existence of

America, what other changes in the world would we see today? Yes, this is all only speculation. And speculation is problematic, although arguably worthwhile. But we can safely say that without Joan of Arc the world would have been a very different place from the one we know today.[33]

In Jesus' case, God's people would rally around His sacrifice, and the Christian church would be born. Although this cosmic battle continues to rage on, Satan will eventually lose his kingdom on earth, never to claim it again (see Revelation 20: 10). Through His Son Jesus, God has thus provided us a way out of this world of sin, pain, and death. In short, the importance of His appearance cannot be overstated. The world has never been the same since His coming, nor will it ever be again. He has made all things new! *"He who was seated on the throne said, 'I am making everything new!'"* Revelation 21: 5

"Therefore, if anyone is in Christ, he is a new creation; the old has gone, the new has come!" 2 Corinthians 5: 17

"Sign, sign, everywhere a sign..."
Les Emmerson, Five Man Electrical Band, 1970

You and I may not be talking directly with angels. And maybe God has not given us a sign of such world changing proportions, as He did with Joan of Arc. Still, we are all made in the image of God (Genesis 1: 26- 27), and we all have our own unique talents and calling. Whether we know it or not, we all have a sign, or signs, that reflect God's presence within us to others. Even small signs are most worthy in God's eyes, and can be very powerful, as Sainte Therese of Lisieux discovered.

Sainte Therese was a young French girl who, like Joan of Arc, died at a very young age. She was a great admirer of Joan. She wrote, directed and starred in her own play about her entitled <u>Saint Joan of Arc</u>. *"Therese died when she was twenty-four (1873-1897), after having lived as a cloistered Carmelite for less than ten years. She never went on missions, never founded a religious order, and never performed great works. The only book of hers, published after her death, was a brief edited version of her journal called <u>Story of a Soul</u>...But within 28 years of her death, the public demand was so great that she was canonized. Generations of Catholics have called her the 'Little Flower.'"*[34] She is now known throughout the world for her 'little way'. And all this without ever leaving her small monastery. She understood that it wasn't necessary to accomplish heroic deeds or perform great actions to be a person of holiness and express her love of God. She writes:

"Love is proven through actions. So how can I show great love when great actions are not permitted for me to do? The only way is to pluck the petals from flowers, one by one. These petals represent every small sacrifice, each look, each word...and doing all these smallest of actions with love."[35]

"Jesus doesn't ask great actions from us, but rather that we give ourselves to Him with gratefulness."[36]

"You can see that I am only a very small soul and that I can offer God only very little things."[37]

"I rejoice in being so small."[38]

Following *'her little way'*, her *'very little things'* led all the way to her canonization on May 17, 1925 by Pope Pie XI.

"Be faithful in small things because it is in them that your strength lies." Mother Teresa (1910-1997)

Wrap Up

We've now come full circle in this chapter, and are back to the original question: "Like, Dude (and/or 'Dudess'), what's your sign?"

No, not your astrological sign. But your <u>sign</u>! The sign of God's presence in you. Can people see this sign in you? Could it be...

-Spreading the word about God and His Son?
-A life of prayer?
-Your love for others?
-Praising God through all your daily activities?
-An interior life transformed by God, shining through from the inside-out?
-Fill in the blank: _____

If you don't know what your sign is yet, then a prayerful search may be rewarding to both you and those around you. For many, a daily time of prayer and Bible reading helps to enter into the presence of the Living God. And it is only there that we find *"the peace of God which transcends all understanding..."* Philippians 4:7

---

[1]The classical Biblical example of a witch and witchcraft is found in the 'Witch of Endor': 1Samuel 28: 7-25
[2]For example: Acts 3: 1-10; Acts 4: 30-31; Acts 8: 5-8; Acts 9: 32-35.
[3]Régine Pernoud, <u>Jeanne d'Arc par elle-même et ses témoins,</u> Editions du Seuil, Paris, 1996, p. 57

[4]Joan of Arc translated by Willard Trask, Joan of Arc: In Her Own Words, Turtle Point Press, New York, 1965, p. 34
[5]Ibid, p. 73
[6]Régine Pernoud, Jeanne d'Arc par elle-même et ses témoins, Editons du Seuil, Paris, 1996, p. 215
[7]Joan of Arc translated by Willard Trask, Joan of Arc: In Her Own Words, Turtle Point Press, New York, 1965, p. 108
[8]In his era, 'Bastard of Orleans' was a term of respect since it acknowledged him as a first cousin to the king and acting head of a branch of the royal family. He was entrusted with the care of the town of Orleans and was Lieutenant-General of the King in affairs of war. He was also one of Joan of Arc's trusted friends, and helped her relieve the siege of Orléans. He also joined her on the military campaigns of 1429, and took part in the coronation of Charles VII. In 1436 he aided in the capture of Paris. http://www.stjoan-center.com/Trials/null06.html
[9]Régine Pernoud, Jeanne d'Arc par elle-même et ses témoins, Editions du Seuil, Paris, 1996, p. 60
[10]From the *Journal of the Siege*; Régine Pernoud, Joan of Arc By Herself and Her Witnesses, Scarborough House, Lanham, MD, 1982, p. 82-84
[11] *"When Jeanne was come into the City, she exhorted us all to hope in God; saying that, if we had good hope and trust in God, we should escape from our enemies...I believed, like all in the town, that, had the Maid not come in God's Name to our help, we should soon have been, both town and people, in the hands of the enemy: we did not believe it possible for the army then in the town to resist the power of the enemy who were in such force against us."* Jean Luillier, Burgher of Orleans, Trial of Nullification
[12]Here are two examples: a) *"As Joan had done wonders in the war, and as the English are commonly superstitious, they reckoned that there was something supernatural about her. That, in my opinion, is why in all their counsels and in other places they desired her death."* Thomas Marie, a Benedictine Monk, Trial of Nullification - Régine Pernoud, The Retrial of Joan of Arc, Ignatius Press, San Francisco, 2007, p. 199; b) *"If she had not been harmful to the English she would never have been treated and condemned as she was. But they were more afraid of her than of a large army...I heard an English knight say that the English feared her more than a hundred men at arms. They said that she used spells and feared her on account of the victories she had won..."* Pierre Miget, a former Assessor, Trial of Nullification - Régine Pernoud, The Retrial of Joan of Arc, Ignatius Press, San Francisco, 2007, p. 200
[13]As Winston Churchill wrote: *"Upon her invocation the spirit of victory changed sides, and the French began an offensive which never rested till the English invaders were driven out of France."* Winston Churchill, HISTORY OF THE ENGLISH SPEAKING PEOPLES, Book Three, Chapter Twenty-Six
[14]Jean d'Aulon, Trial of Nullification, 1456
[15] Régine Pernoud, The Retrial of Joan of Arc, Ignatius Press, San Francisco, 2007, p. 149
[16] Adolf Hitler, Mein Kamp, Houghton Mifflin, New York: Hutchinson Publ. Ltd., London, 1969, p. 60
[17]Willard Trask, Joan of Arc: In Her Own Words, Turtle Point Press, New York, 1996, p. 6
[18]This was no off the cuff remark. Fr. Pasquerel was Joan's chaplain, spiritual adviser, confessor and secretary. According to his own testimony, he was instructed to follow her everywhere. He was able to observe her actions and words in all areas of her life, and knew her heart as well as, if not better than, anyone else. He was present at many of her meetings with royalty, the military, and interactions with the common people. He was at all the battles in which she participated, and when wounded, she called for him. He heard

her confession nearly every day. Toward the end of her life she made him promise to stay with her always as her confessor, which he faithfully did up to the time of her capture by the English.

[19] From the Trial of Condemnation; Régine Pernoud, Jeanne d'Arc par elle-meme et ses témoins, Editions du Seuil, Paris, 1996, p. 225

[20] From the city journal of Orleans, Journal of the Siege, as quoted from: Régine Pernoud et Marie-Véronique Clin, Jeanne d'Arc, Editions Fayard, Mesnil-sur-l'Estrée, 2001, p. 40-41

[21] *"Hosanna"* is an exclamation of praise. It means, *"the Savior comes!"* They were right. And they came to welcome Him, and give thanks for His long awaited arrival.

[22] Régine Pernoud et Marie-Véronique Clin, Jeanne d'Arc, Editions Fayard, Mesnil-sur-l'Estrée, 2001, p. 40-41

[23] His humble entrance was itself a great sign to the people, one that had been prophesied 600 years earlier by the prophet Zechariah: *"Rejoice greatly, O daughter of Zion! Shout Daughter of Jerusalem! See, your king comes to you, righteous and having salvation, gentle and riding on a donkey..."* Zechariah 9: 9

[24] May 8 was an Ecclesiastical Sunday called *Exaudi*. *Exaudi* means "LISTEN". According to all reports that have come down to us, this day the people were listening. What did they hear? A great celebration! Shouts of joy, laughter and church bells ringing throughout the city announced this great victory of God, led by their earthly "savior", Joan of Arc.- Régine Pernoud et Marie-Véronique Clin, Jeanne d'Arc, Editions Fayard, Mesnil-sur-l'Estrée, 2001, p. 49

[25] Régine Pernoud et Marie-Véronique Clin, Jeanne d'Arc, Editions Fayard, Mesnil-sur-l'Estrée, 2001, p. 50; See Chapter 11

[26] Willard Trask, Joan of Arc-Self Portrait, The Telegraph Press, New York, New York, 1936, p. 50; See Chapter 11

[27] Said to Gerardin d'Epinal of Domremy, at Chalons, July 14-15, 1429; Willard Trask, Joan of Arc-Self Portrait, The Telegraph Press, New York, New York, 1936, p 80

[28] *"During the Ancien Régime* (roughly from the 15th to the 18th century under the late Valois and Bourbon dynasties), *France had traditionally been considered the Church's eldest daughter, and the King of France always maintained close links to the Pope."* http://en.wikipedia.org/wiki/Religion_in_France, January 2012

[29] France remains the largest country in Western Europe, has the fifth largest population (63 million), is the number one tourist destination in the world, and possesses the world's fifth largest economy (measured by GDP). However it has grown more slowly than any other developed country in the world. In 2006, its 2% growth was the worst in Europe. It also has one of the highest unemployment rates - 9.8% - of any European country. http://news.bbc.co.uk/2/hi/africa/6547841.stm; http://www.bonjourlafrance.com/france-facts.htm, accessed January 16, 2012 *"The welfare system and the state are heading toward bankruptcy, and all they can promise is still more public and social spending...European statistics reveal a decline in the French standard of living that dropped from 3rd to 12th place among EU countries in just ten years...The last balanced budget was in 1973... The French state has had a deficit for more than 30 years...and has the largest deficit of all EU members: over 4.1 percent of GNP."* http://www.ideasinactiontv.com/tcs_daily/2004/04/old-europe-looking-older.html, accessed Jan. 2012

[30] *"Of the developed nations, people in the United States were most sure of the existence of God or a higher power (2% atheist, 4% agnostic), while France had the most skeptics (19% atheist, 16% agnostic).* http://en.wikipedia.org/wiki/Demographics_of_atheism, January 2012 *Religious observance* (in France) *nowadays is generally low...A poll published early 2010, presented following figures. Whilst, in 1965, 81% of the French declared themselves as*

Catholics, they were no more than 64% in 2009, the reduction in active Catholics was even more profound whilst 27% of the French went to Mass once a week or more in 1952, there are no more than 4.5% in 2006...A 2006 poll published by Le Monde and Le Monde des Religions in January 2007 found that 51% of the French population describe themselves as Catholics (and only half of those said they believed in God), 31% as atheists, between 4% as Muslims, 3% as Protestants and 1% as Jews."
http://en.wikipedia.org/wiki/Religion_in_France, January 2012

[31] The French Muslim population is now estimated to be the largest in Western Europe, and growing steadily. The number of mosques in 1985 was 913, and in 2006 was 2,147. http://news.bbc.co.uk/2/hi/africa/6547841.stm; http://www.bonjourlafrance.com/france-facts.htm; http://gayandright.blogspot.com/2008/03/growth-of-islam-in-france.html- accessed in January 2012. *"Migration trends are to intensify over the coming thirty years...There will be an overall mingling of cultures and civilizations that may lead, as far as France is concerned, to the emergence of a predominantly African population and to rapid Islamization."* Interview with Jean-Claude Chesnais, Valeurs Actuelles, Oct. 6, 1996. Mr. Chesnais is one of France's leading demographers at the National Institute for the Study of Demographics (Ined). Similar anxieties are voiced by many others, including Jean-Claude Barreau, a former government official in charge of immigration and the author of several books on Islam and the Middle East.

[32] a) *"There is no doubt that America would not have won the Revolutionary War without France's financial and military aid..."* A quote from a PBS special entitled BENJAMIN FRANKLIN, which premiered November 19 and 20, 2002. See http://www.pbs.org/benfranklin/l3_world_france.html; Twin Cities Public Television, Inc., accessed January 2012

b) *"French support of the American colonists was, of course, a significant factor in how the American Revolution turned out. Without French support, it's unlikely the Americans could've sustained a long war effort against the British Empire. Trapping Cornwallis at Yorktown certainly would not have happened, were it not for the French...Once the French recognized the United States and entered the war, the American Revolution became a world war for the British."* http://americanrevolutionblog.blogspot.com/2009/03/why-did-british-lose-american.html, accessed January 2012; also see http://www.americanrevolution.org/frconfiles/fr1.html

[33] See also Chapter 13-Joan's France?
[34] www.catholic.org, June 2010
[35] www.wikipedia.org, accessed August, 2008
[36] James Grundl, This Child, Carmel of Port Tobacco, La Plata, 2004, p. 12
[37] Ibid, p. 22
[38] www.wikipedia.org, accessed August, 2008

Chapter 3
The Call to Serve

"The call of God is not just for a select few but for everyone. Whether I hear God's call or not depends on the condition of my ears, and exactly what I hear depends upon my spiritual attitudes."
Oswald Chambers [1]

Ring-g-g...ring-g-g-...ring-g-g...

Bill: *"Hell-o."*

Nancy: *"Hi Bill, this is Nancy. Hey, did you get my message from last night?"*

Bill: *"Message?"*

Nancy: *"Yeah, this guy called looking for you."*

Bill: *"Guy? What guy?"*

Nancy: *"Not sure. He had a really deep voice. Let's see, he said his name was...uh... Grog?...er...Fog...Dod... er...maybe it was...God?...well, something like that."*

Bill: *"God?!! Nah-h-h. That just couldn't be. I got a cell phone with me all the time."*

Nancy: *"Well, have you been trying to reach Him?"*

Bill: *"Yeah, kind of. I've been praying to Him for a long time now, but...called by God? Nah, I don't think so. That just couldn't be. Those kinds of things don't really happen... Do they??"*

  I have heard some Joan admirers say that she must have been inspired by some kind of cosmic 'force'....or perhaps her own 'higher consciousness'. Maybe some kind of a 'universal connection'? In any case, they feel quite sure that it wasn't God who called her. At least not the God of the Bible. Of course, many of them don't believe in God in the first place. At least not as He is described in the Bible. Joan, on the other hand, always claimed that it was only through His power that she was able to do all she did. She believed this deeply and proclaimed it steadfastly up to the day of her death. And as we'll see, there is much evidence to support such a claim. Those who choose to reject her explanations must have their reasons. Nonetheless, it is curious. Although claiming to be great admirers of Joan, her own beliefs and statements made under oath seem to carry little weight with them.

Although Joan didn't receive a phone call from God, she did say that she was called by Him: *"When I was thirteen, I had a voice from God…"*.[2] Now we are all 'called' in our daily lives to be His followers.[3] But in this chapter, when I speak of being 'called', I mean called to a specific mission. Like Joan of Arc.

Any Questions about the Call of God?

Well, actually I have quite a few, including the following:

-How is someone 'called' by God?
-How does God manifest Himself to someone He has chosen?
-How would we react if suddenly, out of the blue, we came into direct contact with an angel/messenger from God?
-Having only earthly terms, vocabulary and experiences, would we be able to explain such a supernatural encounter accurately?
-And why does He choose whom He does?

Let's take a look in the Bible at God's calling of some of His servants:

1) God called Abraham, told him to pack up everything, *"…and go to the land I will show you. I will make you into a great nation and I will bless you; I will make your name great and all peoples on the earth will be blessed through you."* Gen. 12:1-3 God tells him, *"Do not be afraid."* Gen. 15: 1 He says that He will be with him. Abraham did what was asked of him. It is from Abraham that the Hebrews will become the Jewish people of Israel, and the spiritual light for the entire world. They will point the way to the only true God. First through their Scriptures (the Bible), and then through the Messiah Himself. And it is the Messiah (Jesus Christ) that will provide, for those willing to accept Him, the way to salvation.

2) Moses saw a bright light *"in the flames of fire from within a bush…God called to him from within the bush, 'Moses! Moses! And*

Moses said, 'Here I am'" Exodus 3: 2, 4 God tells him that he is sending him to deliver a message to mighty Pharaoh of Egypt. The message? To let the Hebrews go (they were slaves at that time), so that they may go worship Him. This seemed to be an impossible task. But God assures him, *"I will be with you."* Ex 3: 12 In spite of his fears, Moses does as God requests. After Moses' death, Joshua is then chosen to continue on with God's plan. God tells Joshua, *"As I was with Moses, so I will be with you; I will never leave you nor forsake you.*" Joshua 1: 5

As we see with Abraham, Moses and Joshua, God's plans are compassionate and intricately involved in the destiny of both individuals and nations (see Chapter 10). We see both of these aspects in the story of Joan of Arc.

3) The prophet Ezekiel had a vision. He looked up and saw *"...a windstorm coming with flashing lightning and surrounded by brilliant light. The center of the fire looked like glowing metal... and high above on the throne was a figure like that of a man. I saw that from what appeared to be his waist up he looked like a glowing metal, as if full of fire, and that from there down he looked like fire; and brilliant light surrounded him. Like the appearance of a rainbow in the clouds on a rainy day, so was the radiance around him. This was the appearance of the likeness of the glory of the LORD. When I saw it, I fell facedown, and I heard the voice of one speaking... Do not be afraid."* Ezekiel 1: 4-5, 25-28; 2: 6

4) The great prophet Daniel also had visions. He tells us, *"...as I was standing on the bank of the Tigris, I looked up and there before me was a man dressed in linen, with a belt of the finest gold around his waist. His body was like chrysolite, his face like lightning, his eyes like flaming torches, his arms and legs like the gleam of burnished bronze, and his voice like the sound of a multitude...a hand touched me and set me to trembling on my hands and knees. He said, '...Do not be afraid, Daniel...I have come to explain to you what will happen to your people in the future'...while he was saying this to me, I bowed with my face toward the ground and was speechless."* Daniel 10

5) The New Testament also gives some interesting accounts: *"And there were shepherds living out in the fields nearby, keeping watch over their flocks at night, when an angel of the Lord appeared to them. The glory of the LORD shone around them, and they were terrified. But the angel said to them, 'Do not be afraid...'"* Luke 2: 8-10

6) Paul was on his way to persecute the new fledgling Christian church, when *"suddenly a light from heaven flashed around him."* Acts 9: 3 He heard the voice of Jesus asking him why he was persecuting Him, and then telling him to *"...go in to the city, and you will be told what you*

must do." Acts 9: 4-6 From the zealous Christian persecutor, Paul would become the great world evangelist.

7) While John the apostle was a prisoner on the island of Patmos, Jesus sent an angel to him (Rev. 1: 1). John heard a voice, and *"...turned around to see the voice that was speaking to me...I saw seven golden lampstands, and among the lampstands was someone 'like a son of Man', dressed in a robe reaching down to his feet and with a golden sash around his chest. His head and hair were white like wool, as white as snow, and his eyes were like blazing fire. His feet were like bronze glowing in a furnace, and his voice was like the sound of rushing waters. In his right hand he held seven stars, and out of his mouth came a sharp double-edged sword. His face was like the sun shining in all its brilliance. When I saw him, I fell at his feet as though dead. Then he placed his right hand on me and said: 'Do not be afraid. I am the First and the Last. I am the Living one...Write, therefore, what you have seen...'"* Revelation 1 12-17, 19

If Joan was being used as an agent of the God of the Bible, then we would expect to see some similarities between her and those listed above. Fortunately, we have her own words on this. Notaries during her first trial took down her sworn testimony verbatim. Here are some excerpts:

"When I was thirteen, I had a voice from God to help me govern my conduct. And the first time, I was very fearful. And came this voice, about the hour of noon, in the summer-time, in my father's garden; I had not fasted on the eve preceding that day. I heard the voice on the right-hand side towards the church; and rarely do I hear it without a great light...He told me that I, Jeanne, should come into France...He taught me to behave rightly and to go often to church...I saw him afterwards several times before knowing that it was Saint Michael. I knew it by his speech and by the language of the Angels, and I believe firmly that they were Angels...before all things he told me to be a good child and that God would help me...He told me that Saint Catherine and Saint Margaret would come to me, and that I should act by their advice, that they were bidden to lead me in what I had to do and that I should believe in what they would say to me and that it was by God's order." [4]

"He (St Michael) *was not alone, but duly attended by heavenly angels...I saw them with the eyes of my body as well as I see you. And when they left me I wept, and I wished that they might have taken me with them...And I kissed the ground where they had stood, to do them reverence."* [5]

"...The name by which they often called me was 'Joan the Maid, Daughter of God'...They told me that my King would be restored to his

Kingdom despite his enemies. They promised to lead me to Paradise, for that was what I asked of them…And when I have made my prayer to God, I hear a voice that says to me: 'Daughter of God, go, go, go! I shall be with you to help you. Go!' and when I hear that voice I feel a great joy. Indeed, I would that I might ever be in that state." [6]

As you see, the Biblical accounts and Joan's testimony have many things in common, including:

1. The visions are often accompanied by great light.
2. Hearing the voice of God is an unnerving experience for all.
3. God, or His messenger, often tells the person to not be afraid.
4. In general, God doesn't give the details; only what the mission is, and that they should go.
5. When the Lord calls, there's no doubt it's Him.
6. All are obedient to God's call. Turning down the Boss seems to hold little promise.
7. When God chooses someone, He doesn't target just the person chosen. Rather, it's always for some common interest. A 'call' only acquires its full meaning when seen in the context of the universal design of the Creator.
8. Those called become themselves a 'Living Call' to others.
9. God says that He will be with them.

This last one is key. When God calls someone to a specific mission, He does not send them out alone. He is with them. In fact, one of the great themes running all through the Bible is God's promise to be with us. Here are a couple of examples:

"Fear not for I have redeemed you. I have summoned you by name; you are mine… When you walk through the fire, you will not be burned; the flames will not set you ablaze. For I am the Lord, your God, the Holy One of Israel, Your Savior…Do not be afraid, for I am with you." Isaiah 43: 1-3

Jesus says, *"All authority in heaven and on earth has been given to me…and surely I am with you always, to the very end of the age."* Matt. 28: 18-20

One other important thing to mention here is that throughout Scripture we are told that God is FAITHFUL. He keeps His promises, and we can count on Him (e.g. compare Gen. 12: 2-3 with the history of the Jews). When He says He will be with us, He will be with us.

These days, we often hear how God is a God of love. Occasionally we might also hear how He is a God of justice. While both are true, we should not forget this other quality held in high esteem by God's chosen people: His faithfulness. Here are some examples:

"Know therefore that the Lord your God is God; he is the faithful God, keeping his covenant of love to a thousand generations of those who love him and keep his commands." Deut. 7: 9

"For the word of the Lord is rich and true; He is faithful in all he does. The Lord loves righteousness and justice; the earth if full of his unfailing love." Psalm 33: 4-5

"If we are faithless, He will remain faithful, for He cannot disown himself." 2 Tim. 2: 13

So, why does God call who He does? Well, God alone knows.[7] However we can see some similarities among the called. Although they are quite different from each other, they all share some similar characteristics. Such as…

-A strong will.
-No pretensions.
-Usually living a simple life.
-An active prayer life.
-The desire to do God's will.
-Obedience.
-The sure belief that evil exists.
-The belief in an after-life and that God will judge all people.
-They all knew and loved God.
-They chose to believe in God's word and promises, and then acted on that belief. As Joan said during her Trial of Condemnation, *"I had the will to believe."*[8] Does she share any other of these characteristics? Yes, every one.

How many of these characteristics do you have? Personally, I know that I need work on many of them! Surely this list is one we can learn from and aim for.

"The place God calls you to is the place where your deep gladness and the world's deep hunger meet." Frederick Buechner[9]

[1]Oswald Chambers (1874-1917), My Utmost for His Highest: Traditional Updated Edition, Discovery House Publishers, Grand Rapids, MI, 1992
[2]Trial of Condemnation, Feb. 22, 1431
[3]Here is one of many examples: Jesus said, *"Come, follow me…"* Matthew 4: 19; see also 1 Corinthians 1: 9
[4]Régine Pernoud (translated from the French by Edward Hyams), Joan of Arc, By

Herself and Her Witnesses, Scarborough House, Lanham, MD, 1982, p. 30-31
[5]Régine Pernoud, La Spiritualite de Jeanne d'Arc, Editions Mame, Saint-Amand-Montrond (Cher), 1992, p. 54 and 58
[6]Joan of Arc translated by Willard Trask, Joan of Arc: In Her Own Words, Turtle Point Press, New York, 1996, p.7 and 41
[7]Paul has an appropriate comment about this: *"He has saved us and called us to a holy life—not because of anything we have done but because of his own purpose and grace."* 2 Timothy 1: 9
[8]Régine Pernoud, Jeanne d'Arc par elle-memes et ses témoins, Editions du Seuil, Paris, 1996, p. 31
[9]Frederick Buechner, Wishful Thinking: A Theological ABC, Harper & Row; New York, 1973; Mr. Buechner (1926-) is a well-known American writer, theologian, ordained Presbyterian minister and the author of more than thirty published books.

Chapter 4
Her Time Had Come

Jimmy, not especially inventive and tongue tied as usual, was hoping to make time with the firms newest and prettiest young lawyer. As she was passing his desk he spoke up, "Uh, Emily...er... do you have the time by any chance?"

Happy to show off her new watch from her new boyfriend, Emily immediately stopped and with a flick of her wrist said, "Well, let me just take a look at my Rolex...hmm...let's see...well, it's 19:47, military time, Central Standard Time. Or maybe you needed the time in Paris?"

Jimmy thought about that. He was encouraged, but...a little confused.

"What then is time? If no one asks me, I know what it is. If I wish to explain it to him who asks, I do not know." Saint Augustine [1]

If you take the time to think about it, time is a little confusing for all of us. Even the concept of time is a difficult one to get hold of. And it seems to go by so quickly sometimes. *"How did it get so late so soon. Its night before its afternoon. December is here before its June. My goodness how the time has flewn. How did it get so late so soon?"* Dr. Suess [2]

These days we tend to break time down into small units. From years to months, then months to weeks, weeks to days, to hours, to minutes, seconds, mini-seconds...and so on. But time is also measured in seasons:

"There is a time for everything, and a season
For every activity under heaven;
A time to be born and a time to die...
A time to plant and a time to uproot,
A time to kill and a time to heal,
A time to tear down and a time to build..."
Ecclesiastes 3: 1-3

Man's perception of time seems to change according to the times. And God's perception of time is not the same as man's: *"But do not forget this one thing, dear friends: With the Lord a day is like a thousand years, and a thousand years are like a day."* 2 Peter 3:8; see also Psalm 90: 4
A quick look at the way Joan perceived time, and the times she lived in, may be helpful at this point.

Joan's Time

"Joan was a being so uplifted from the ordinary run of mankind that she finds no equal in a thousand years." Winston Churchill [3]

Did Joan perceive time as Emily did? No, I would think not. Joan, and many of her contemporaries, seemed to measure time more in terms of church seasons, holidays and festivals. "God's Time" we might say. For example, at Melun during the week of April 16, 1429 she said, *"**Last Easter week**, I was standing near the moat at Melun, and my voices told me that I would be taken prisoner **before Saint John's Day**, and that it must be so, and that I must not be frightened but accept it willingly, and God would help me."* [4] Many other examples could be cited, but this will suffice for the point I'm making.

Joan's time, the Middle Ages, were of course, another time entirely. One far removed from our 'modern' contemporary world. Here are two interesting observations:

"If we are typically modern, we are bored, jaded, cynical, flat, and burnt out...If we were not so bored and empty, we would not have to stimulate ourselves with increasing dosages of sex and violence---or just constant busyness. Here we are in the most fantastic fun and games factory ever invented---modern technological society---and we are bored, like a spoiled rich kid in a mansion surrounded by a thousand expensive toys. Medieval people in comparison were like peasants in toyless hovels---and they were fascinated. Occasions for awe and wonder seemed to abound: birth and death and love and light and darkness and wind and sea and fire and sunrise and star and tree and bird and human mind—and God and heaven. But all these things have not changed, we have. The universe has not become empty and we full; it has remained full and we have become empty, insensitive to it fullness, coldhearted." Peter Kreeft [5]

"Our 'modern' society is a by-product of materialistic, rationalistic notions, and since there is no longer encouragement for us to accept heaven as a natural continuation of our existence, it is no wonder that our hearts struggle to keep our attention fixed on the world to come. As the German theologian Karl Rahner laments, 'Belief in eternal life has grown weaker in the consciousness of modern people.'" Joseph M. Stowell [6]

Of all the false philosophies/religions prevalent today, the one thing they hold in common is the worship of self instead of God. They do not promote a relationship with the real God of the universe who will judge the living and the dead. It is as though contemporary culture has decided what people were created for, and then designed the world around those illusions. But the Bible makes very clear that God is personal and Heaven is real.

As we continue to make 'progress' in the world, we follow our own schedule, and our own time. I would dare say that many people from the Middle Ages knew what time it is better than ourselves. Joan lived in 'God's Time', His ever-present present, centering her life in Him. Without this perception and approach to life, she could never have done all she did.

What time do you live in? Sad to say, too often we live in 'Me-Time'. May we venture more often into 'God's Time'.

[1] Saint Augustine (354-430), Bishop of Hippo Regius (present-day Annaba, Algeria), was a Latin philosopher and theologian from Roman Africa. His writings were very influential in the development of Western Christianity.
[2] Dr. Seuss, a.k.a. Theodor Seuss Geisel (1904-1991), was an American writer, poet, and cartoonist most widely known for his children's books written under the pen names Dr. Seuss.
[3] Winston Churchill, HISTORY OF THE ENGLISH SPEAKING PEOPLES, Book Three, Chapter Twenty-Six. Winston Churchill (1874-1965) is widely regarded as one of the greatest wartime leaders of the century. He served as British Prime Minister twice (1940–45 and 1951–55). A noted statesman and orator, Churchill was also an officer in the British Army, a historian, a writer, and an artist. He is the only British prime minister to have received the Nobel Prize in Literature.
[4] Régine Pernoud, Jeanne d'Arc, Editions Fayard, Mesnil-sur-l'Estrée, 2001, p. 143; emphasis by author. See Chapter 11 for this prophecy's fulfillment.
[5] Peter Kreeft, Everything You Ever Wanted to Know about Heaven, Ignatius Press, San Francisco, 1990, p. 20-21
[6] Joseph M. Stowell, Eternity, Moody Press, Chicago, 1995, p. 77

Chapter 5
God's Time

"Pray, and let God worry." Martin Luther [1]

"...True prayer is measured by weight, not by length. A single groan before God may have more fullness of prayer in it than a fine oration of great length." C.H. Spurgeon [2]

The evening news always got her attention, and now Wanda had a troubled look on her face. She grabbed the remote, clicked the TV off, and began looking for Killer. She needed to talk. Then she saw him. He was sitting in the den, right in front of the fireplace, staring intently into the fire. She could tell he was preoccupied, and so began speaking softly at first. "Oh my God, Killer. It's so terrible. Things are just getting worse and worse. What's going to happen next? I get so nervous when I watch the news! You know, last night little Billy took the car to visit a friend, and I couldn't stop worrying about him. What if he has a wreck? Sometimes, I can't even sleep anymore. Did I tell you about my boss, Rumpy? Well, he's still having an affair with Uncle Bill's wife. Yeah, every other Tuesday right after the Oprah re-run...Oh, and her brother, Doofus? I'm so afraid he'll kill 'em all if he finds out...And what if he does? That reminds me! What's going to happen in Afghanistan now...and goodness! Israel! ...and don't forget Iran!... and...for gosh sakes ... do you think that this could be the end of the world? I saw on TV the other day how Nostradamned-us predicted the end, and it was supposed to happen really soon... and ...What do **you** think, Killer!?"

Killer took it all in, and gave his usual response: *Ruff, Ruff! Ruff-f-f!!"*

Our imagination is a gift from God. But like a premium racehorse, to unleash its power in winning fashion it must be guided skillfully. Wanda has a very active imagination, but it is greatly based on her own fears and anxieties. Is this the best use of her imagination? Probably not. Indeed, it's probably harmful to her health.

What if we guided our imagination towards the glories and wonders of a God that loves and cares for us? As Dr. Seuss tells us, *"Oh the places we would go!"* [3]

But Planet Earth can be a pretty scary place. And leaving our fears and anxieties may be easier said than done. Perhaps we could replace at least some of them with something else. Prayer, for example. If we could make prayer the center post of our life, then surely our fears, anxieties, and other harmful uses of our imagination would decrease.

All though Scripture we see the importance of prayer. It is the center post for all prophet/servants of God:

"Be still and know that I am God." Psalm 46:10

"Come near to God and He will come near to you." James 4: 8

"Is anyone of you in trouble? He should pray. Is anyone happy? Let him sing songs of praise… The prayer of a righteous man is powerful and effective." James 5: 13-16

"Rejoice in the Lord always. I will say it again: rejoice! Let your gentleness be evident to all. The Lord is near. Do not be anxious about anything, but in everything, by prayer and petition, with thanksgiving, present your requests to God. And the peace of God, which transcends all understanding, will guard your hearts and minds in Christ Jesus." Philippians 4: 4-7 (It is interesting to note that when he wrote this, Paul was in prison awaiting his execution.)

"Be joyful always; pray continually; give thanks in all circumstance, for this is God's will for you in Christ Jesus." 1 Thessalonians 5: 16-18

Jesus said, *"And when you pray, do not be like the hypocrites, for they love to pray in the synagogues and on the street corners to be seen by men. I tell you the truth, they have received their reward in full. But when you pray go into your room, close the door and pray to your father, who is unseen…This then is how you should pray;*

> *'Our Father in Heaven,*
> *Hallowed be your name.*
> *Your Kingdom come,*
> *Your will be done on earth as it is in heaven.*
> *Give us today our daily bread.*
> *Forgive us our debts as we also have forgiven our debtors.*
> *And lead us not into temptation, but deliver us from the evil one.'"* Matthew 6: 5-13

What about Joan? Like Jesus, she was often seen going off by herself to pray (e.g. see Mark 1: 35). Sometimes she'd even do this on the battlefield.[4]

Here are a couple of examples of her speaking about prayer:

"Whenever I am unhappy, because men will not believe me in the things

that I say at God's bidding, I go apart and pray to God, complaining to him that those to whom I speak do not easily believe me. And when I have made my prayer to God, I hear a voice that says to me: 'Daughter of God, go, go, go! I shall be with you to help you. Go!' and when I hear that voice I feel a great joy. Indeed, I would that I might always be in that state."[5]

To one of her captains before the battle of Orleans, she said, *"You have been with your counsel and I have been with mine. Believe me that the counsel of my Lord will be accomplished and will stand, and this counsel of yours will perish."*[6]

After winning the battle of Orleans, what was the first thing she did? High fives with her generals? No. Champagne toasts with her friends? Not so much. Party down at the local disco? *"The Maid and the other lords and men-at-arms reentered Orleans to the great rejoicing of the clergy and the people, who together rendered humble thanks to Our Lord along with the well-deserved praise for the very great aid and victories that He had given and sent them against the English, ancient enemies of the kingdom..."*[7]

Later, she refused to attend an elaborate banquet, which had been planned in her honor. Instead, she passed nearly all her time that evening in prayer. For Joan, entering into God's time was the center post of her life.[8]

Renewing Our Mind with Prayer
"Prayer does not fit us for the greater work, prayer is the greater work." Oswald Chambers [9]

As with Wanda, our imagination is influenced by all sorts of things, both consciously and unconsciously. Imagination running free may not be as free as we might think. Misdirected imagination generates an excess of worry, fear and anxiety. And eventually it will make us sick, in one form or another. Medical studies show that unchecked anxiety is directly related to an increased risk of many problems, including but not limited to: heart disease, stroke, severe problems of the digestive system, skin disorders, psychiatric problems and some cancers. Although there are some medications and treatments that are helpful in dealing with such problems, not including God in the treatment plan is both short sighted and less effective.[10] And substituting prayer for misdirected imagination will at least point us in the right direction.

"Do not conform any longer to the pattern of this world, but be transformed by the renewing of your mind. Then you will be able to test

and prove what God's will is-his good, pleasing and perfect will."
Romans 12: 2

[1]Martin Luther (1483-1546) was a German priest, professor of theology and iconic figure of the Protestant Reformation. Luther taught that salvation is not earned by good deeds but received only as a free gift of God's grace through faith in Jesus Christ. His theology challenged the authority of the Pope by teaching that the Bible is the only source of divinely revealed knowledge. His translation of the Bible from Latin into the language of the people made it more accessible, causing a tremendous impact on the church and on German culture.
[2]C.H. Spurgeon (1834-1892) was a British Baptist preacher, and remains highly influential among Christians of different denominations, among whom he is known as the "Prince of Preachers". In his lifetime, Spurgeon preached to around 10,000,000 people.
[3]Dr. Seuss, "Oh, the Places You'll Go!", Random House Children's Books, New York, 1960
[4]E.g. see Régine Pernoud and Marie-Véronique Clin, Joan of Arc-Her Story, St Martin's Griffin edition, New York, New York, 1998, p. 47
[5]Joan of Arc translated by Willard Trask, Joan of Arc: In Her Own Words, Turtle Point Press, New York, 1996, p. 41
[6] Régine Pernoud, Jeanne d'Arc par elle-meme et ses temoins, Editions du Seuil, Paris, 1996, p. 103
[7]From the Journal of the Siege: Régine Pernoud and Marie-Véronique Clin, Joan of Arc-Her Story, St Martin's Griffin edition, New York, New York, 1998, p. 49
[8]For Joan's only recorded prayer, see Chapter 12-*"If you love me..."*.
[9]Mr. Chambers (1874-1917) was a prominent early twentieth century Scottish Christian minister and teacher, best known as the author of the widely-read devotional My Utmost for His Highest.
[10]There is ample proof that prayer works. Many scientific studies have been conducted that validate this observation. An Israeli survey following 10,000 civil servants for 26 years found that Orthodox Jews were less likely to die of cardiovascular problems than "nonbelievers." And a study from Dartmouth College in Hanover, N.H., monitoring 250 people after open-heart surgery concluded that those who had religious connections and social support were 12 times less likely to die than those who had none...Certainly, following a spiritual or religious lifestyle might lead to better health. However, for the non-believers, it is hard to understand how intercessory or non-local prayer works. This is the situation when the sick persons are prayed for and don't even know it. In widely publicized studies of the effect of intercessory prayer, cardiologist Randolph Byrd studied 393 patients admitted to the coronary-care unit at San Francisco General Hospital. Some were prayed for by home-prayer groups, others were not. All the men and women got medical care. In this randomized, double-blind study, neither the doctors and nurses nor the patients knew who would be the object of prayer. The results were dramatic and surprised many scientists. The men and women whose medical care was supplemented with prayer needed fewer drugs and spent less time on ventilators. They also fared better overall than their counterparts who received medical care but nothing more. The prayed-for patients were: significantly less likely to require antibiotics (3 patients versus 16), significantly less likely to develop pulmonary edema-a condition in which the lungs fill with fluid because the heart cannot pump properly (6 versus 18), significantly less likely to require insertion of a tube into the throat to assist breathing (0 versus 12), less likely to

die. Even more incredible experiments in distance healing involve nonhuman subjects. In a survey of 131 controlled experiments on spiritual healing, it was found that prayed-for rye grass grew taller; prayed-for yeast resisted the toxic effects of cyanide; prayed-for test-tube bacteria grew faster. Dr. Larry Dossey says, *"Because they don't involve humans, you can run them with fanatical precision and you can run them hundreds of times. It's the best evidence of all that prayer can change the world. And it operates as strongly on the other side of the Earth as it does at the bedside."* In his book, Healing Words, Dr. Dossey, M.D., co-chair of the Panel on Mind-Body Interventions of the Office of Alternative Medicine at the National Institutes of Health in Washington, D.C., reviewed over 100 experiments, most published in parapsychological literature on the effects of prayer. More than half showed an effect on everything from seed germination to wound healing. At the Mind Science Foundation in San Antonio, Texas, researchers took blood samples from 32 volunteers, isolated their red blood cells (RBCS) and placed the samples in a room on the other side of the building. Then the researchers placed the RBCs in a solution designed to swell and burst them, a process that can be measured extremely accurately. Next the researchers asked the volunteers to pray for the preservation of some of the RBCS. To help them, the researchers projected color slides of healthy RBCS. The praying significantly slowed the swelling and bursting of the RBCS. These experiments have shown that prayer can take many forms. Results occurred not only when people prayed for explicit outcomes, but also when they prayed for nothing specific. The experiments showed that a simple "Thy will be done" approach was as powerful as when specific results were held in mind. A simple attitude of prayerfulness, an all pervading sense of holiness and a feeling of empathy, caring, and compassion for the entity in need, seemed to set the stage for healing. Experiments also showed that prayer positively affected: high blood pressure, wounds, heart attacks, headaches and anxiety. The processes that had been influenced by prayer were: activity of enzymes, the growth rate of leukemic white blood cells, mutation rates of bacteria, germination and growth rates of various seeds, firing rate of pacemaker cells, healing rates of wounds, the size of goiters and tumors, time required to awaken from anesthesia, autonomic effects such as electrodermal activity of the skin, rates of hemolysis of red blood cells and hemoglobin levels. It did not matter whether the praying person was with the person who was prayed for the power of prayer to work. You can pray for someone who is far away and still will have an influence on the outcome. Nothing seems to block or stop the effects of prayer - the object in one study was placed in a lead-lined room and in another in a cage that shielded it from all known forms of electromagnetic energy, the effect still go through. Given the scientific evidence, Dossey and several other researchers now admit that withholding prayer from an ailing patient is downright irresponsible. *"It became an ethical issue for me,"* says Dossey. Certainly, the idea of distance healing is catching on even today. Cyberspace is full of fellow believers who post their requests on daily prayer chains. Of course, the ancient stories of the Bible, and of Jesus link healing with faith. So, it is reasonable to assume that something such as prayer that provides comfort and peace would influence the propensity for you to get disease or how you recover from a disease. A study of 91,000 people in rural Maryland showed that weekly church attendees had 50 percent fewer deaths from heart disease than non-churchgoers and 53 percent fewer suicides. Churchgoers have lower blood pressure levels than

nonbelievers, even after smoking and other known risk factors are taken into consideration. Many doctors believe that if they prayed with their patients before and after surgery or before administering a course of powerful drugs, this treatment might assist in the patient's recovery. Thirty medical schools in America are now offering courses in faith and medicine. *"Prayer works,"* says Dr. Matthews, associate professor of medicine at Georgetown University School of Medicine in Washington, D.C., and senior research fellow at the National Institute for Healthcare Research in Rockville, Maryland. Dr. Matthews has reviewed more than 200 studies linking religious commitment and health, cited in his book, 'The Faith Factor'. Dr. Matthews cites studies suggesting that people who pray are less likely to get sick, are more likely to recover from surgery and illness and are better able to cope with their illnesses than people who don't pray. Some evidence indicates that sick people who are prayed for also fare significantly better than those who aren't. In fact, some physicians report that people who are prayed for often do better even if they don't know they're being prayed for.
http://www.dosseydossey.com/larry/healingwords.html; accessed Jan. 2014

Chapter 6
A Lifelong Pilgrimage

"Blessed are those whose strength is in you, who have set their hearts on pilgrimage." Psalm 84: 8

I approached the luminescent, other-worldly lights with a sense of reverence and awe. For nearly 40 minutes, my entire being had been focused on this one event. I had survived one difficulty after another (cut off twice on the freeway, running low on gas, and nearly missed my exit), when I finally saw the ethereal illuminations in the sky boldly proclaiming, '7/Eleven'. Once there, I felt an enormous sense of gratitude and relief. I immediately gave thanks and praise to God for my safe arrival. It seemed like I had been preparing for this for so long, and now that I was finally here, I knew it was time to take the next step. I walked to the third aisle with purposeful step, and with heartfelt love and devotion, began inspecting the myriad choices of cat food. The colors were so beautiful, and as I glided up to the counter, there was a peace in my heart that I had not felt in such a long time. That's when I knew that it had all been worth the price ($1.89 per can) and that Sylvester (our cat) would reward me with his all-knowing 'Me-o-o-o-o-w', as if to say, 'Well done, good and faithful human.' My journey was at an end.

Could this qualify as a pilgrimage? Well-l-l ... The essence of pilgrimage must take into consideration the goal, approach, perception and preparation of the experience. It could be looked at from several different viewpoints. It might take forty minutes, or forty years (e.g. Numbers 32: 13) to complete the experience. For some, the destination might be a sacred site that has been frequented by pilgrims for centuries. For others, perhaps even a one night visit to their local 7/Eleven convenience store might qualify. In any case, for most of us, pilgrimage always has a spiritual connotation.

Some believe their life is a daily pilgrimage with God. Others believe that their life is a pilgrimage back to God. Some believe that God has called them for a very specific purpose, and everything in their life is tied to that purpose. They believe that to fulfill that calling is the very reason God gave them life. Their whole life becomes a daily pilgrimage to this calling God has entrusted to them. The dictionary gives us a definition that fits this idea:

Pilgrimage: *The course of life on earth.*[1]

Encyclopedia Britannica gives a more common perspective:

Pilgrimage: *A journey to a shrine or other place undertaken to gain divine aid, as an act of thanksgiving or penance, or to demonstrate devotion.*[2]

What was Joan's perspective? She falls into the first category. She saw her life as a lifelong pilgrimage from, with and back to God. As she said, *"I was born for this."*[3] And Jesus? *"You are right in saying I am a king. In fact, for this reason I was born, and for this I came into the world, to testify to the truth. Everyone on the side of truth listens to me."* John 18: 37

A Lifelong pilgrimage
"We see in these swift and skillful travelers a symbol of our lives, which seeks to be a pilgrimage and a passage on this earth for the way of heaven." Pope Paul VII [4]

Moses and Joan of Arc are good examples of those following a **lifelong pilgrimage**. At first glance, these two don't seem to have much in common. There are approximately 2,700 years between them. One was an illiterate, thirteen-year-old French peasant girl when first called. She would be only nineteen when her pilgrimage was completed and the Lord called her home. The other was a Hebrew man who was raised in the Egyptian royal family of Pharaoh. He was eighty years old when he got the call. He would die at the ripe old age of 120. Could there be *any* similarities between these two? Actually there are several, as we'll see.

The similarities began when God first called them. At that time, they were both given a specific task to accomplish. But simultaneously there was always a deeper, parallel mission present: a lifelong pilgrimage with God. Perhaps at first they were so focused on their immediate task, that they didn't realize the lifelong pilgrimage aspect inherent in their mission. If so, we might have something in common with them. We are often so focused on our immediate mission, whatever it may be, that we tend to lose sight of the big picture. For most of us, it's only in retrospect that we come to see that, from the very beginning, our immediate task, our day-to-day calling, was also in fact an integral part of our lifelong pilgrimage. Whether losing sight of our lifetime walk, or feeling unsure of our day-to-day task, our mission remains the same: come what may, one step at a time towards God's light, to His glory. *"So, whether you eat or drink, or whatever you do, do all to the glory of God."* 1 Corinthians 10: 31 Such was both Joan's and Moses' approach. Let's take a look…

1. Joan's calling was quite dramatic. An angel of the Lord (St. Michael) appeared to her. There was light all around, and it was quite unnerving to her at first. *"When I was thirteen, I had a voice from God to help me govern myself. The first time, I was terrified…I heard the voice on my right hand, towards the church. There was a great light all about."* From the 1431 Trial of Condemnation [5]

Moses calling was quite dramatic. An angel of the Lord appeared to him. There was light all around, and it was quite unnerving to him at first. *"An angel of the Lord appeared to him in flames of fire from within a bush…"* When Moses realized who it was, he *"…hid his face, because he was afraid to look at God."* Exodus 3 2, 6

2. When in the presence of God's messengers, Joan was in awe and showed them reverence. *"He* (i.e. the Archangel St Michael) *was not alone, but duly attended by heavenly angels. I saw them with the eyes of my body as well as I see you. And when they left me, I wept, and I wished that they might have taken me with them. And I kissed the ground where they had stood, to do them reverence…"* Trial of condemnation of 1431[6]

When Moses realized he was in the presence of God, he was in awe and showed Him reverence. He *"…hid his face, because he was afraid to look at God…"* then took off his sandals *"…for the place where you are standing is holy ground."* Ex 3: 5-6

3. Joan was custom-made for her lifetime mission. She said that she was chosen by God to save France, and that she was the only one who could: *"…I must be with the King before mid-Lent, though I wear my legs to the knees on the road. For there is none in this world-neither kings, nor dukes, nor the king of Scotland's daughter, nor any other who can recover the Kingdom of France. Nor is there any succor for it but from me."* Spoken to Jean de Metz at Vaucouleurs, Feb. 1429[7] Indeed, for such a mission she appears to have had just the right psychological make-up, courage, physical stamina and constitution, common sense, intelligence and leadership qualities. On top of these attributes, she had a deep belief in God, and desire to do His will. Being brought up in a small village and raised in a Godly atmosphere also helped to prepare her. She was well chosen!

Moses was custom-made for his lifetime mission. Although born a Jew, he was adopted by Pharaoh's daughter (see Ex. 2: 1-10 for the divine circumstances). Consequently he was raised in the royal court of Egypt. He saw up close how the Egyptians mistreated his own people. Later he killed an Egyptian while defending one of his own (Ex 2: 11-15), and was forced to flee and live in exile several years. Hardships would make him grow stronger. He would need all the strength he had. After all, he would soon be put to the test against mighty Pharaoh, and then lead his people through the desert for forty years! For such a mission, his previous hardships had prepared him well. He appears to have had just the right psychological make-up, courage, physical stamina and constitution, common sense, intelligence and leadership qualities. On top of these attributes, he would develop a deep belief in his God, and desire to do His will. He was well chosen!

4. The Lord chose Joan for a specific mission: to free the French from their English occupiers, and put Charles VII on the throne. In the course of history, countries come and go, and at that time the French people saw no hope for their future. France was on the edge; a country whose fragile life appeared close to the end. However, for His own good purpose, God still had future plans for France. As Joan said, *"The voice has told me that it is God's will to deliver the people of France from the calamity that is upon them."*[8] Another example: *"He told me of the pitiful state of the Kingdom of France. And he told that I must go to succor the King of France...Twice and thrice a week the voice told me that I must depart and go into France... and the voice said that I would raise the siege before Orleans."*[9]

The Lord chose Moses for a specific mission: to free the Israelites from Egyptian slavery, and then lead them to their new home. At that time the Israelites saw no hope for their future. They had been slaves in Egypt for some 400 years. However, for His own good purpose, God still had plans for them. He would deliver them from their pitiful state, and then from them the Messiah, the Savior of all Mankind, would come. *"The Lord said* (to Moses)*, 'I have indeed seen the misery of my people in Egypt... and I am concerned about their suffering ... the cry of the Israelites has reached me... So now, go. I am sending you to Pharaoh to bring my people the Israelites out of Egypt.'"* Exodus 3: 7, 10

5. When first called Joan did not want to do this. Surely this was a job for anyone but her. *"And I answered to the voice that I was a poor girl who knew nothing of riding and warfare."*[10]

When first called Moses did not want to do this. Surely this was a job for anyone but him. *"...Moses said to God, 'Who am I, that I should go to Pharaoh and bring the Israelites out of Egypt? ...O Lord, I have never been eloquent, neither in the past nor since you have spoken to your servant...Please send someone else to do it.'"* Ex 3: 11; 4: 10, 13

6. Joan was unsure of herself, but God simply told her she must go, and that He would be with her: *"And when I have made my prayer to God, I hear a voice that says to me: 'Go, go, go, Daughter of God. I will be with you to help you. Go!'"*[11]

Moses was unsure of himself, but God simply told him he must go, and that He would be with him: *"So now, go. I am sending you to Pharaoh'...And God said, 'I will be with you.'"* Ex 3: 10, 12

7. Although the mission was specific, few details on how to accomplish it were given. Only the final goal was clear, and that seemed totally impossible. She was to meet and then convince the King that she, Joan, had been sent by God to deliver Orleans from the English siege? And then escort him through enemy territory to Reims (the 'Promised Land'), where he would be crowned and anointed King of France? Were the French people about to be reborn? Yes! *"I am come from the King of Heaven to raise the siege of Orleans and to lead the Dauphin to Reims to be crowned and anointed."*[12]

Although the mission was specific, few details on how to accomplish it were given. Only the final goal was clear, and that seemed totally impossible. He was to convince Pharaoh that he, Moses, had been sent by God to deliver the Hebrew people out of Egyptian bondage? And then escort them through enemy territory to the "Promised Land"? Were the Hebrew people about to be reborn? Yes! *"So now, go. I am sending yon to Pharaoh to bring my people the Israelites out of Egypt."* Ex 3: 10

8. The Lord had explained to her that earthly kingdoms all belonged to Him, but He was putting the Kingdom of France in the hands of the Dauphin, Charles VII. *"The Kingdom of France is not the Dauphin's but my Lord's. But my Lord wills that the Dauphin shall be made king and have the Kingdom in custody."*[13]

The Lord had explained to him that earthly kingdoms all belonged to him, but He was putting the land of Israel in the hands of His chosen people, the Israelites. He said, *"The land must not be sold permanently, because the land is mine and you are but aliens and my tenants."* Leviticus 25: 23 *"...I have come down to rescue them (the Israelites) from the hand of the Egyptians to bring them up out of that land into a good and spacious land, a land flowing with milk and honey...so now, go...bring my people the Israelites out of Egypt."* Exodus 3: 8, 10[14]

9. Joan knew many would probably not belief her message. But the Lord provided her with two signs. As noted in Chapter 2, Joan delivered the first one to Charles the first time she met him:

Prosecutor: *"What sign did you give your King that you came from God?"*

Joan: *"I have always answered that you will not drag this from my lips. Go and ask it of him."*

Prosecutor: *"Have you not sworn to reveal what shall be asked of you touching the Trial?"*

Joan: *"I have already told you that I will tell you nothing of what concerns my King. There on I will not speak."*

Prosecutor: *"Do you not know the sign that you gave to the King?"*

Joan: *"You will not know it from me."*

Prosecutor: *"But this touches on the Trial."*

Joan: *"Of what I have promised to keep secret, I will tell you nothing. I have already said, even here, that I could not tell you without perjury."*

Prosecutor: *"To whom have you promised this?"*

Joan: *"To Saint Catherine and Saint Margaret; and this had been shown to the King..."* Trial of Condemnation, March 1, 1431[15]

Whatever it was, it convinced Charles that she was indeed God-sent, and upon hearing it he immediately provided quarters for her in the castle. The second sign was "the impossible" liberation of Orleans (again, see Chapter 2).

Moses knew that many would probably not believe his message. He asked the Lord, *"What if they do not believe me or listen to me and say, 'The Lord did not appear to you.'?"* Ex. 4:1 Then the Lord gave Moses two signs (see Ex. 4: 1-9).

10. In spite of her fears, she would go. To royalty. And she would simply and directly communicate God's message to Charles VII. *"I bring you news from God, that our Lord will give you back your kingdom; bring you to be crowned at Reims, and drive out your enemies. In this I am*

God's messenger. Do set me bravely to work, and I will raise the siege of Orleans."[16]

In spite of his fears, he would go. To royalty. And he would simply and directly communicate God's message to Pharaoh. *"... Moses and Aaron went to Pharaoh and said, "This is what the Lord, the God of Israel, says: Let my people go..."* Exodus 5: 1

11. Unsure of herself at first, once she committed herself to doing God's will, Joan went boldly forward. Without knowing how on earth she would be able to accomplish her task, she focused rather on how in heaven this would be done through her.

Unsure of himself at first, once he committed himself to doing God's will, Moses went boldly forward. Without knowing how on earth he would be able to accomplish his task, he focused rather on how in heaven this would be done through him.

12. In spite of the apparent impossibility of the mission, she was obedient. God had asked her to free the key city of Orleans from the mighty English. And within a few days God had accomplished this through her. Next she was to escort the Dauphin to the 'Promised Land' (i.e. Reims) to be crowned and anointed King of France. In the weeks to come, this too would be done through her.

In spite of the apparent impossibility of the mission, Moses was obedient. God had asked him to free His people from mighty Pharaoh. And within a short time God had accomplished this through him. Next he was to lead them to the 'Promised Land'. This too would be done through him, but this mission would take forty years! (See Ex. 12: 31-Deuteronomy 34:12)

13. Did Joan long to return home to Domremy after the King was crowned and anointed at Reims? From the beginning she had talked about missing her simple life with family and friends: *"Far rather would I sit and sew beside my poor mother, for this thing is not of my condition."*[17] This would be a recurring theme in her short life: *"Would it might please God, my Creator, that I might retire now, abandon arms and return to serve my father and mother and to take care their sheep with my sister and my brothers, who would be so happy to see me again!"*[18] In any case once she embarked on her **Lifelong Pilgrimage**, it would be just that. And now there was no turning back.

Did Moses long to return home to Midian after his people were freed from mighty Pharaoh? Perhaps, but Scripture is silent on this. He knew from the very beginning that he was to lead the people to *'a land flowing milk and honey'* Ex. 3: 7-8. But he had no idea that this would be a 40-year journey through a desert wilderness with a demanding and discontented people (Ex 15: 22-Deut. 34: 12). In any case once he embarked on his **Lifelong Pilgrimage**, it would be just that. And now there was no turning back.

14. What Joan couldn't know at the beginning of this strange and miraculous journey, was that what had begun as a specific God-given mission would also become a **Lifelong Pilgrimage** with God. In Joan's case, her **Lifelong Pilgrimage** (i.e. counting from her calling to her death) would last no more than seven years.

What Moses couldn't know at the beginning of this strange and miraculous journey, was that what had begun as a specific God-given mission would also become a **Lifelong Pilgrimage** with God. In Moses' case, his **Lifelong Pilgrimage** would take more than 40 years.

15. The outcome of her pilgrimage would ultimately be the rebirth of a great nation, France. This would have worldwide ramifications down through time. After all, France would play a pivotal role in world events for centuries. By the time Joan was approaching the end of her earthly existence, this concept of **Lifelong Pilgrimage** with God must have been crystal clear. At her Trial of Condemnation, on Feb. 24, 1431, she said, *"I come sent by God. I have no* (further) *business here. I pray you, send me back to God from whom I am come."*[19]

The outcome of his pilgrimage would ultimately be the birth of a great nation, Israel. This would have worldwide ramifications down through time. After all, the Jews had been chosen to be a light to the world, pointing to the only true God. Through them would come first God's word (the Bible), and then the Messiah Himself. God's last command to Moses was to climb Mount Nebo. He wanted him to see the 'Promised Land' before dying (Deut. 34: 1-10). As he was sitting on top of this mountain, approaching the end of his earthly existence, this concept of a **Lifelong Pilgrimage** with God must have been crystal clear.

Other Similarities…

-Both Moses and Joan came from tending their flocks to dealing with royalty.

-Both believed that their talents and calling came from above, and were to be shared with us here below.

-Both consistently claimed to have had an ongoing **Close Encounter of the God Kind**.

-Both were sent to serve others, not to be served.

"Whoever wants to become great among you must be your servant, and whoever wants to be first must be your slave---just as the son of man did not come to be served, but to serve, and to give his life as a ransom for many." Messiah Jesus, Matthew 20: 28

A High-Profile-Position

The Marines say they're looking for 'a few good men'. But the Boss looks at it differently. Basically, He's looking for everyone.[20] Why? Well, for one thing, have you ever tried to find 'a few good men'? They're really hard to find. In fact, to tell the truth, there aren't any.[21] That is, not according to God's standard of perfection: *"There is no one righteous, not even one; there is no one who understands, no one who seeks God. All have turned away, they have together become worthless; there is no one who does good, not even one... for all have sinned and fall short of the glory of God."* Romans 3: 10-12, 23

Since *"all have sinned and fall short of the glory of God"*, the boss simply works with what He's already put into motion. After all, He's the one with the Master plans. And in His plans, everyone has a part to play. Everyone. That includes, as Clint Eastwood might say, the good, the bad and the ugly.

Sometimes His plans will include a **High-Profile Position**. Moses, Abraham, David, Isaiah, Peter, Paul, Constantine, Joan of Arc, Martin Luther, Mother Teresa, Billy Graham, Brother Roger of Taize, John Paul II and many others, were all chosen for a **High-Profile-Position**. And it wasn't a headhunters company that chose them. No, it was the Boss Himself. Often, those already living a **Lifelong Pilgrimage** were the ones selected for such a mission. Joan falls in this category. *"I often heard her say of her work, that it was her mission."*[22]

Now it is true that these **High-Profile-Positions** can be very demanding. There are no part-time positions available, and the hours can be long. However, the benefits are exceptional, including: Eternal Medical Insurance with no deductibles (although truth be told, you'll never need it), Death Insurance, and a retirement plan that is out of this world! Also, you can count on seeing the light at the end of the tunnel.

Has the Boss chosen you for a **High-Profile-Position**? For most of us, the answer to this question would be no. Have you been chosen for a really important job while here? A mission? One so important, that you had to be custom-made according to your own time, circumstances, and God's good purpose? My belief is yes, you have. We all have. It is undeniable that we all find ourselves in circumstances that no one else can affect quite like we can. In fact, the Lord has given us all a job/mission to do while here. Just as everyone has a sign (or signs) that reflect God to others, so too do we all have a job/mission to do for the Lord. The search for it may be part of your own lifelong pilgrimage.

> *"God has created me to do him some definite service; has committed some work to me which he has not committed to another. I have my mission-I may never know it in this life, but I shall be told it in the next."*
> John Herny Newman [23]

A Little about the Boss

"I believe God is managing affairs and that He doesn't need any advice from me. With God in charge, I believe everything will work out for the best in the end. So what is there to worry about." Henry Ford [24]

For those who have chosen to make a lifelong pilgrimage, the central question then becomes with whom? The object of such a commitment becomes of greatest importance. History is littered with many who made a lifetime commitment, often with disastrous consequences, to someone or something that was not worthy of such an investment. Moses and Joan of Arc, like so many others, chose the Boss, the God of the Bible.

Now, the Boss is something else! He's awesome. He's the epitome of love and justice. He's known worldwide, and those who have signed on with Him have no regrets. They know that they're with THE very best. Although slandered by many of His competitors (e.g. materialism, secularism, atheism, false religions, "self-absorptionism" etc.), His history, i.e. the Bible, is unmatched and speaks for itself. He has lots of experience. In fact, He's been in business longer than anyone knows.

It's curious though. Although you never really see Him, He always seems to know what you're up to. He must have some outstanding video and surveillance equipment.

He's different from other bosses, and working for Him has some real advantages. For one thing, you can always depend on Him. He always keeps His word, and is faithful to His employees.[25] He's unbiased and completely fair[26], and you always know where you stand.

Job descriptions, benefits, rules, regulations, compensation, protocols, etc. are all in the Employee Manuel (the Bible). It's very comprehensive. It took 1500 years to write, and will answer many of your questions.

Another thing: He truly only wants what's best for you.[27] And you can call Him, 24/7. He's always there to at least listen to your concerns.[28] In fact, the Boss want to get to know you, and have a real relationship with you. He even sent us His Son so that we could get to know Him better. How many other bosses can claim all of this?

Now it's true that He expects the best from His employees. Qualities that He values include faith, hope, love, compassion and perseverance. Experience is not a must. However, many of those chosen for a High-Profile-position had been devoted to the Boss for years, and were already very active in their Lifelong Pilgrimage before getting the call.

Still, not everyone wants to work for Him. In fact, some people run away so fast, they don't even take the time to check out the Job Descriptions. Maybe they're afraid that the Boss is too hard to work for? To tell the truth, working that closely with someone as powerful as He, is kind of scary. But if they would take a little time to get to know Him, their life would just light up, and they'd find the peace *"...which transcends all understanding."* Philippians 4: 7

Nonetheless, some only want to work for themselves. They don't want to have any kind of boss at all. And while self-employment might be a good idea for some of us here on planet earth, when dealing with the boss, SELF-employment misses the big picture completely. After all, it's not about us. It's all about the Boss. Indeed, the Boss is the only one worthy of such a serious commitment as a Lifelong Pilgrimage. If you miss this foundational point, your life can become pure hell.

Worthy of Consideration

The vast majority of us have not had an encounter with God as dramatic as Moses or Joan. Nor will we be at the center of such earth changing evens. However, we don't have to be written about in the Bible or history books for our mission to have great importance in God's eyes. Even if we don't yet know exactly what our mission is, Jesus did give us the universal two-part Mission Statement. The first part says, *"...Love the Lord your God with all your heart and with all your soul and with all your mind and with all your strength.' The second is this: 'Love your neighbor as yourself.' There is no commandment greater than these'".* Mark 12: 30-31 This puts us on the right path, as we search for more details. All through Joan of Arc's and Moses' life, we see them faithfully following this Mission Statement.

As we saw in #7 above, although the details of our mission may not at first be clear, God puts us to work just as we are. Then as we do the work given, the details of our mission become clearer. As we go through this day by day process, our Lifelong Pilgrimage takes on more depth and clarity, just as our daily mission does. Indeed, as mentioned above, it's often only when we look back on this process that the tapestry of God's plans stand out. In the beginning of Joan's story, she wasn't given any details for her High-Profile-Position. Rather she underwent a preparation period of training, strengthening and encouragement, which lasted at least a couple of years. *"When I was thirteen, I had a voice from God to help me govern my conduct* [29] *... Above all Saint Michael told me that I must be a good child, and that God would help me. He taught me to behave rightly and to go often to church..."* [30]

Where can we go to get our training? As close to God as we can get. In fact, our Lifelong Pilgrimage might consist of nothing less than our daily walk with Him. As they say, 'the trip is the destination.' In any case, prayer[31] and Scripture will light our way from [32], to and with the Boss. And the closer we get to Him, the clearer our vision will become for what he has in mind for us.

Some believe that the creation of life was random. They've heard that we came from some murky 'primordial soup'. Others, including Moses and Joan, were convinced of the reality of God, the supreme creator of everything. They believed *"...that they were aliens and strangers on the earth."* Hebrews 11: 12-13 Merely pilgrims en route to a better country. They lived lives rooted in faith and hope, and trusted God to the end of their days. In spite of their own flaws and falls, their Lifelong Pilgrimage never came to a halt. The same can be said for so many others. History books and the Bible are full of such examples. Case in point: the prophet Jeremiah (circa 600BC). One of the major prophets of the Bible, he certainly had his share of difficulties and suffering. So much so that scholars now refer to him as the "Weeping Prophet". He was attacked by his own brothers (Jeremiah 12:6), beaten and put into the stocks by a priest and false prophet (Jer. 20: 1-4), imprisoned by the king (Jer. 37:18), threatened with death (Jer. 38: 28), thrown into a cistern by Judah's officials (Jer. 38: 4), opposed by a false prophet (Jer. 38:6)... Undeterred, he stuck to his lifelong path with God. And now through him, the Lord encourages us to do the same:

> *"Yet the Lord pleads with you still: Ask where the good road is, The godly paths you used to walk in, in the days of long ago. Travel there, and you will find rest for your souls."*
> Jeremiah 6:16

[1]http://www.merriam-webster.com/dictionary/pilgrimage, August, 2009
[2]http://www.britannica.com/bps/search?query=pilgrimage&blacklist=460445, August, 2009]
[3]Joan of Arc translated by Willard Trask, Joan of Arc: In Her Own Words, Turtle Point Press, New York, 1006, p. 19
[4]Pope Paul VI (1897-1978) was Pope of the Catholic Church from 1963 until his death in 1978. He fostered improved ecumenical relations with Orthodox and Protestants, which resulted in many historic meetings and agreements.
[5]Régine Pernoud, Jeanne d'Arc par elle-meme et ses témoins, Editions du Seuil, Paris, 1996, p. 30. Also, see Chapter 2.
[6]Joan of Arc translated by Willard Trask, Joan of Arc: In Her Own Words, Turtle Point Press, New York, 1996, p. 6; Also see Chapter 2.
[7]Régine Pernoud, Jeanne d'Arc par elle-meme et ses témoins, Editions du Seuil, Paris, 1996, p. 36
[8]Joan of Arc translated by Willard Trask, Joan of Arc: In Her Own Words, Turtle Point Press, New York, 1996, p. 25; said to her examiners at Poitiers in March 1429
[9] Ibid, p. 6-7; Trial of Condemnation
[10]Joan of Arc translated by Willard Trask, Joan of Arc: In Her Own Words, Turtle Point Press, New York, 1996, p. 7; Trial of Condemnation, 1431
[11]Joan of Arc translated by Willard Trask, Joan of Arc: In Her Own Words, Turtle Point Press, New York, 1996, p. 41
[12]Joan of Arc translated by Willard Trask, Joan of Arc: In Her Own Words, Turtle Point Press, New York, 1996, p. 25; said to her examiners in Poitiers, March 1429
[13]Joan of Arc, translated by Willard Trask, Joan of Arc: In Her Own Words, Turtle Point Press, New York, 1996, p. 15; Joan's words to Robert de Baudricourt, March 1429
[14]God had promised this land to the Israelites some 450 years before Moses, beginning with Abraham: *"All the land you see I will give to you and your offspring forever."* Genesis 13: 15 This passage (Exodus 3: 8, 10) was just the continuation of fulfilling that promise.
[15]http://www.stjoan-center.com/Trials/sec05.html, accessed January 21, 2012
[16]Régine Pernoud, Jeanne d'Arc par elle-meme et ses témoins, Editions du Seuil, Paris, 1996, p.51; Joan of Arc translated by Willard Trask, Joan of Arc: In Her Own Words, Turtle Point Press, New York, 1996, p. 21
[17]Régine Pernoud et Marie-Véronique Clin, Jeanne d'Arc, Editions Fayard, Mesnil-sur-l'Estrée, 2001, p. 33; said to Jean de Metz at Vaucouleurs, February 1429.
[18]Jean, Count of Dunois, Bastard of Orleans, Trial of Nullification; Joan said this on August 11, 1429.
[19]Joan of Arc translated by Willard Trask, Joan of Arc: In Her Own Words, Turtle Point Press, New York, 1996, p. 95
[20]*"The Lord...is patient with you, not wanting anyone to perish, but everyone to come*

to repentance." 2 Peter 3: 9

[21] Abraham learned this the hard way. Hoping to save the city of Sodom, he bargained with God, that if He could find but ten righteous people there, God would spare Sodom. The ten could not be found, and Sodom was destroyed. See Genesis 18: 16 - 19: 28

[22] Father Jean Pasquerel, Trail of Nullification; www.stjown-center.com/Trails/null07.html, 2011, Joan's Friends-Part 2, p.2; accessed June 2010

[23] Mr. Newman (1801-1890) was an important figure in the religious history of England in the 19th century. His beatification was officially proclaimed by Pope Benedict XVI on September 19, 2010.

[24] https://www.goodreads.com/author/quotes/203714.Henry_Ford, accessed Jan, 2014. Mr. Ford (1863-1947) was the founder of the Ford Motor Company, and sponsor of the development of the assembly line technique of mass production. His introduction of the Model T automobile revolutionized transportation and American industry.

[25] *"I will praise you with the harp for your faithfulness, my God..."* Psalm 71: 22

[26] *"For God does not show favoritism."* Romans 2: 11; *"The LORD does not look at the things man looks at. Man looks at the outward appearance, but the LORD looks at the heart."* 1 Samuel 16: 7

[27] *"For I know the plans I have for you," declares the Lord, "plans to prosper you and not to harm you, plans to give you hope and a future.* Jeremiah 29: 11

[28] *Then you will call upon me and come and pray to me, and I will listen to you. You will seek me and find me when you seek me with all your heart."* Jeremiah 29: 12-13

[29] Régine Pernoud (translated from the French by Edward Hyams), <u>Joan of Arc, By Herself and Her Witnesses</u>, Scarborough House, Lanham, MD, 1982, p. 30-31

[30] Willard Trask, <u>Joan of Arc-Self Portrait</u>, The Telegraph Press, New York, New York, 1936, p. 29

[31] *"If any of you lacks wisdom, he should ask God, who gives generously to all without finding fault, and it will be given to him."* James 1: 5

[32] *"Your word is a lamp to my feet and a light for my path."* Psalm 119: 105

Chapter 7
Remarkable Obedience

"It is necessary that I should go to the noble Dauphin;
my Lord the King of Heaven wills that I should go;
I go in the name of the King of Heaven; even if I have
to drag myself thither on my knees, I shall go!" Joan of Arc [1]

"He is no fool who gives what he cannot keep
to gain what he cannot lose." Jim Elliot [2]

Angry, indignant, and self-righteous, Carrie had finally had enough. She decided to set the record straight once and for all. She looked him right in the eye and said, "No!! I will not! You think you can tell me what to do?! I have the 'Right' to do what I want. It's my life! Who do you think you are, anyway? God Almighty? You don't own me!" With that she stomped out of the house, slamming the door behind her. Then, without even a moment's hesitation, she hopped on her bright red tricycle and sped off down the sidewalk.

Goodness. Do you know Carrie? Have you ever acted like Carrie? To your parents? Maybe to your spouse or significant other? How about to a teacher or boss? Many of us have, or at least wanted to. There's just something that really irritates us when someone plays the "authority-figure" card on us.

I know this isn't some great new revelation. It's as old as man himself. We seem to have an innate problem with authority. With obedience. Sylvester, our cat, provides an object lesson. He hardly ever seems happy anymore, and he's not shy in expressing his feelings. "Meow! ME-O-O-O-W-W-W!!" He used to go outside all the time, and he ruled (i.e. terrorized) the neighborhood with a firm paw. But about two years ago, he started coming home on a regular basis all beat up. We'd patch him up, and he'd rest indoors a couple of days. Then he'd be ready to go out again, determined to reclaim his kingdom one more time. However, as time went on, he came home more and more often a bloody mess. Trips to the vet became more frequent. The sad truth eventually became inescapable: Sylvester couldn't rule his territory anymore. He was getting too old. The new, younger cats on the block were taking over. He just couldn't stop them anymore.

But try telling Sylvester that! Even though his wounds were

becoming more serious all the time, he remained convinced that he was the King of his kingdom. Finally, we felt forced to step in to protect him from himself. Yes, that's when Sylvester became an indoor cat.

He didn't like that at all, and he let us know about it. He began making weird noises and destroying as much as he could in the house and, in general, making life hell for everyone living there. You see, Sylvester wants what he wants. Even if it kills him. He screams at us, "Nobody owns me! I have the right to do whatever I want! It's my life!"

Well, actually, there's part of the problem. Sylvester's life is not his alone. His life belongs to God. And just like Sylvester, our life doesn't belong completely to us either. *"Behold, all souls are mine, the soul of the father as well as the soul of the son is mine."* Ezekiel 18: 4

According to the Bible, it's God who gives us life: *"The spirit of God has made me; the breath of the Almighty gives me life."* Job 33: 4 Or: *"...the LORD...the Creator of the heavens ...gives breath to its people, and life to those who walk on it ... "* Isaiah 42: 5 Or: *"...God, who gives life to everything... "* 1 Tim 6: 13 Life is God's gift, not our "right".

Without this understanding, it's very difficult to cultivate an attitude of gratitude. Without gratitude for the gift of life, obedience to our Creator becomes impossible. Without obedience to the One who made us, how can we ever get to know Him? And if we don't know Him, life's incessant difficulties and injustices eventually just wear us down, leading to feelings of depression, anxiety, frustration, and anger; feelings of being unjustly attacked. In short, we are likely to become like a spoiled and rebellious child. Somewhat like Carrie... or our cat Sylvester. And if that happens...well...we want what we want. Even if it kills us.

Obedience has never been one of man's most popular concepts (see Adam and Eve in Genesis 2-3). But during the last forty or fifty years its popularity has plummeted even lower than usual. These days, many have decided that they are their own "higher power". After all, we want what we want. The advertisement world has figured this out, and is tapping into it for all its worth. How many times do we hear: "Buy our product! After all, you deserve it!" Does the advertising world really know what you or I deserve?

The truth is that obedience is a difficult concept to accept, much less do.

~~~~~~~~~~~~

Was Joan of Arc obedient to her God? Yes, at His request, she left family, friends, and home for an unknown and improbable future.[3] How did she feel about obedience? Well, she came from a time when most

people held more to the idea of "Father Knows Best". Just as some do today, many believed that following the will of God is what would lead them to their greatest level of joy. Why? Because God created us and knows what's best for us. And He <u>wants</u> what's best for us. These two verses from the previous chapter footnotes are worth repeating here:
"For I know the plans I have for you," declares the Lord, *"plans to prosper you and not to harm you, plans to give you hope and a future. Then you will call upon me and come and pray to me, and I will listen to you. You will seek me and find me when you seek me with all your heart."* Jeremiah 29: 11-13

Rightly understood and followed, God's commandments bring great joy and freedom, not a sense of oppression.[4] Jesus said, *"Come to me, all you who are weary and burdened, and I will give you rest. Take my yoke upon you and learn from me, for I am gentle and humble in heart, and you will find rest for your souls. For my yoke is easy and my burden is light."* Matthew 11: 28-30 The apostle John tells us, *"this is love for God: to keep his commands. And his commands are not burdensome."* 1 John 5: 3 So obedience to God's will is one of our greatest blessings, both in this life and in the one to come. This is the principle behind the Ten Commandments (Exodus 20). And this was part of the worldview from which Joan operated:

"I do best by serving my sovereign Lord-that is, God." Joan of Arc, Trial of Condemnation[5]

"I did not talk of my visions...I feared that my father would prevent me (from going into France)...But since God had commanded me to go, I must do it. And since God had commanded it, had I had a hundred fathers and hundred mothers, and had I been a king's daughter, I would have gone." Joan of Arc, Trial of Condemnation[6]

"Far rather would I sit and sew beside my poor mother, for this thing is not of my condition. But I must go, and I must do this, because my Lord will have it so." Joan of Arc, Trial of Condemnation[7]

"All that I have done is by our Lord's bidding. And if he had bid me put on other clothing I should have put it on because it was at his bidding. All that I have done at our Lord's bidding I believe that I have done rightly. And I expect good protection for it and good succour." Joan of Arc, Trial of Condemnation[8]

"I carry out our Lord's command, given me by my voices, with all my might-so much of it as I can understand. And they command me nothing

save at our Lord's good pleasure." [10]

Hear some of her words to her companions:

"Fear not: what I do, I do by commandment. My brothers in Paradise tell me what I must do. It is four or five years since my brothers in Paradise and My Lord first told me that I must go to restore the Kingdom of France." [11]

"My Lord has sent me to succour this good town of Orleans." Said April 29, 1429 [12]

This is consistent with what we see in Scripture:

"Does the Lord delight in burnt offerings and sacrifices as much as in obeying the voice of the Lord? To obey is better than sacrifice..."
1 Samuel 15: 22

"Christ Jesus...taking the very nature of a servant, being made in human likeness...he humbled himself and became obedient to death, even death on a cross! Therefore God exalted him to the highest place and gave him the name that is above every name..." Philippians 2: 5-9

"And this is love: that we walk in obedience to his commands. As you have heard from the beginning, his command is that you walk in love."
2 John 1: 6

There are many other quotes that could be cited from both the Bible and Joan of Arc, but the above quotes are sufficient to see the emphasis they both placed on obedience to God. And being obedient is both a commandment and our blessing.

"My God, I love you!"
The last words of St. Therese of Lisieux,
given from her death-bed on September 30, 1897 [13]

Of course, recognizing and acknowledging the importance of God's commandments is one thing, but actually doing them is quite another. It's easier said than done. If fact, we can't do them! At least, not on our own. This aspect deserves a closer look...

First of all, as we saw in the previous chapter, Jesus gave us God's greatest commandment (what I described as His "Mission Statement"):

"'...Love the Lord your God with all your heart and with all your soul and with all your mind'. This is the first and the greatest commandment. And the second is like it: 'Love your neighbor as yourself.' All the Law and the Prophets hang on these two commandments." Matthew 22: 37-40
But is this kind of love even possible? At first glance, it sounds impossible. I think I might have a little problem here.

Some might say, "Well, sure I love God. No problem." Really? How would God know that? Would a bumper sticker saying "What Would Jesus Do" be sufficient? Jesus said, *"Whoever has my commands and obeys them, he is the one who loves me. He who loves me will be loved by my Father, and I too will love him and show myself to him."* John 14: 21 Now I know I've got a problem. Do I obey all of the Lord's commands all the time? Well, no. Am I obedient all the time? Uh-h...no. The truth is none of us are. Even the great saints of the Bible were unable to remain obedient all the time. They all sinned, and sometimes did so BIG TIME. Just take a quick look at three of the greatest Biblical heroes:

1. King David, *"the apple of God's eye"* Psalm 17: 8, slept with the wife of one of his soldiers. He then saw to it that the woman's husband was killed so he could keep her for himself (2 Samuel 11).

2. Before his conversion, Paul (the great apostle to the gentiles) was personally responsible for zealously persecuting to death many in the new Christian church (Acts 7: 1 - 8: 3).

3. Peter (the Lord's disciple), even though he knew that Jesus was the Messiah (Matthew 16: 13-20), denied even knowing Him three times (John 18: 15-27). Then later on, even after Jesus' resurrection, we find him again inconsistent in his obedience (Galatians 2: 11-21).

What do David, Peter, Paul, you and I all have in common? We are all deeply flawed. As we just saw in Chapter 6, *"...all have sinned and fall short of the glory of God."* Romans 3: 23 Indeed. Nonetheless, through perseverance and with Jesus' help, we will get there!

1. Through Perseverance (Blessed Cussedness)
"He conquers who endures."
Persius (34–62 AD), was a Roman poet and satirist

Perseverance is defined as: *steady persistence in adhering to a course of action, a belief, or a purpose; a state of quality of being insistent...cussedness.*[14] Hmm...cussedness, huh. That sounds suspiciously like a kind of stubbornness to me. Maybe we could call perseverance a blessed cussedness.

"Blessed is the man who perseveres under trial, because when he has stood the test, he will receive the crown of life that God has promised to those who love him." James 1: 12

"Perseverance must finish its work so that you may be mature and complete, not lacking anything." James 1: 4

We are called to persevere. It is through perseverance that we display our faith. And true faith is not a single event, but a way of life. It endures.

2. With Jesus' Help
"Know Jesus, Know peace. No Jesus, No peace." [15]

Jesus has already paid the price for our sins. Past, present and future. I don't think that this side of heaven, living in this fallen world, we'll become the perfect vessels that God requires. But when we turn to Jesus, He helps us with our myriad imperfections and chronic disobedience. And His blood has taken away all of our sins. Now for me, this is a difficult concept to get a hold of... For one thing, just *"How far has the LORD taken our sins from us?"* The next line gives the answer: *"Farther than the distance from east to west!"* Psalm 103:12-13 (CEV) Now that's a long ways.

"Jesus is the God whom we can approach without pride and before whom we can humble ourselves without despair." Blaise Pascal

Wrap Up
"In His will is our peace." Dante [16]

Let me see if I got this right. By nature (i.e. our fallen nature), man rebels against authority.[17] He wants to be his own god. But without turning to the one true God, and striving to be obedient to His will, we can never fulfill our purpose of communion with Him. Without this communion, we never find peace, nor our true identity. Nor genuine enduring joy.[18] Scripture and prayer help us to better understand what His will is for us. But we find that obedience seems at times humanly impossible. However...

1) Jesus has prepared our way, and if we turn to Him, He will help us with this.

2) If we keep persevering...stubbornly...cussedly...one step at a time...day-by-day...always going toward His light in spite of our flaws and falls...come what may...we <u>will</u> get there! God will help us.[19] And when in God's light, we lack nothing.

THE WITCH THAT WASN'T

Joan of Arc was not perfect. At one point during her tortuous trial, hoping to escape further brutality of the English, she signed a document admitting her own "guilt".[20] However, within a couple of days, she recanted that document, and thereby knowingly ensured her own death by fire.[21] Her perseverance carried her to the end. She was obedient to God. Obedient to death. But she was also obedient in her daily life. Obedient in the small things as well as the large. With both the large and small, she kept the big picture in view. This is the pattern we see with the believers and prophets of the Bible.

David was not perfect. However, when confronted with his sins of murder and adultery, he admitted them and repented (2 Samuel 12). Of course, there were serious consequences for such sins. But David hung in there and persevered in his walk with God to the end.

Paul was not perfect. He was responsible for the deaths of innocent people. After being called by Jesus on the Damascus Road (Acts 9), he changed his life and forged ahead. He was beaten many times, left for dead, whipped, stoned, shipwrecked, persecuted in many ways, went hungry, was imprisoned, brought to trial, and eventually executed (2 Corinthians 11: 23-27). However he continued to talk about Jesus, persevered to the end, and surely is in God's presence now.

Peter was not perfect. Yes, he denied his Lord. Three times. Yes, he was inconsistent in his dealings with the new church (Galatians 2: 11-21). Still, Peter had a lot of stubborn cussedness in him. Blessed cussedness. He became a fearless witness for Jesus (e.g. Acts 2: 14-41; 3: 11-26; 4: 1-21...), leader of the other apostles, fought many battles for the faith, and persevered to the end.

This is the pattern seen consistently throughout Scripture, Christian history and daily life. Abraham, Moses, David, Peter, Paul, Francis of Assisi, Joan of Arc, Mother Teresa, Brother Roger of Taize...the list goes on and on. Anybody perfect on this list? No, not one. There is only one exception to this rule. Jesus Christ was completely obedient to His Father. Obedient in daily life. And obedient in death. Perfectly.

Our question then becomes, can we be obedient in the small things of daily life? Can we just stubbornly persevere? Yes, with God's help, we can. If we will continue to turn to Him one step at a time, the rest will take care of itself.

> *"True holiness consists in doing God's will with a smile"*
> Mother Teresa

[1] Quoted by Henri LeRoyer of Vaucouleurs, Trial of Nullification
[2] Mr. Elliot (1927-1956) was an evangelical Christian who was one of five missionaries killed while participating in Operation Auca, an attempt to evangelize the Waodani people of Ecuador.
[3] For a Biblical parallel, see Abraham's story: Genesis 12: 1-4
[4] Crossway Bibles. *ESV Study Bible-English Standard Version*, Good News Publishers, Wheaton IL, 2007, notes from p. 2,436
[5] Joan of Arc translated by Willard Trask, Joan of Arc: In Her Own Words, Turtle Point Press, New York, 1996, p. 107
[6] Régine Pernoud, Jeanne d'Arc par elle-meme et ses témoins, Editions du Seuil, Paris, 1996, p.32
[7] Régine Pernoud et Marie-Véronique Clin, Jeanne d'Arc, Editions Fayard, Mesnil-sur-l'Estrée, 2001, p. 33
[8] Régine Pernoud, Jeanne d'Arc par elle-meme et ses témoins, Editions du Seuil, Paris, 1996, p.219
[9] Willard Trask, Joan of Arc: In Her Own Words, Turtle Point Press, New York, 1996, p. 112
[10] Ibid, p. 120
[11] Ibid, p. 19-20
[12] Joan of Arc, translated by Willard Trask, Joan of Arc: In Her Own Words, Turtle Point Press, New York, 1996, p. 34
[13] http://en.wikipedia.org/wiki/Th%C3%A9r%C3%A8se_of_Lisieux, accessed May, 2012
[14] http://www.thefreedictionary.com/perseverance, March, 2014-Underlining by author.
[15] Found on a car bumper sticker.
[16] Dante (Alighieri), c1265-1321, was an Italian poet, prose writer, literary theorist, moral philosopher, and political thinker. He is best known for the monumental epic poem *La divina commedia* (Divine Comedy), considered the greatest literary work composed in the Italian language and a masterpiece of world literature.
[17] Cat too. Like man, we often saw Sylvester sneaking around, trying to get away with whatever he could. He seemed well aware of his disobedience.
[18] Chuck Colson said, *"Knowing that we are fulfilling God's purpose is the only thing that really gives rest to the restless human heart."* Mr. Colson (October 16, 1931-April 21, 2012) was a Christian leader, cultural commentator, and former Special Counsel for President Richard Nixon from 1969 to 1973. He converted to Christianity in 1973. He served seven months in the federal Maxwell Prison as the first member of the Nixon administration to be incarcerated for Watergate-related charges. He created Prison Fellowship in 1976, which today is the nation's largest outreach to prisoners, ex-prisoners, and their families. He was also well known as a public speaker and author.
[19] See Chapter 9-God's Help
[20] Joan of Arc, Trial of Condemnation, March 12, 1431; see Daniel Hobbins, The Trial of Joan of Arc, Harvard University Press, Cambridge, MA, 2005, p. 92
[21] Francis Winwar, The Saint and the Devil-Joan of Arc and Gilles de Rais, Harper & Brothers Publishers, New York and London, 1948, p. 210-211

Chapter 8
Enduring Persecution

"Blessed are those who are persecuted because of righteousness, for theirs is the kingdom of heaven."
Jesus Christ, the Sermon on the Mount, Matthew 5: 10

Here is my own informal 'one-question-survey', given to a group of eighty-five Americans:

What are three things a Christian might encounter in the world today?

How would you answer? Although obviously not an in-depth survey, the results were interesting. Here are the top five answers:

1. another Christian
2. love
3. misunderstanding regarding Christianity
4. sin
5. non-believers

How many times do you think persecution was listed? Just once out of 255 answers. Had this survey been conducted in most other times or places throughout history, I believe it would have been listed quickly and often. Could this indicate that persecution no longer exists today? No, it doesn't mean that. In fact, we will see just the opposite.

Historically in America, a nation born of religious freedom, it has not been socially acceptable to overtly demonstrate one's hatred of Christianity. Until recently, most seemed hesitant to openly attack it. But this has been changing, especially these last thirty-forty years. From the relentless attack on Christmas, to the obsessive attempt to excise anything referring to God or Jesus from public life (as if this was what the founders had in mind at the birth of the nation!), the drum beat for getting rid of God grows louder all the time. But Christian persecution is as old as its founder. Jesus was well aware of the price to follow him:

"Blessed are you when men hate you, when they exclude you and insult you and reject your name as evil, because of the Son of Man. Rejoice in that day and leap for joy, because great is your reward in heaven." Luke 6: 22-23

It's interesting to note that the two messengers sent by God to counsel Joan of Arc, Saint Catherine and Saint Margaret, were themselves victims of persecution. And like Joan, they both died at a young age...

According to tradition, Saint Catherine of Alexandria was a young girl who like Joan of Arc, pledged her virginity to God. She was renowned for her great intelligence and faith in God. She used these tools in trying to dissuade Emperor Maxentius (279-312 AD) from his persecution of Christians. This eventually led to her being thrown into prison, tortured and then beheaded at the age of eighteen.[1]

Saint Margaret of Antioch also consecrated her virginity to God. According to tradition, she was the daughter of a pagan priest, Aedisius of Antioch. She became a Christian and was thereby disowned by her father. She then lived as a shepherdess. Known for her great beauty, she refused marriage to Olybrius, governor of Antioch. When she wouldn't renounce her faith, she was tortured. Still she refused to renounce her God or accept the Roman gods as her own. Thrown into prison, she continued to preach the word, and consequently converted large numbers to Christianity. She was eventually beheaded during the Great Persecution of Diocletian (303-305AD).[2]

We are not surprised to see persecution from such evil tyrants as a Diocletian, Nero, Stalin or Hitler. As non-believers, they hated Christianity, and persecuted to death millions of Jews and Christians alike. As John Calvin said, *"Against the persecution of a tyrant the godly have no remedy but prayer."*[3] But some of the worst cases of persecution come from within the faith itself. In this context, the similarities between Joan and Jesus are striking...

"...Persecuted Because of Righteousness..." Mt. 5: 10

*"Wicked men seem to bear great reverence
to the saints departed; they canonize dead saints,
but persecute the living."* Thomas Watson [4]

1. After the highpoint of Orleans, when Joan was welcomed as a great prophetess and the savior of the city[5], who could have imagined that in less than a year she would be captured, persecuted, and killed?

After the highpoint of the first Palm Sunday in Jerusalem, when Jesus was welcomed as a great prophet and the long-awaited Savior[6], who could have imagined that in just one short week He would be captured, persecuted, and killed?

2. Her own King would betray her.[7] Although it was Joan who was most responsible for the King finally obtaining his crown, his gratitude would be short lived. He would abandon her as soon as she was captured.

One of His own disciples would betray him. *"While he was still speaking Judas, one of the Twelve, arrived. With him was a large crowd armed with swords and clubs, sent from the chief priests and the elders of the people. Now the betrayer had arranged a signal with them: The one I kiss is the man; arrest him. Going at once to Jesus, Judas said, Greetings, Rabbi, and kissed him."* Matthew 26: 47-50

3. She would then be subjected to an illegal and prejudiced "trial" that was engineered and conducted by the religious authorities, but which was primarily for political reasons.[8] Joan was not allowed to have a lawyer, or any legal representative. On the other hand, a multitude of church authorities (nearly ninety lawyers, clerics and scholars) had gathered together, looking for some way to put her to death. Joan stood alone against them. *"I do not know whether she asked for counsel, but I think no one would have dared to counsel or defend her, nor would they have been permitted."*[9] *"Jeanne had no director, Counsel, nor defender, up to the end of the Process, and no one would have dared to offer himself as her counsel, director, or defender, for fear of the English. I have heard that those who went to the castle to counsel and direct Jeanne, by order of the Judges, were harshly repulsed and threatened."*[10]

He would then be subjected to an illegal and prejudiced "trial" that was engineered and conducted by the religious authorities, but which was primarily for political reasons. Jesus was not allowed to have a lawyer, or any legal representation. On the other hand, a multitude of religious authorities, i.e. *"the chief priests and the whole Sanhedrin"*[11], had gathered together, looking for some way to put Him to death. Jesus stood alone against them. *"The chief priests and the whole Sanhedrin were looking for false evidence against Jesus so that they could put him to death. But they did not find any, though many false witnesses came forward."* Matthew 26: 59-61

4. They would make an example of her. It was imperative for the English that they "prove" Joan to be a "witch", an agent of the devil.[12] Otherwise they feared that the people would think that God was with her,

and therefore against them.[13] So they accused her of witchcraft and being an agent of the devil. In the first paragraph of their first document against her (The Seventy Articles), they listed their official charges, which include *"...heresies, witchcrafts, superstitions..."*[14]

They would make an example of Him.[15] It was imperative for the *"the chief priests and the whole Sanhedrin"* that they "prove" Jesus to be a "demon", an agent of the devil. Otherwise they feared that the people would think that God was with Him, and therefore against them. So they accused Him of being a demon, an agent of the devil. They said, *"It is only by Beelzebub, the prince of demons, that this fellow drives out demons."*[16]

5. The religious authorities, not secular, were the ones primarily responsible for her prosecution.[17]

The religious authorities, not secular, were the ones primarily responsible for His prosecution. *"But some of them went to the Pharisees and told them what Jesus had done. Then the chief priests and the Pharisees called a meeting of the Sanhedrin..."* John 11: 46-47

6. They were willing to do whatever was necessary in order for her to die. And they did this in the name of God![18]

They were willing to do whatever was necessary in order for Him to die. And they did this in the name of God! *"Again the high priest asked him, 'Are you the Christ, the Son of the Blessed One?' 'I am,' said Jesus, 'And you will see the son of Man sitting at the right hand of the Mighty One and coming on the clouds of heaven.' The high priest tore his clothes. 'Why do we need any more witnesses?' he asked...They all condemned him as worthy of death."* Mark 14: 61-65

7. After being found guilty by the religious authorities, she would immediately be turned over to the secular authorities (soldiers), and then quickly led to her death, and this in a most cruel and public way. In fact, as soon as the church passed sentence on her, she was taken by soldiers to the stake and burned to death. The church part of the trial was illegal from several standpoints, and reflects the hatred and fear the religious authorities had for her. *"The sentence was pronounced as though Joan had been abandoned to secular justice. Immediately after that sentence, she was put in the hands of the bailiff, and before the bailiff or I, to whom it belonged to pronounce such a sentence, had the chance to pronounce*

one, the executioner seized Joan without further ado and led her to the place where the wood had been prepared and she was burned."[19]

After being found guilty by the religious authorities, He would immediately be turned over to the secular authorities (soldiers), and then quickly led to His death, and this in a most cruel and public way. In fact, as soon as Pilot passed sentence on Him, He was taken by soldiers to Golgotha and crucified to death.[20] The Jewish part of the trial was illegal from several standpoints[21], and reflects the hatred and fear the Jewish religious authorities had for Him.

8. They put a hat on her with her "crimes" written on it: *"Heretic, relapsed, apostate, idolatress"*.[22] They also had a painted board placed right in front of the stake that said, *"Jehanne who called herself the Maid, liar, pernicious, deceiver of the people, sorceress* (i.e. a witch), *superstitious blasphemer of God, presumptuous, disbeliever in the faith of Jesus Christ, boastful, idolatrous, cruel, dissolute* (meaning immoral), *invoker of devils, apostate, schismatic, and heretic."*[23]

They put a sign over His head with His "crimes" written on it. *"Above his head they placed the written charge against him: 'This is Jesus, the King of the Jews'."* Mark 15: 26; Matthew 27: 37; John 19: 19-22

9. Even from the stake she was heard asking for the forgiveness of those who were executing her, as well as for her own sins.[24] *"She also most humbly begged all manner of people, of whatever condition or rank they might be, and whether of her party or not, for their pardon and asked them kindly to pray for her, at the same time pardoning them for any harm they had done her. This she continued to do for a very long time, perhaps for half an hour and until the end. The judges who were present, and even several of the English, were moved by this to great tears and weeping* (see also # 12 below), *and indeed several of these same English, recognized God's hand and made professions of faith when they saw her make so remarkable an end."*[25]

Even from the cross Jesus was heard asking for the forgiveness of those who were executing Him. *"Jesus said, 'Father, forgive them, for they do not know what they are doing.'"* Luke 23: 34

10. She would be lifted up high for all to see. At this time it was the custom, as an act of mercy, for the executioner to strangle the person before the flames reached them. In Joan's case however, they built her

platform much higher than usual. In fact, it was so high that the executioner was unable to reach her before the flames did. Consequently, she was indeed burned to death.[26]

He would be lifted up high for all to see. *"Here they crucified him, and with him, two others-one on each side and Jesus in the middle."* John 19: 18

11. In Joan's case, when all the people who had gathered to witness this sight saw what took place, many broke into tears. *"...Once in the fire, she cried out more than six times, 'Jesus!'...so that everyone present could hear it; almost all wept with pity."*[27]

In Jesus' case, *"When all the people who had gathered to witness this sight saw what took place, they beat their breast and went away."* Luke 23: 48

12. Even John Tressart, secretary to the King of England, seeing what had happened exclaimed, *"We are lost, we've burned a Saint!"*[28]

Even a Roman soldier, *"...seeing what had happened, praised God and said, 'Surely this was a righteous man.'"* Luke 23: 47

13. She had prophesied her martyrdom more than once. Here's one example:
Joan: *"Saint Catherine told me that I will have help...that I will be delivered by a great victory, and then my voices told me, 'Take everything serenely, do not shrink from your martyrdom; from that you will come finally to the kingdom of paradise.' And this my voices have told me simply and absolutely, that is, assuredly. I call it martyrdom because of the pain and oppression that I suffer in prison. I do not know if I shall suffer a greater pain yet; that I leave with our Lord."*
Response from one of the church authorities: *"That is an answer of great weight."*
Joan: *"I hold it also to be a great treasure."*[29]

He had prophesied His martyrdom more than once. Very early in His ministry He said, *"Destroy this temple, and I will raise it again in three days.' The Jews replied, 'It has taken 46 years to build this temple, and you are going to raise it in three days?' But the temple he had spoken of was his body. After he was raised from the dead, his disciples recalled what he had said. Then they believed the Scripture and the words that*

Jesus had spoken." John 2: 19-22

Again, just before going to Jerusalem for the last time, Jesus told His disciples this: *"We are going up to Jerusalem, and everything that is written by the prophets about the Son of Man will be fulfilled. He will be handed over to the Gentiles. They will mock him, insult him, spit on him, flog him and kill him. On the third day he will rise again."* Luke 18: 31-33. See also Matthew 20: 17-19 and Mark 10: 32-34

14. Her enemies had believed that by killing her, they would be rid of her once and for all. *"I know well that these English will put me to death, thinking that after I am dead they will win the Kingdom of France. But even if they were a hundred thousand more that they are now they shall not have the kingdom."* Joan of Arc[30]

His enemies had believed that by killing Him, they would be rid of Him once and for all. *"Now the Feast of Unleavened Bread, called the Passover, was approaching, and the chief priests and the teachers of the law were looking for some way to get rid of Jesus, for they were afraid of the people."* Luke 22: 1-2

15. But her death was not the end of this amazing story, but rather the beginning of a new one. Around this one event France would rally to a new hope and future.[31]

But His death was not the end of this amazing story, but rather the beginning of a new one. Around this one event mankind would rally to a new hope and future. *"The angel said to the women, 'Do not be afraid, for I know that you are looking for Jesus, who was crucified. He is not here; he has risen, just as he said. Come and see the place where he lay. Then go quickly and tell his disciples: He has risen from the dead...'"* Matthew 28: 5-7

16. Through her France would be resurrected. Although England's power over France would continue for a season, ultimately the English would be kicked out of France, never to reclaim it again.[32]

Through His power and grace, Jesus the Messiah would be resurrected.[32] Although Satan's power would continue for a season (until the second coming of Christ), ultimately he will be kicked out of this earthly kingdom, never to reclaim it again.[33]

17. On May 30, 1431, the day of her death, she spoke of paradise. After

being told she was to be immediately burned to death, she asked Master Pierre Maurice: *"'Master Pierre, where shall I be this night?'" And Master Pierre answered her, 'Do you not have good hope in God?' She answered him, 'Yes, and by God's grace I shall be in Paradise.'"*[34]

On the day of His death, He spoke of paradise. While they were both hanging on a cross, the thief said to Him, *"'Jesus, remember me when you come into your kingdom.' Jesus answered him, 'I tell you the truth, today you will be with me in paradise.'"* Luke 23: 42-43

Just a few other notes:

A) An irony: the same church that had put her to death in 1431 would canonize her nearly five hundred years later. On May 16, 1920 Joan of Arc became not only the heroine of France, but also France's patron Saint.

B) Irony of ironies: under the pretext of saving the Jewish faith from yet another false prophet, religious authorities had Jesus killed. But instead of the movement dissolving, the Christian church was born from His death. It would become more powerful and influential than the Sanhedrin would have ever dreamed.

C) How did Joan view her time of persecution? *"I believe, since it pleases our Lord, that it is best that I am a prisoner."*[35]

Asked if her angels had not failed her, since she was now a prisoner, she replied, *"How could they fail me, when they comfort me each and every day?"*[36]

D) They could not destroy Joan's heart. Neither literally, nor figuratively. When she was dead, the executioner was asked to destroy every part of her body that might remain. To his great surprise, he found Joan's heart still intact, and filled with liquid blood. During the Trial of Nullification, Friar Isambart testified to what the executioner had revealed to him about this: *"...despite the oil, the sulfur, and the carbon that he had applied to the entrails and the heart of Joan, he still could not make them burn in any way, nor could he reduce her entrails and her heart to ashes, at which he was as astonished as if by a confirmed miracle."*[37]

It has been reported by some that Joan's remains have recently been discovered. Given the historical record, this seems unlikely. Jean Massieu, a bailiff during the Trial of Condemnation, also testified to what the executioner told him: *"...although her body had been burned in the fire and reduced to ashes, her heart remained intact and full of blood, and he was told to gather the ashes and everything that remained of her and to throw them in the Seine River, which he did."*[38]

An interesting analogy to the above can be drawn: they (i.e. the forces of evil down through the centuries) have not been able to destroy the heart of Jesus (i.e. the church of faith), despite the millions of Christians who have been persecuted to death in the attempt.

~~~~~~~~~~~~~

Christian Persecution: Then and Now
"If the Tiber rises too high, or the Nile too low, the remedy is always feeding Christians to the lions." Tertullian (c. 160-c. 225 AD)

In its first three centuries, the Christian church endured frequent persecution at the hands of the Roman authorities. Although the Roman Empire was usually tolerant in its treatment of other religions, Christianity fell under a different category. In general, the imperial policy was one of incorporation: i.e. the local gods of a newly conquered area were simply added to the Roman pantheon, and often even given Roman names. Even the Jews with their one God were mostly tolerated. So why the persecution of Christians?

For the Romans, religion was first and foremost a social activity that promoted unity and loyalty to the state. Christianity however was viewed as a superstition, or as Pliny the Younger (a Roman governor circa 110 AD) said in his letter to Emperor Trajan, *"...a superstition taken to extravagant lengths"*. The Roman historian Tacitus called it *"...a deadly superstition."*[39] Gaius Suetonius Tranquillus, commonly known as Suetonius (circa 69/75 – after 138), was an official under the emperor Hadrian from 117 to 138 AD, and a Roman historian in the early Imperial era. He called Christians *"...a class of persons given to a new and mischievous superstition."*[40] In short, Christianity was seen as something strange, foreign and bad for society.

The Romans believed that the gods helped to sustain the well-being of their cities and people. They believed that bad things would happen if the gods were not respected and worshiped properly. Many thought that the neglect of the old gods, who had made Rome strong, was responsible for the disasters which were overtaking their world.[41]

On a more practical level, Christians were also distrusted because of the secret and misunderstood nature of their worship. Words like "love feast" and talk of "eating Christ's flesh" sounded suspicious to the pagans, and Christians were suspected of cannibalism, incest, orgies, and all sorts of immorality. All of this contributed to the many Christian persecutions in Rome. Recant your faith or suffer the consequences was the message repeatedly given and applied.

Besides being put to death, Christians were used as objects of amusement.[42] Such as dressing them up in the hides of animals, and then throwing them to the dogs to be torn to pieces. Others were crucified. When night came on, some were set on fire to illuminate the darkness.[43] For such displays, Nero (37- 68 AD; Roman Emperor 54-68 AD) would open to the public his personal grounds. He organized "shows" in his "circus", during which he'd drive around in his chariot dressed up as a charioteer, mingling with the people.[44] Quite a party, huh.

Did persecution of believers end this new religion? Quite the contrary: *"Though beheaded, and crucified, and thrown to wild beasts, and chains, and fire, and all other kinds of torture, we don't give up our confession; but, the more such things happen, the more do others in larger numbers become faithful."*[45] As Tertullian said, *"The blood of the martyrs is the seed of the Church."*[46]

Christian persecution and its resulting martyrs would have significant consequences for the developing faith. Including among other things, the rapid growth and spread of Christianity, and well thought out explanations of what the faith is really all about. By the time Joan of Arc came on the world stage, Christianity had established itself as the principal faith of Europe. But just as today, you could always choose a different "god" if you so desired. The love of money, power, and even Satanism were all alive and well during the Middle Ages. The case of Gilles de Rais provides a frightening example. One of Joan's companions in arms, he was one of the most infamous serial killers of children in recorded history. We'll take a closer look at his case in Chapter 13.

Some claim that man is making great progress towards world peace. That man's "spiritual evolution" is blossoming worldwide, and that persecution will soon just be a faded memory.[47] A quick look at world history books, or the morning newspapers, should give them second thoughts. In any case, it would seem that with a 'blossoming worldwide spiritual evolution', we should have at least made some progress reducing man's inhumanity to man.[48] Alas, statistics don't support this.[49] Everywhere we look today, people are at war[50], and persecution is alive and well on Planet Earth.

In fact, Christian persecution has increased. According to a Regent University study done in 1999, there were close to 156,000 Christians martyred around the world in 1998. In 2006, according to Gordon-

Conwell Theological Seminary, 171,000 Christians were martyred for their faith. This, according to the authors, compares to 34,400 at the beginning of the 20th century. If current trends continue, Barrett, Johnson and Crossing estimate that by 2025, an average of 210,000 Christians will be martyred annually. On April 8, 2002, the United Nations Commission on Human Rights reported: *"We estimate that today there are more than 200 million Christians in at least 60 countries who do not have full human rights as defined by the UN Declaration of Human Rights, simply because they are Christians. We believe that this is the largest group in the world without full human rights because of their beliefs."* [51] What's the bottom line? *"There have been <u>more than 100,000,000 people</u> martyred for their faith in Jesus Christ in the 20th century; more than in all the previous nineteen centuries combined."* [52]

Let's recall Jesus' words about persecution of believers: *"If the world hates you, keep in mind that it hated me first. If you belonged to the world, it would love you as its own. As it is, you do not belong to the world, but I have chosen you out of the world. That is why the world hates you…If they persecuted me, they will persecute you also…They will treat you this way because of my name, for they do not know the One who sent me."* John 15: 18-21

The Bible has some words of comfort for all those enduring persecution today, no matter what form it may take: *"Do not be afraid of what you are about to suffer. I tell you, the devil will put some of you in prison to test you, and you will suffer persecution…Be faithful, even to the point of death, and I will give you the crown of life. He who has an ear, let him hear what the Spirit says to the churches. He who overcomes will not be hurt at all by the second death."* Revelation 2: 10-11

---

[1] http://www.catholic.org/saints/saint.php?saint_id=341, accessed Jan. 2012; http://www.newadvent.org/cathen/03445a.htm, accessed Jan-Feb 2012
[2] Ibid.
[3] http://www.persecution.net/pray1.htm, accessed Jan. 2014. John Calvin (1509-1564) was an influential French theologian and pastor during the Protestant Reformation.
[4] Thomas Watson 1620-1686 was an English, non-conformist, Puritan preacher and author.
[5] Régine Pernoud and Marie-Véronique Clin, Jeanne d'Arc, Editions Fayard, Mesnil-sur-l'Estrée, 2001, p. 80-81
[6] *The next day the great crowd that had come for the Feast heard that Jesus was on his way to Jerusalem. They took palm branches and went out to meet him shouting, 'Hosanna! Blessed is he who comes in the name of the Lord! Blessed is the King of Israel!'…So the Pharisees said to one another, 'See how the whole world has gone after him!'"* John 12: 12-13, 19

[7] V. Sackville-West, Saint Joan of Arc, Country Life Press, Garden City, N.Y., U.S.A, 1936, p. 265

[8] *"I marvel much that such great Clerks as those who caused her death at Rouen should have dared such a crime as to put to death so poor and simple a Christian, cruelly and without cause-sufficient for death. They might have kept her in prison or elsewhere; but she had so displeased them that they were her mortal enemies; and thus, it seems, they assumed the responsibility of an unjust court."* Father Pasquerel, Trial of Nullification

[9] Brother Pierre Migier, Prior of Longueville, Trial of Nullification, Second Examination, May 9, 1452; www.stjoan-center.com, St Joan of Arc Center, Albuquerque, New Mexico, accessed June, 2011

[10] Brother Martin Lavenu, Trial of Nullification, May 3, 1452; www.stjoan-center.com, Ibid.

[11] The Sanhedrin was the "supreme court" of ancient Israel, and was made up of 71 members.

[12] John of Lancaster, the English Duke of Bedford (1389-1435), sent Charles VII an angry letter in early August of 1429. Ben Kennedy (MaidOfHeaven.com) tells us that the Duke *"...was a wily and unscrupulous leader who used whatever means available to him to obtain his objective. The letter...gives an early hint of how Bedford planned to destroy Joan and reverse her successes by calling her a witch. When Joan was captured the following spring by Bedford's Burgundian allies it was the chance Bedford had prepared for to have Joan convicted of heresy by the Church so as to discredit Charles VII hoping people would believe he had obtained his crown by the aid of witchcraft. Joan's trial and ultimate execution under the auspices of the Church was carefully orchestrated and paid for by Bedford who was in complete control of the entire proceedings."* Ben Kennedy, www.maidofheaven.com/joanofarc_duke_bedford.asp. Accessed March 2012

[13] Régine Pernoud and Marie-Véronique Clin. Joan of Arc-Her Story, St Martin's Griffin, New York, New York, 1998, p. 142

[14] From The Promoter Presents His Petition and The Seventy Articles as found at: www.stjoan-center.com, St Joan of Arc Center, Albuquerque, New Mexico. Accessed May, 2010

[15] *"Then ...the high priest, Caiaphas spoke up, '...It is better...that one man die for the people than that the whole nation perish.'"* John 11: 49-50

[16] Matthew 12: 24; See Matthew 12: 22-28

[17] Régine Pernoud and Marie-Véronique Clin, Jeanne d'Arc, Editions Fayard, Mesnil-sur-l'Estrée, 2001, p. 105

[18] Régine Pernoud and Marie-Véronique Clin, Jeanne d'Arc, Editions Fayard, Mesnil-sur-l'Estrée, 2001, p. 133

[19] Laurent, bailiff of Rouen, Trial of Nullification; Régine Pernoud and Marie-Véronique Clin, Jeanne d'Arc, Editions Fayard, Mesnil-sur-l'Estrée, 2001, p. 215

[20] *"...Pilot handed him over to them to be crucified. So the soldiers took charge of Jesus. Carrying his own cross, he went out to the place of the Skull (which in Aramaic is called Golgotha). Here they crucified him..."* John 19: 16-18. Crucifixion was the most painful and humiliating form of death conceived up to this point in history.

[21] http://www.netbiblestudy.com/00_cartimages/illegaltrialofjesus.pdf; Accessed March 2012

[22] Martin Ladvenu, Trial of the Nullification

[23] Clement de Fauquemberque, Trial of Nullification, Proces-Vol. IV, p 459

[24] Ibid

[25] Régine Pernoud and Marie-Véronique Clin, Jeanne d'Arc, Editions Fayard, Mesnil-sur-l'Estrée, 2001, p. 80-81; Francis Gies, Joan of Arc-The Legend and the Reality, Harper and Row publishers, New York, 1981, p. 223; John Holland Smith, Joan of Arc, Sidgwick & Jackson, London, 1973, p.173; V. Sackville West, Saint Joan of Arc, Country

Life Press, Garden City, N.V., 1936, p. 340-342
[26] Jean Massieu, Trial of Nullification. He served as usher during the Trial of Condemnation. Also see Ann W. Astell, Political Allegory in Late Medieval England, Cornell University Press, Ithaca, N.Y., 1999, p. 145
[27] Régine Pernoud and Marie-Véronique Clin, Jeanne d'Arc, Editions Fayard, Mesnil-sur-l'Estrée, 2001, p. 136-137
[28] Régine Pernoud, Jeanne d'Arc par elle-meme et ses témoins, Editions du Seuil, Paris, 1996, p. 276
[29] Trial of Condemnation; Régine Pernoud and Marie-Véronique Clin, Jeanne d'Arc, Editions Fayard, Mesnil-sur-l'Estrée, 2001, p. 190
[30] Joan of Arc's words to Jean de Luxembourg while in prison. Régine Pernoud and Marie-Véronique Clin, Jeanne d'Arc, Editions Fayard, Mesnil-sur-l'Estrée, 2001, p. 204
[31] Régine Pernoud and Marie-Véronique Clin, Joan of Arc-Her Story, St Martin's Griffin, New York, New York, 1998, p. 139, 142, 146-147, 149
[32] *"For what I received I passed on to you as of first importance: that Christ died for our sins according to the Scriptures, that he was buried, that he was raised on the third day according to the Scriptures, and that he appeared to Peter, and then to the Twelve. After that he appeared to more than five hundred of the brothers at the same time..."* 1 Corinthians 15: 3-6
[33] *"And the devil, who deceived them, was thrown into the lake of burning sulfur, where the beast and the false prophet had been thrown. They will be tormented day and night for ever and ever."* Revelation 20: 10 (Future prophecy yet to be fulfilled.)
[34] Régine Pernoud, Jeanne d'Arc par elle-meme et ses témoins, Editions du Seuil, Paris, 1996, p. 275
[35] Joan of Arc translated by Willard Trask, Joan of Arc: In Her Own Words, Turtle Point Press, New York, 1996, p. 112
[36] Trial of Condemnation, March 12, 1431
[37] Régine Pernoud and Marie-Véronique Clin, Jeanne d'Arc, Editions Fayard, Mesnil-sur-l'Estrée, 2001, p. 219
[38] Ibid. p. 218
[39] Annals 15-44, c. AD 115.
[40] Lives of the Caesars, 26:2.
[41] At home things had been deteriorating for the Romans. The wealth that now flowed into Rome from her overseas territories, in the form of war booty and taxes, increased social tensions, as the rich got richer and the poor got poorer. This poisoned the politics of Rome, and led to political extremism and violence.
[42] *"...Nero ...inflicted the most exquisite tortures on a class hated for their abominations, called Christians by the populace."* Tacitus' Annals XV.44. Tacitus (AD 56-AD 117) was a senator and a historian of the Roman Empire.
[43] *"... in their deaths they were made the subjects of sport; for they were wrapped in the hides of wild beasts and torn to pieces by dogs, or nailed to crosses, or set on fire, and when day declined, were burned to serve for nocturnal lights."* Ibid.
[44] Ibid.
[45] Justin Martyr (martyred for the faith in 165 AD), Ante-Nicene Fathers Vol. I, Dialogue with Trypho, Chapter CX
[46] Tertullian (160-225 AD), was a prolific early Christian author from Carthage in the Roman province of Africa, and a notable early Christian apologist and a polemicist against heresy.
[47] www.gurusoftware.com/GuruNet/Articles/Pages/Societys.htm. Accessed Jan. 2012. This is just one of many sites easily found on the web.
[48] Will Rogers' humoristic perception is otherwise: *"You can't say civilization don't advance...in every war they kill you in a new way."* Mr. Rogers (1879-1935) was a well-

known humorist, social commentator, vaudeville performer, and motion picture actor.
[49]Two examples: a) *"In the last 3 centuries there have been 286 wars on the continent of Europe alone."* J.K. Laney, Marching Orders, p 50. b) *"The Personnel Journal reported this incredible statistic: since the beginning of recorded history, the entire world has been at peace less than eight percent of the time! In its study, the periodical discovered that of 3530 years of recorded history, only 286 years saw peace. Moreover, in excess of 8000 peace treaties were made--and broken."* Moody Bible Institute, Today In The Word, June, 1988, p.33
[50]According to Wikipedia twenty-seven ongoing conflicts existed in the world as of 04-09-10: http://wiki.answers.com/Q/How_many_wars_are_currently_going_on_in_the_world_today. Accessed March 2011
[51]Johan Candelin, Director to the WEA Religious Liberty Commission WFA, www.worldevangelicals.org
[52]James & Marti Hefley, <u>By Their Blood</u>, Baker Book House Co, Grand Rapids, 2004, back book cover. Underlining by author.

For those wanting to know more about Christian persecution today, go to Voice of the Martyrs: www.persecution.com They are, *"...a non-profit interdenominational organization with a vision for aiding Christians around the world who are being persecuted for their faith in Christ."*

Chapter 9
God's Help Ever-Present
"...God sent me to the help of the King of France."
Joan of Arc, Trial of Condemnation, March 17, 1431

"Help! I need somebody. Help! Not just anybody. Help! You know I need someone...Help!!" Lennon/McCartney 1965

Did John Lennon have 'God's Help' in mind when he wrote this song? Nah. I don't think so.[1] But looking at these lyrics today, it does seem that they could be directed towards Him. Certainly they express feelings we can all identify with. We all need some help. Fortunately, help is available. The Bible says, *"...do not fear, for I am with you; do not be dismayed, for I am your God. I will strengthen you and help you; I will uphold you with my righteous right hand."* Isaiah 41: 10

For Joan of Arc, God's help was not something obscure or difficult to grasp. She experienced it first hand, and recognized it as such. From the time she was a child, it was a natural part of her life: *"Above all, Saint Michael told me that I must be a good child, and that God would help me."*[2] As time passed, her implicit trust in Him and His help continued to grow and be strengthened. Before her examination by church authorities in Poitiers, she said, *"I know that I shall have much to do in Poitiers. But my Lord will help me. In God's name, let us go on!"*[3] During her Trial, she again spoke of God's help. And, of leaving up to Him the form it should take:

Question: *"Did you ask your saints if ... you would win every battle you entered, and be victorious?"*
Joan: *"They told me to take it up bravely and God would help me."*[4]

And here's an interesting quote: *"My voices have told me that, if I want our Lord to help me, I must lay all my deeds before Him."*[5] This calls to mind a verse from 1 John: *"If we confess our sins, he is faithful and just and will forgive us our sins and purify us from all unrighteousness."* 1 John 1: 9 Joan took this to heart. Wishing to help the people of Compiegne who were under English siege, she made an unsuccessful prison escape when she jumped from a seventy foot high wall! She survived, but this easily could have killed her. Her messengers had forbidden her many times to jump. She testified that after this ill-conceived attempt, she *"...confessed it and begged our Lord to forgive me for it, and I have our Lord's pardon for it. And I think it was not right for me to jump-it was wrong."*[6]

But what about us? What about the great majority of people who are not having daily conversations with angels?[7] How exactly does God help us? Well, in many ways. Let's take a look at seven of them, and Joan's willingness to gratefully make use of them all.

1) The Church

"She was the most perfect daughter of her Church; to her its sacraments were the very Bread of Life; her conscience, by frequent confession, was kept fair and pure as the lilies of Paradise."
Speaking about Joan of Arc, Andrew Lang [8]

When stocking up on 'God's Help', a home church is essential. God often speaks and acts through other believers and clergy. Paul tells us to *"Bear one another's burdens."* Galatians 6: 2 In 2 Corinthians he says, *"Praise be to the God and Father of our Lord Jesus Christ...who comforts us in all our troubles, so that we can comfort those in any trouble with the comfort we ourselves receive from God."* 2 Corinthians 1: 3-4

Once upon a time, I believed it best to look for God strictly through His creation. Nature, for example. I didn't need, nor want, to go to any "@#$%&!" organized church! I had my own ideas about 'those church people', and I didn't want to be around a bunch of hypocrites. It took me years to figure out that I was one of them. In fact, at one time or another, in one way or another, we all qualify as hypocrites.[9] Adding hypocrisy to my already long and still growing list of sins finally brought me to a better understanding of just who these church people were, who I was, and the value of the church. *"The Church is the only fellowship in the world where the one requirement for membership is the unworthiness of the candidate."*[10] Churches are not fortresses for 'good people'. Far from it. These 'good people' are the sinful, the imperfect, the fallen, the very sick.[11] As Jesus said *"It is not the healthy who need a doctor, but the sick. I have not come to call the righteous, but sinners to repentance."* Luke 5: 31-32 Indeed, may we put our faith not in the flawed efforts of frail Christians, but rather in the powerful and proven person of Jesus the Messiah. The church is simply all these extremely flawed people worshipping God with others equally diseased. As has often been said, the church is the hospital for the spiritually sick. And the disease we all have is sin, and we can't cure ourselves. In fact it's a terminal condition.[12] Although I still love nature, and try to spend as much time as possible in the great outdoors, it can't take the place of communal worship. It was never meant to: *"Let us not give up meeting together, as some are in the habit of doing, but let us encourage one another..."* Heb. 10: 25

Joan of Arc certainly knew the importance of the church. Even as she was being persecuted by it, she loved the church with her whole heart: *"As for the Church, I love it and I would wish to support it with all my might for the sake of our Christian faith; it is not I who should be prevented from going to church and hearing mass!"*[13] Those who knew her often testified to her love and devotion to the church. Here's a sampling:

"Jeanne often attended Church. Sometimes, when the village bell rang for service, I saw her kneel down and pray with great devotion."[14]

"Often did she confess her sins. Every day, when he (i.e. Messire Guillaume Fronte, Cure of Domrémy) *celebrated Mass, she was there."*[15]

"Joan the Maid...went frequently to church and frequently confessed. The cause of my knowing this is that I was, in those days, churchwarden at the church of Domrémy and often did I see Joan come to church, to Mass and to Compline. And when I did not ring the bells for Compline, Joan would catch me and scold me saying that I had not done well; and she even promised to give me some wool if I would be punctual in ringing for Compline..."[16]

"I was brought up with Jeannette, close to her house. I know that she was good, simple and pious, and that she feared God and the Saints. She loved Church and the Holy places; she was very charitable, and liked to take care of the sick. I know this of a surety, for, in my childhood, I fell ill, and it was she who nursed me. When the church bells rang, I have seen her kneel down make the sign of the Cross..."[17]

"My father's house joined the house of Jacques d'Arc: so I knew her well. We often spun together, and together worked at the ordinary house-duties, whether by day or night. She was a good Christian, of good manners and well brought up. She loved the Church, and went there often, and gave alms from the food of her father. She was a good girl, simple and pious so much so that I and her companions told her she was too pious."[18]

"She was a good girl, simple and gentle; she went willingly and often to Church, and holy places. Often she was bashful when others reproached her with going too devotedly to church...I did not know of Jeanne's departure; I wept much, I loved her dearly for her goodness and because she was my friend."[19]

"She was simple and good, frequenting the Church and Holy places. Often, when she was in the fields and heard the bells ring, she would drop to her knees."[20]

"Joan was of good behavior, devout, patient, going readily to church, willingly to confession, and gave alms to the poor when she could, as I witnessed, both in the town of Domrémy and at Burey, at my house, where Joan resided during a period of six weeks."[21]

There can be no doubt of Joan's love of the church, and the great role it player in her life. Nonetheless, her first and ultimate allegiance to God was always very clear, as we see from this part of her trial testimony:

"Question: *"If the Church Militant* (i.e. the church on earth) *tells you that your revelations are illusions, somehow diabolic, would you defer to the church?"*
Joan: *"In that case, I would defer as always to God, whose command I have always obeyed, and I know well that what is contained in this trial comes through God's command, and what I have affirmed in the process that I have done by God's command. It would be impossible for me to do the contrary. And should the Church Militant command me to do otherwise, I would not defer to any man of the world, other than our Lord, whose good command I have always done."*
Question: *"Do you believe that you are subject to the church of God that is on earth, that is to say, to our lord the pope, to the cardinals, Archbishops, bishops, and other prelates of the church?"*
Joan: *"Yes, so long as our Lord is first served."*
Question: *"Have you received the command from your voices not to submit to the Church Militant, which is on the earth, nor to her judgment?"*
Joan: *"I shall not answer anything that comes in to my head, but what I do answer is at the command of my voices; they do not command me not to obey the church, God being first served."*[22]

This is line with what the Bible teaches. When there is a contradiction between authority (i.e. any authority, be it church, government, or other) and God, that *"...We ought to obey God rather than men."* Acts 5: 29 KJV Ideally of course, there should be no contradiction between God's word and the church. But fallible man being what he is, this has not always been the case. Joan, the illiterate peasant girl, uncluttered with 'great learning', again gets to the heart of the matter here: *"It seems to me that our Lord and the Church are one and the same, and that no one should make difficulties about that. Why do you make difficulties about it not being one and the same?"* [23]

On matters of theology and doctrine, there has always been debate and often great discord within the church.[24] Joan's time was no exception. From 1378 to 1417 there was a split within the Church, which came to be known as the papal Schism. This was based on two men who both claimed to be the true pope. At one time there were actually three popes simultaneously![25] A century later, the birth of the Protestant Church (1517) led to even more intense disagreement, increasing violence and eventually war.[26] And so it goes. Today the Catholic church claims Joan of Arc as their own.[27] Others call her 'the first Protestant'.[28] Admirers from the Feminist movement proclaim her their female mystic.[29] Some of the New Age Movement saw her playing a central part in their 2012 end of the world predictions.[30] And so on... whatever our position regarding Joan, keeping our eyes on the Savior, come what may, is the ticket. If we do that, the love of Jesus will spur us on to *"a profound love for the church".*[31] As Pope Benedict XVI said so well: *"...In Jesus, Joan contemplated the whole reality of the Church, the 'Church triumphant of Heaven, as well as the 'Church militant' on earth. According to her words, 'About Jesus Christ and the Church, I simply know they're just one thing.' This affirmation, cited in the Catechism of the Catholic Church (n. 795), has a truly heroic character in the context of the Trial of Condemnation, before her judges, men of the church who were persecuting and condemning her. In the love of Jesus Joan found the strength to love the Church to the very end, even at the moment she was sentenced... Dear brothers and sisters, with her luminous witness St. Joan of Arc invites us to a high standard of Christian living: to make prayer the guiding motive of our days; to have full trust in doing God's will, whatever it may be, to love charity without favoritism, without limits and drawing, like her, from the Love of Jesus a profound love for the Church."*[32] And in His true church, God's help is present in spades.

2) God's Word

Question: *"Do you believe that the Holy Scriptures have been revealed by God?"*
Joan of Arc: *"You know it well; I know it well!"*
Trial of Condemnation, April 18, 1431

"The Bible is no mere book, but a Living Creature, with a power that conquers all that oppose it." Napoleon Bonaparte (1769-1821)

The authentic Christian church will always be focused on God's word. We know from experience that reading His word brings a sense of peace and purpose. *"For everything that was written in the past was written to teach us, so that through the endurance taught in the Scriptures and the encouragement they provide we might have hope."* Romans 15: 4 Even in this crazy world, seemingly totally out of control, the Scriptures provide us tangible help. They explain the meaning of life, and reveal the way to life beyond death. They help us understand that we will have to suffer, but that our suffering is temporary, and that good can result from it. They strengthen our faith, and give us assurance that we can endure and persevere, like so many before us have done. They give evidence of God's love, wisdom, power, and faithfulness to His promises. And in times of need, they reinforce that God can and will help us.[33]

"I am busily engaged in the study of the Bible. I believe it is God's Word because it finds me where I am." Abraham Lincoln (1809-1865)

3) Prayer
"Work as if you were to live a hundred years, pray as if you were to die tomorrow." Benjamin Franklin (1706-1790)[34]

"Often when we were all at play, Jeannette would retire alone to 'talk with God'. I and the others laughed at her about this."
Jean Waterin of Greux, laborer, Trial of Nullification

Prayer too brings us into His presence. It is He who *"...is our refuge and strength, a very present help in trouble."* Psalm 46: 1 With Joan of Arc, we see a life from beginning to end centered in prayer (as we saw in Chapter 5). A prayerful person is a strong witness to others in itself. And as we see from the following, Joan made a strong impression in this regard to many who knew her:

"She was no dancer; and, sometimes, when the others were singing and dancing, she went to prayer."[35]
"She was not fond of playing, at which we, her companions, complained... she was more often in Church at prayer."[36]
"Sometimes when the village bell rang for church service, I saw her kneel down and pray with great devotion."[37]
*"I was... attached to the Chapel of the Blessed Mary at Vaucouleurs, I often saw Jeanne in this Chapel; she behaved with great

piety, attended Mass in the morning, and remained a long time in prayer."[38]

"Every day after dinner she was for a long time on her knees, and also at night; and she often went into a little Oratory in the house and there prayed for a long time."[39]

No matter what we are facing, prayer leads us right to His side. Even in the midst of intense suffering. *"Is anyone among you suffering? Let him pray."* James 5: 13 (ESV) He will never abandon us. *"Never will I leave you; never will I forsake you."* Hebrews 13: 5 And He is with us everywhere. Be it the highest mountain, the deepest sea, or the moon above.[40]

"Be strong and courageous. Do not be terrified; do not be discouraged, for the LORD your God will be with you wherever you go." Joshua 1: 9

4) Eternal Life
"Death gives us sleep, eternal youth, and immortality." Jean Paul [41]

"Jesus said to her, 'I am the resurrection and the life. The one who believes in me will live, even though they die; and whoever lives by believing in me will never die. Do you believe this?'"
John 11:25-26

Still another help we receive from God, is the knowledge of eternal life with Him. On the day of his death, John Newton said, *"I am still in the land of the dying; I shall be in the land of the living soon."*[42] We all suffer. But Christians have the assurance that we can endure, that God will help us, that the result will be for our good, and that in the end we will have eternal life in Heaven. Jesus said, *"For God so loved the world that he gave his one and only Son, that whoever believes in him shall not perish but have eternal life."*[43] As we saw in the previous chapter, this 'eternal life knowledge' was a big comfort to Joan of the day of her death: *"Master Pierre, where shall I be this night?'* And Master Pierre answered her, *'Do you not have good hope in God!* She answered him, *'Yes, and by God's grace I shall be in Paradise.'"*[44] Whatever our situation is, we can carry on, knowing that one day we too will find ourselves at the gates of Heaven.

"I consider that our present sufferings are not worth comparing with the glory that will be revealed in us." Romans 8: 18

In the meantime, we are told to tell the world about, God, and His Son Jesus, who offers us eternal life.[45] And then one day, this 'testimony shoe' will be on the other foot:

> *"Whoever confesses Me before men, him the Son of Man also will confess before the Angels of God."* Luke 12: 8

5) "…the Angels of God." Luke 12: 8

"See, I am sending an angel ahead of you to guard you along the way and to bring you to the place I have prepared." Exodus: 23: 20

"Do not forget to show hospitality to strangers, for by so doing some people have shown hospitality to angels without knowing it."
Hebrews 13: 2

For a few, like Joan of Arc, God's help may come in the form of direct intervention. Angels are spiritual beings created by God to serve Him. The Bible mentions them nearly 300 times. The author of Hebrews describes them as, *"ministering spirits, sent out to render service for the sake of those who will inherit salvation…"* Heb 1: 14 (NAS) As you see, angels are not directed to render service to 'everyone', but rather specifically to believers in God. Joan of Arc made an interesting comment in this regard. *"They* (i.e. angels) *often come among Christian people and are not seen. I have seen them many times among Christians."*[46]

Some angels joined Satan during his rebellion in heaven, and so were expelled from heaven with him (see Isaiah 14: 12-20; Ez. 28: 1-19; Rev. 12: 7-9). The Bible calls these fallen angels 'demons' (e.g. Deut. 32: 17, Ps. 106: 37, Mt. 7: 22, Mt 12: 24, Mark 16: 17…). They now stand in active opposition to God's work and plans.

Those who remained loyal to God, carry out His will. They protect (e.g. Ex. 23: 20…), direct (e.g. Mt 1: 20-21…), and provide (e.g. Ex 23: 20…). They reveal God's word (e.g. Acts 7: 38, 53; Gal. 3: 19; Heb. 2: 2) [47], punish evildoers (e.g. Mt. 13: 40-42), and carry out His judgments (e.g. Rev. 6-17…). The Psalmist says: *"Bless the LORD, you His angels. Mighty in strength, who perform His word, obeying the voice of His word!"* Ps. 103: 20

For the most part they remain unseen by human eyes. Personally, I have never seen one. Have you? I have met only one person who did. And for her, it was an unforgettable experience. Holy angels never draw attention to themselves. Typically, they do their work and disappear. Most of their ministry is done without us even being aware of their presence. But their presence is assured, and powerful. *"For he will command his angels concerning you, to guard you in all your ways; they will lift you up in their hands, so that you will not strike your foot against a stone."* Psalm 91: 11-12

When determining if angels are Heaven-sent, there are three things we can look for:

1) their ministry would never contradict the Bible.

2) their actions would always be consistent with the character of Jesus.

3) an angel from God would always glorify God, not themselves. And Scripture tells us that they are never to be worshipped. Jesus said, *"It is written: 'Worship the Lord your God and serve Him only."* Luke 4: 8 (see also Ex. 20: 3; Deut. 6: 5, 13) Here's an object lesson regarding this: *"Then the angel said to me, 'Write this: Blessed are those who are invited to the wedding supper of the Lamb!' And he added, 'These are the true words of God.' At this I fell at his feet to worship him. But he said to me, 'Don't do that! I am a fellow servant with you and with your brothers and sisters who hold to the testimony of Jesus. Worship God! For it is the Spirit of prophecy who bears testimony to Jesus.'"* Rev. 19: 9-10

If we are not to worship angels, then it follows that we aren't to pray to them either. In the Bible we find no precedent, no example, no suggestion, no encouragement, no hint nor permission for doing so. *"For these is one God and one mediator between God and men, the man Christ Jesus."* 1 Tim. 2: 5 Angels are God's servants, and our prayers and worship should go to Him, not His servants. God says, *"I will not share my glory with another."* Is. 42: 8 Joan of Arc is a good example in this regard. When faced with God's holy messengers, she shows them proper reverence, but never speaks of praying to or worshiping them in any way"

Question: *"Your King and you, did you do reverence to the Angel who brought the sign?"*

Joan of Arc: *"Yes, I made a salutation, knelt down, and took off my cap."*[48]

During her Trial of Condemnation, Joan often spoke of angels. For her, they were as real as anything in this world. *"I saw them with the eyes of my body as well as I see you."*[49] All through the trial, her adversaries went to great lengths trying to connect her 'voices' with the dark side. But from the beginning of her trial, Joan identified this 'voice' as an angel: *"...I believe it was sent to me from God. When I heard it for the third time, I recognized that it was the voice of an angel. It has always guarded me well.....*"[50] Five days later (Feb. 27, 1431) she added some further information: *"It was* (the Angel) *Saint Michael. I saw him before my eyes. He was not alone, but duly attended by heavenly angels..."*[51] Nonetheless the prosecutors, following their own agenda, nearly always referred to Joan's angels or messengers as *'Your voices'*.

6) Holy Spirit

"The Wizard of Oz says look inside yourself and find self. God says look inside yourself and find the Holy spirit. The first will get you to Kansas. The latter will get you to heaven. Take your pick." Max Lucado [52]

"I used to ask God to help me. Then I asked if I might help Him. I ended up by asking God to do His work through me."
Hudson Taylor (1832-1905) was a British Protestant Christian missionary to China.

When we become believers and followers of His Son, Jesus, God sends us His Holy Spirit to help us. In fact, Jesus actually refers to Him as the 'Helper'. Sometimes, in times of great need, I have felt an overwhelming sense of joy in God's presence. I don't know how else to describe it. I believe that this is indeed one manifestation of His Holy Spirit. The Holy Spirit wants to help us, and will if we allow Him to do so. Jesus said: *"And I will pray to the Father, and He will give you another Helper, that He may abide with you forever, even the Spirit of truth, whom the world cannot receive, because it neither sees Him, nor knows Him; but you know Him, for He dwells with you and will be in you. I will not leave you orphans; I will come to you."* John 14: 16-18 NKJ

According to the Bible, the Spirit of God helps us in many ways, including...

-with prayer: *"Likewise the Spirit also helps in our weaknesses. For we do not know what we should pray for as we ought, but the Spirit Himself makes intercession for us with groanings which cannot be uttered."* Romans 8: 26 NKJ

-testifying about Jesus: *"But you shall receive power when the Holy Spirit has come upon you; and you shall be witnesses to Me in Jerusalem and in all Judea and Samaria, and to the end of the earth."* Acts 1: 8 NKJ

-encouraging us: *"The Spirit Himself bears witness with our spirit that we are children of God..."* Romans 8: 16

-guiding us: *"However, when He, the Spirit of truth, has come, He will guide you..."* John 16: 13

Joan allowed herself to be guided by the Spirit of God from beginning to end, as several testified:

"Jeanne was led by the Spirit of God." Husson Le Maitre of Viville[53]

"I never observed in her nothing deserving reproof, and from her manner of life and actions I believe she was inspired by God." Maître Reginal Thierry[54]

"When Jeanne was in her lodging, she, being led by the Spirit, cried out: 'In God's Name! our people are hard pressed.' ...arming herself, she went to the Fort of Saint Loup, where there was an assault being made by the King's people on the English; and no sooner had Jeanne joined in the attack, than the fort was taken." Simon Baucrix[55]

7) Keeping our eyes on the Savior

"Jesus, Jesus, Jesus...!!" Joan of Arc, at the stake, May 30, 1431

"And everyone who calls on the name of the Lord will be saved."
Acts 2: 21

Of course, God's greatest help presents itself in His son, Jesus. After all, He comes not just to help us, but ultimately to save us. Joan of Arc understood this to the core of her being. As she was being burned alive at the stake, *"...she cried out more than six times, 'Jesus!' ...so that everyone present could hear it; almost all wept with pity."*[56] No doubt, she was literally calling out to the Son of God, that He deliver her from her agony. For centuries people have called out to Him by name, often in times of desperation. For others, the name of Jesus is used at best as a simple sentence-filler or an exclamation. Or perhaps worse, such as an epithet or obscenity. And this with no apparent concern over any possible misuse of His holy name. For some this reflects a willful ignorance. For others, simply a deep animosity. What is it about this man that stirs up such powerful feelings among both believers and unbelievers? Just who is this Jesus? Although questions about His identity will certainly continue, one day there will be no more questions. As Paul says, *"...God exalted him to the highest place, and gave him the name that is above every name, that at the name of Jesus every knee should bow, in heaven and on earth and under the earth, and every tongue acknowledge that Jesus Christ is Lord, to the glory of God the Father."* Philippians 2: 9-11

Joan for her part had no questions: *"...I believe that our Savior Jesus Christ suffered death, and passion for us. And that which makes me believe it, is the good counsel, comfort and good doctrine which he has given me."*[58] On the day of her death she said, *"I believe that He alone can deliver me."*[59] And during her Trial of Condemnation: *"I have a*

good master-that is, our Lord-to whom only I look, and to none other."
Joan of Arc, Trial of Condemnation, May 2, 1431

This is consistent with the Bible. Jesus said, *"I am the way and the truth and the life. No one comes to the Father except through me."* John 14: 6 And speaking about Jesus, *"...Peter, filled with the Holy Spirit..."* echoed this: *"Salvation is found in no one else, for there is no other name under heaven given to mankind by which we must be saved."* Acts 4: 8, 12

Even chained to the stake, Joan became one last time a powerful witness to Jesus: *"With great devotion, Joan asked to have the cross, and when an Englishman who was present there heard her, he made her a little one in wood from the end of a stick, which he handed to her, and she took it devoutly and kissed it, making a pious lamentation to God, our redeemer, who had suffered on the cross...and she put that cross in her bosom, between her flesh and her garments."*[60] Then she said to Brother Isambard (who served as an assessor at her trial), *"I pray you, go to the nearest church, and bring me the cross, and hold it up level with my eyes until I am dead, I would have the cross on which God hung be ever before my eyes while life lasts in me."*[61] Her request was granted. *"Brother Isambard hurried to the church and came back with the processional crucifix. Mounting the scaffold with it, for she was now chained to the stake, he held it to her lips. But now the fire was lighted and as the flames crept up she begged him to descend, holding it always before her."*[62] *"Friar Isambart ...attested that Joan, being already surrounded by the flame, never ceased up to the end to proclaim and to profess in a high voice the holy name of Jesus..."*[63] For Joan, as well as believers throughout the ages, He is *"...King Jesus, King of Heaven and of all the world, my rightful and sovereign Lord."*[64]

He strikes a deep chord with many non-believers also. Here are some examples:

"I am a Jew, but I am enthralled by the luminous figure of the Nazarene... No one can read the Gospels without feeling the actual presence of Jesus. His personality pulsates in every word. No myth is filled with such life." Albert Einstein [65]

"I am a historian, I am not a believer, but I must confess as a historian that this penniless preacher from Nazareth is irrevocably the very center of history. Jesus Christ is easily the most dominant figure in all history." H.G. Wells [66]

"A man who was completely innocent, offered himself as a sacrifice for the good of others, including his enemies, and became the ransom of the world. It was a perfect act." Mahatma Gandhi [67]

"I know men and I tell you that Jesus Christ is no mere man. Between Him and every other person in the world there is no possible term of comparison. Alexander, Caesar, Charlemagne, and I have founded empires. But on what did we rest the creation of our genius? Upon force. Jesus Christ founded His empire upon love; and at this hour millions of men would die for Him." Napoleon Bonaparte [68]

May we, like Joan, keep our eyes fixed on Jesus to the very end.

"...let us throw off everything that hinders and the sin that so easily entangles. And let us run with perseverance the race marked out for us, fixing our eyes on Jesus...so that you will not grow weary and lose heart." Hebrews 12: 1-3

Cosmic Battle

"We are engaged in a Cosmic Battle to define the truth. But truth does not wait on reason of man to be defined, truth is simply reality from God's perspective, His opinion and the intentional design of all He created." Douglas L. Thompson [69]

The Bible says that there is a war going on. One that goes beyond what we can experience with the five senses. When the Bible mentions angels, demons, spiritual forces in heavenly places, or Satan, it is referring to this unseen reality. Although we only get a veiled picture of this world, we do get a few glimpses. Such as: *"...For our struggle is not against flesh and blood, but against the rulers, against the authorities, against the powers of this dark world and against the spiritual forces of evil in the heavenly realms. Therefore put on the full armor of God, so that when the day of evil comes, you may be able to stand your ground..."* Ephesians 6: 10-20

Joan of Arc seems to have experienced some of this ongoing, unseen battle first hand. At the siege of Saint-Pierre-le-Moutier, the French army's assault was failing. Their retreat was already under way when Jean d'Aulon saw the Maid. She was *"...surrounded by a very small group of her men and a few others. Riding toward her, I asked what she was doing alone and why she did not withdraw like the others. She removed her helmet from her head and answered that she was not alone and that she still had in her company fifty thousand of her men and that she would not depart from there until she had taken the city. At that time, despite what she said, she did not have with her more than four or five men...I said to her directly that she should leave and retire as the others had done; and then she said that I should bring some bundles of sticks and wicker hurdles to make a bridge over the town moat so that they could approach better. Having just given me that instruction, she cried out in a loud voice: 'To the bundles and the hurdles, everybody, make a bridge!'---which was prepared swiftly and then accomplished. I was entirely amazed, for the city was taken all at once by her assault, without finding therein very much resistance."*[70]

This brings to mind a passage from 2 Kings: *"When the servant of the man of God* (i.e. Elisha) *got up and went out early the next morning, an army with horses and chariots had surrounded the city. 'Oh no my lord! What shall we do?' The servant asked. 'Don't be afraid', the prophet answered. 'Those who are with us are more than those who are with them.' And Elisha prayed, 'Open his eyes, Lord, so that he may see.' Then the Lord opened the servant's eyes, and he looked and saw the hills full of horses and chariots of fire all around Elisha."* 2 Kings 6: 15-17

Espionage, double-agents, treason…all play a part in wars waged here on earth. So too in this cosmic war between good and evil. We must remember that Satan has his own fallen 'angels'. And the world is full of double-agents, i.e. false Christs, false believers and false angels…all spouting false doctrine.[71] The Bible says as much. Some *"…people are false apostles, deceitful workers, masquerading as apostles of Christ. And no wonder, for Satan himself masquerades as an angel of light. It is not surprising then, if his servants also masquerade as servants of righteousness. Their end will be what their actions deserve."* 2 Cor. 11: 12-15

"The Spirit clearly says that in later times some will abandon the faith and follow deceiving spirits and things taught by demons." 1 Tim. 4 Discernment is essential. But how? Paul gives us one important way: we must know what God's word says. *"But even if we or an angel from heaven should preach a gospel other than the one we preached to you, let them be under God's curse! As we have already said, so now I say again: if anybody is preaching to you a gospel other than what you accepted, let them be under God's curse!"* Galatians 1: 8-9 Strong words!

As we all know, God does not always use supernatural ways to help us or take away our suffering or problems. In fact, He may allow these things as a tool for growth, to witness to others, to show the character of Christ… Paul provides us an object lesson on this. He prayed three times that God take away his 'thorn'. Instead of giving him what he wanted, God gave him what he needed: *"Therefore in order to keep me from becoming conceited, I was given a thorn in my flesh, a messenger of Satan to torment me. Three times I pleaded with the Lord to take it away from me. But he said to me, 'My grace is sufficient for you, for my power*

is made perfect in weakness.' Therefore I will boast all the more gladly about my weaknesses, so that Christ's power may rest on me. That is why, for Christ's sake, I delight in weaknesses, in insults, in hardships, in persecutions, in difficulties. For when I am weak, then I am strong."
2 Corinthians: 7-10

We probably won't see the whole picture until we get to Heaven. So until then, we must remember that Father Knows Best, and that He will provide the help and strength needed to endure whatever we face. As we've seen, God's help is plentiful and diverse. But will we make use of the help available? It seems that too often we do not. Joan of Arc, on the other hand, took full advantage of everything offered. During these turbulent times, we'd be well served to do as she, and latch on to all the help we can get.

"So we say with confidence, 'The Lord is my helper; I will not be afraid. What can mere mortals do to me?" Hebrews 13: 6

---

[1] Lennon wrote the lyrics of 'Help' to express his stress after the Beatles' quick rise to success. *"I was fat and depressed and I was crying out for 'Help'."* Playboy, Interview with John Lennon and Yoko Ono, January, 1981 issue. Ironically he died on December 8th, 1980, shortly before this interview was published. See http://en.wikipedia.org/wiki/Help!_%28song%29#cite_note-FOOTNOTESpitz2005555-3; Dec 2011.

[2] Joan of Arc translated by Willard Trask, Joan of Arc: In Her Own Words, Turtle Point Press, New York, 1936, p. 29

[3] Ibid., p. 47

[4] Joan of Arc, Trial of Condemnation, March 17, 1431

[5] Joan of Arc translated by Willard Trask, Joan of Arc: In Her Own Words, Turtle Point Press, New York, 1936, p. 171

[6] Ibid., p. 121

[7] *"There is no day that I do not hear the voice. And indeed I need it. I have never asked it for any other reward than, in the end, the salvation of my soul."*: Joan of Arc, Trial of Condemnation, February 22, 1431

[8] The Maid of France, Longmans, Green, and CO, London, 1908, p. iii. Mr. Lang was a 19th Century Scottish Writer and Historian.

[9] Although this observation is as old as man himself, for many years I was too proud and arrogant to accept it! Here are some relevant quotes: a) *"We are all hypocrites. We cannot see ourselves or judge ourselves the way we see and judge others."* José Emilio Pacheco, Battles in the Desert and Other Stories, New Directions Publishing Corporation, New York, 1987. Mr. Pacheco (1939-), is a Mexican essayist, novelist and short story writer, and is regarded as one of the major Mexican poets of the second half of the 20th century. b) *"Forbear to judge, for we are sinners all."* William Shakespeare (1564-1616), Henry VI.

c) *"Nothing that we despise in other men is inherently absent from ourselves. We must learn to regard people less in the light of what they do or don't do, and more in light of what they suffer."* Dietrich Bonhoeffer (1906-1945). Mr. Bonhoeffer was a German Lutheran pastor, theologian, and anti-Nazi. He was involved in plans to assassinate Adolf

Hitler. He was arrested in April 1943 by the Gestapo and executed by hanging in April 1945, 23 days before the Nazis' surrender. His view of Christianity's role in the secular world has since become very influential. d)And here's Mark Twain's tongue-in-cheek observation: *"Nothing so needs reforming as other people's habits."* Mark Twain (1835-1910), Pudd'nhead Wilson's Calendar, 1894.

[10]Charles H. Talbert, Reading Luke: a literary and theological commentary, Smyth and Helwys Publishing, Inc., Macon, Georgia, 2002, p. 66

[11]Romans 3: 10-12, 23

[12]*"For the wages of sin is death, but the gift of God is eternal life in Christ Jesus our Lord."* Romans 6: 23

[13]Trial of Condemnation, March 17, 1431-Joan of Arc-Self Portrait, Willard Trask, The Telegraph Press, Harrisburg, Pa, 1936, p. 157

[14]Dominique Jacob, Cure of the Parish Church of Montier-sur-Saulx, Trial of Nullification; www.stjoan-center.com/Trials/null03.html; accessed Dec. 2011

[15]Dominique Etienne of Sionne, Curé of the Parish Church of Roncessey-sous-Neufchâteau, Trial of Nullification; www.stjoan-center.com/Trials/null03.html, accessed Dec. 2011

[16]Dominique Perrin Drappier, churchwarden of Domremy in Joan's childhood, Trial of Nullification; www.stjoan-center.com/Trials/null03.html; www.stjoan-center.com/Trials/null03.html; accessed Dec. 2011

[17]Dominique Simonin Musnier, farmer and childhood friend of Joan, Trial of Nullification; www.stjoan-center.com/Trials/null03.html, accessed Dec. 2011

[18]Dominique Mengette, wife of Jean Joyart, laborer, childhood friend of Joan, Trial of Nullification; www.stjoan-center.com/Trials/null03.html; accessed Dec. 2011

[19]Dominique Hauviette, wife of Gerard of Sionne, a childhood friend of Joan, Trial of Nullification; www.stjoan-center.com/Trials/null03.html, accessed Dec. 2011

[20]Dominique Jean Waterin, laborer of Greux, Trial of Nullification; http://www.stjoan-center.com/Trials/null03.html, accessed Dec. 2011

[21]Durand Laxart, Joan's uncle, Trial of Nullification; www.stjoan-center.com/Trials/null03.html; accessed Dec. 2011

[22]Trial of Condemnation, April 18, 1431; Régine Pernoud and Marie-Véronique Clin, Joan of Arc-Her Story, St Martin's Griffin, New York, New York, 1998, p. 124

[23]Trial of Condemnation, March 17; Joan of Arc-Self Portrait, Willard Trask, The Telegraph Press, Harrisburg, Pa, 1936, p. 157-158

[24]Here is a relevant Bible verse from Paul regarding God's authentic church: *"By the grace God has given me, I laid a foundation as a wise builder, and someone else is building on it. But each one should build with care. For no one can lay any foundation other than the one already laid, which is Jesus Christ."* 1 Corinthians 3: 10-11

[25]The schism was ended by the Council of Constance (1414–1418).

[26]The birth of the Reformation and the Protestant Church can be traced to Martin Luther, who posted his ninety-five theses on the door of the Castle Church of Wittenbergn on October 31, 1517.

[27]Joan was canonized a Catholic saint on May 16, 1920 by Pope Benedict XV.

[28]For example, the Irish playwright George Bernard Shaw (1856-1950) stated, *"Though a professed and most pious Catholic, and the projector of a Crusade against the Husites, she was in fact one of the first Protestant martyrs."* Saint Joan, George Bernard Shaw, GBS Books, 1924, Preface. Mr. Shaw, the only person to have been awarded both a Nobel Prize in Literature (1925) and an Oscar (1938), was neither Catholic nor Protestant.

[29]E.g. see Journal of Feminist Studies in Religion, Vol. 1, No. 2, Fall, 1985. Here Joan is portrayed as a *"female mystic"*, whose *"...visions led her into central places of*

masculine power."
[30] E.g. see End of the World 2012, Vijay Kumar, http://www.godrealized.com/vijay_kumar.html. Mr. Kumar presents himself as *"The Man who Realized God in 1993".* He tells us, *"I am able to understand the hidden truths of all Scriptures of all Religions of the World...".* He says that he talks *"...to 'God the Creator' every moment of my Life."* and claims that he will show us how to *"Become a living Mahavira, Buddha or Jesus Christ!"* Regarding Joan and the approaching 2012 end of the world, he states, *"2012 is the year of Joan of Arc."*
[31] From the General Audience of Pope Benedict XVI, January 26, 2011
[32] Ibid.
[33] In Chapter 13 we will take a closer look at the Bible, especially regarding two questions: Is the Bible trustworthy? Is it really the word of God?!
[34] Franklin was one of the Founding Fathers of the United States. He was a leading author, printer, political theorist, politician, postmaster, scientist, musician, inventor, satirist, civic activist, statesman, and diplomat.
[35] Jeannette, widow of Thiesselin of Viteaux, formerly clerk at Neufchâteau, Trial of Nullification
[36] Isabellette, wife of Gerardin, laborer, of Epinal, Trial of Nullification
[37] Messire Dominique Jacob, Cure of the Parish Church of Montier-sur-Saulx, Trial of Nullification
[38] Messire Jean Lefumeux, Canon of the Chapel of Saint Mary at Vaucouleurs, and Cure of the Parish Church of Ugny, Trial of Nullification
[39] Maitre Jean Barbin, Doctor of Laws, King's Advocate, Trial of Nullification
[40] In 1971, during the U.S. Apollo 15 space mission, James Irwin (1930-1991) became the eighth person to walk on the moon. For Irwin, this lunar mission was a religious awakening that changed his life. During some mission flight problems, he experienced 'God's Help' through prayer in a tangible way: *"It was almost like a revelation. God was telling me what to do...I didn't have time for Houston to get an answer to me; I needed an immediate answer...I prayed, and immediately I knew the answer. I am not talking about some vague sense of direction. There was this supernatural sensation of His presence. If I needed Him I could call on Him, call on His power...Before the flight, I was really not a religious man, I believed in God, but I really had nothing to share. But when I came back from the moon, I felt so strongly that I had something that I wanted to share with others, that I established High Flight* (see http://highflightfoundation.org), *in order to tell all men everywhere that God is alive, not only on earth but also on the moon."* After his moon trip, Irwin believed that his most important mission in life was to serve God and share his faith in Jesus Christ. He said: *"Jesus walking on the earth is more important than man walking on the moon."* James Irwin and William A. Emerson, Jr., To Rule the Night, A. J. Holman Company, 1973. Here are a couple of appropriate Bible verses: *"The heavens, even the highest heaven, cannot contain You."* 1 Kings 8: 27 *"'Can anyone hide in secret places so that I cannot see him?' declares the LORD. 'Do not I fill heaven and earth?' declares the LORD."* Jeremiah 23: 24
[41] Jean Paul (1763-1825) was a German Romantic writer, best known for his humorous novels and stories.
[42] Mr. Newton (1725-1807) was a British sailor and later an Anglican clergyman. At a young age, he became involved with the slave trade. After experiencing a religious conversion, he became a minister, hymn-writer, and later a prominent supporter of the abolition of slavery. He is the author of many hymns, including "Amazing Grace".
[43] John 3: 16. Revelation gives us a quick glimpse of a part of Heaven: *"After this I looked, and there before me was a door standing open in heaven...then I looked and heard the voice of many angels, numbering thousands upon thousands, and ten thousand times ten thousand....In a loud voice they sang...'To him who sits on the throne and to the*

Lamb be praise and honor and glory and power, for ever and ever!'" Revelation 4: 1, 5: 11, 13
[44] Régine Pernoud, Jeanne d'Arc par elle-meme et ses témoins, Editions du Seuil, Paris, 1996, p. 275; Jean Riquier, a Priest, Trial of Nullification; V. Sackville West, Saint Joan of Arc, Country Life Press, 1936, p.339
[45] *"Then Jesus came to them and said, 'All authority in heaven and on earth has been given to me. Therefore go and make disciples of all nations, baptizing them in the name of the Father and of the Son and of the Holy Spirit, and teaching them to obey everything I have commanded you. And surely I am with you always, to the very end of the age.'"* Matthew 28: 18-20
[46] Joan of Arc, Trial of Condemnation, March 12, 1431; see Daniel Hobbins, The Trial of Joan of Arc, Harvard University Press, Cambridge, MA, 2005, p. 92
[47] Both the Hebrew word for angel (mal'ak,) and the Greek word (aggelos) mean "messenger."
[48] Régine Pernoud, La Spiritualite de Jeanne d'Arc, Editions Mame, Saint-Amand-Montrond (Cher), 1992, p. 54 and 58
[49] Trial of Condemnation, February 22, 1431. This was the second day of the trial.
[50] Trial of Condemnation, February 27, 1431. St. Michael is the Archangel mentioned twice in the Bible: Revelation 12: 7 and Jude 1: 9.
[51] Trial of Condemnation, March 10, 1431. http://www.stjoan-center.com/Trials/sec07.html accessed December 31, 2011.
[52] Experiencing the Heart of Jesus Workbook: Knowing His Heart, Feeling His Love, Thomas Nelson Publisher, 2003. Mr. Lucado (1955-) is a best-selling author and preacher at Oak Hills Church in San Antonio, Texas. He has written more than 50 books with 80 million copies in print.
[53] Husson Le Maitre of Viville, in Bassigny, Trial of Nullification
[54] Maitre Reginald Thierry, Dean of the Church of Meung-sur-Yévre and Surgeon to the King, Trial of Nullification
[55] Simon Baucroix, Squire, Trial of Nullification
[56] Régine Pernoud and Marie-Véronique Clin, Jeanne d'Arc, Editions Fayard, Mesnil-sur-l'Estrée, 2001, p. 136-137
[57] According to the Bible, even His name was given by an angel: *"...an angel of the Lord appeared* (to Joseph) *in a dream and said, ...* (Mary) *will give birth to a son, and you are to give him the name Jesus, because he will save his people from their sins."* Matthew 1: 20-21 Jesus means "God saves".
[58] Joan of Arc, Trial of Condemnation, March 17, 1431
[59] Joan of Arc, Trial of Condemnation, May 30, 1431
[60] Trial of Nullification; Régine Pernoud and Marie-Véronique Clin, Jeanne d'Arc, Editions Fayard, Mesnil-sur-l'Estrée, 2001, p. 136
[61] Trial of Nullification; Joan of Arc, Joan of Arc-Self Portrait, Willard Trask, The Telegraph Press, Harrisburg, Pa, 1936, p. 185
[62] Trial of Nullification; Albert Paine Bigelow, The Girl in White Armor-The Story of Joan of Arc, The Macmillan Company, New York, 1967, p. 206
[63] Trial of Nullification; Régine Pernoud and Marie-Véronique Clin, Jeanne d'Arc, Editions Fayard, Mesnil-sur-l'Estrée, 2001, p. 136
[64] From Joan of Arc's letter to the Duke of Burgundy (July 17, 1429).
[65] From interview with G. S. Viereck on October 26,1929; Isaacson, Walter, 2007, "Einstein and Faith" *Time* 169 (April 5): 47. Albert Einstein (1879-1955) was a German-born theoretical physicist who developed the general theory of relativity, one of the two pillars of modern physics. While best known for his mass–energy equivalence formula $E = mc^2$ (which has been dubbed "the world's most famous equation"), he received the 1921 Nobel Prize in Physics "for his services to theoretical physics, and especially for

his discovery of the law of the photoelectric effect". The latter was pivotal in establishing quantum theory.

[66]This quote is frequently attributed to H. G. Wells from a speech he gave in later years. However, I have not been able to track down the exact speech. Mr. Wells (1866-1946) was an English writer, now best known for his work in the science fiction genre, and is sometimes called "The Father of Science Fiction". His most notable science fiction works include *The War of the Worlds*, *The Time Machine*, *The Invisible Man* and *The Island of Doctor Moreau*. Wells wrote in his book God the Invisible King (1917) that his idea of God did not draw upon the traditional religions of the world: This book sets out as forcibly and exactly as possible the religious belief of the writer. [Which] is a profound belief in a personal and intimate God. ... Putting the leading idea of this book very roughly, these two antagonistic typical conceptions of God may be best contrasted by speaking of one of them as God-as-Nature or the Creator, and of the other as God-as-Christ or the Redeemer. One is the great Outward God; the other is the Inmost God. Later in the work he aligns himself with a *"renascent or modern religion ... neither atheist nor Buddhist nor Mohammedan nor Christian ..."*

[67]Non-Violence in Peace and War, vol. 2, Ch. 16, Mahatma Gandhi, New Directions Publishing Corporation,1964. Gandhi (1869-1948) was an Indian political and spiritual leader. He was the preeminent leader of Indian nationalism in British-ruled India. Employing nonviolent civil disobedience, Gandhi led India to independence and inspired movements for civil rights and freedom across the world.

[68]Christ and the Critics, Vol. 2, Hilarin Felder, Burns, Oates, and Washbourne, 1924, pp. 216-17. Napoleon Bonaparte was a French military and political leader who rose to prominence during the latter stages of the French Revolution. He was Emperor of the French from 1804 to 1814. He implemented a wide array of important reforms across Europe, including the abolition of feudalism and the spread of religious toleration. His legal code in France, the Napoleonic Code, influenced numerous civil law jurisdictions worldwide. He won the majority of his battles and seized control of most of continental Europe in a quest for personal power and to spread the ideals of the French Revolution. Widely regarded as one of the greatest commanders in history, his campaigns are studied at military academies worldwide. He remains one of the most studied political and military leaders in all of history. Whether or not Napoleon ended his days as a Christian has been debated the last couple of centuries, with credible arguments raised for both sides of the issue.

[69]Douglas L. Thompson, http://thecosmicbattle.blogspot.com, accessed Feb. 2012. Mr. Thompson is a Civil Engineer in Chino Hills, CA, and author of several blogs.

[70]Jean d'Aulon (Joan's steward), Trial of Nullification; Regine Pernoud and Marie-Véronique Clin, Joan of Arc-Her Story, St Martin's Griffin, New York, New York, 1998, p. 80-81

[71]*"By mixing a little truth with it, they had made their lie far stronger."* C.S. Lewis, The Last Battle, HarperCollins, 1956. Often false doctrine follows this pattern of mixing a little truth with the lies, to make the lie more powerful. And this is often effective, as many don't know the Bible well enough to recognize the manipulation. Indeed, in order to recognize a counterfeit, we must know what the real thing looks like. Satan himself used distorted or incomplete parts of Scripture, as he tried in vain to manipulate Jesus to his will (see Matthew 4: 1-11).

Chapter 10
A Warrior God

"Jeanne's mission was on the surface warlike, but it really had the effect of ending a century of war, and her love and charity were so broad, that they could only be matched by Him who prayed for His murderers."
Sir Arthur Conan Doyle [1]

"I don't like Joan of Arc. There's too much war and violence in her story. My God isn't like that. My God is a God of love and peace, like Jesus was. God wouldn't have anything to do with war!" So stated Michelle, a very nice French lady we met at a monastery in France. This brings up a number of interesting and worthwhile questions.

The answers to some of these questions are complex, and deserve more than "sound bite" responses. Consequently, for easier reference, here is a small outline for this chapter:

I. Were Joan's actions as a "holy warrior" consistent with what we see in Scripture?
    A. Approach to Combat
    B. Battlefield Conduct and Perspectives
    C. "Thus Saith the Lord..."

II. Isn't war always bad and evil?

III. What does Scripture have to say about war?
    A. Twelve Points
    B. God Is on Our Side?

IV. Jesus: Meek and Mild?

V. Two Gods in the Bible?
    A. Love and Justice
    B. The Amalekites
    C. Nineveh-Belief and Repentance
    D. But isn't the God of the Bible a God of love and peace, not war?

VI. Are there any examples of "holy warriors" in the Bible?
    A. Deborah
    B. Gideon

VII. Other Scriptural Examples of God's Involvement with Nations

VIII. Wrap Up

I. Were Joan's actions as a "holy warrior" consistent with what we see in Scripture?

"I think that Jeanne was sent by God, and that her behavior in war was a fact divine rather than human. Many reasons make me think so."
Jean, Count de Dunois, a.k.a. the 'Bastard of Orleans', Trial of Nullification

A. Her Approach to Combat

a) In Deuteronomy, God tells the Israelites that the numbers and might of the enemy will not determine the winner of the coming battle. He will. He tells them to not be afraid, and that He will be with them. *"When you go to war against your enemies and see horses and chariots and an army greater than yours, do not be afraid of them, because the LORD your God, who brought you up out of Egypt, will be with you."*
Deuteronomy 20: 1

Joan's approach: *"Fear not, however many they be! Neither weigh difficulties. God guides our work. Were I not certain that God guides this work, I would rather keep sheep than expose myself to such perils."*[2]

b) Trust in God is of course a central theme throughout the Bible. He wishes us to turn to Him and have faith, and He has given us His representatives here on earth to help us with this: *"When you are about to go into battle, the priest shall come forward and address the army, 'Hear, O Israel, today you are going into battle against your enemies. Do not be fainthearted or afraid; do not be terrified or give way to panic before them. For the LORD your God is the one who goes with you to fight for you against your enemies to give you victory.'"*
Deuteronomy 20: 2-4

And Joan? *"Trust in God. Make confession, and be forgiven, for in this way God will help you. Being forgiven, you shall have the victory, by God's help."*[3]

Another example: *"Let none tomorrow dare to leave the town and go out to fight, unless he has first gone to confession. And let them beware lest women of evil fame follow them: because, for sin, God will permit the loss of this war."* [4]

Medieval armies were often like a large "moving city". They were accompanied by a large number of cattle and other animals for food and clothing. There would be blacksmiths, cooks, tailors, clergy, musicians, family members, and friends. There were also prostitutes who made their living following the army, and there was always work to be had. When Joan arrived on the scene, she quickly began to chase the prostitutes out of the camp, and placed an emphasis on the soldiers turning to God before battle, instead of their usual diversions.[5]

In a nutshell, here is Joan's approach to battle: *"In God's name! Let us go on bravely!"* She often said something like this to her soldiers during battle.[6]

c) *"When you march up to attack a city, make its people an offer of peace."* Deuteronomy 20: 10 Given the French situation before the Battle of Orleans, it must have seemed a ridiculous waste of time to bother with such empty formalities as an offer of peace. After all, it was the English who had superior forces, supplies and position. And it was the French who were surrounded and under siege from the English, not vice versa. Under such circumstances, surely the English would never consider surrendering. Nonetheless, before attacking Joan offered them peace, as is prescribed in Scripture. This was the pattern she would follow throughout her military career. *"First, I begged them to make peace; and it was only in case they would not make peace that I was ready to fight."* Joan of Arc, Trial of Condemnation, March 27, 1431

At Orleans, she made three offers. Here's part of the first one:

Jesus-Maria,
King of England, and you duke of Bedford, who call yourself regent of the kingdom of France, you, William de la Poule, Sir John Talbot, and you, Sir Thomas of Scales, who call yourself lieutenant of the aforesaid duke of Bedford, render your account to the King of Heaven. Surrender to the Maid, who is sent here from God, the king of Heaven, the keys to all of the good cities that you have taken and violated in France. She has come here from God to proclaim the blood royal. She is entirely ready to make peace if you are willing to settle accounts with her, provided that you give up France and pay for having occupied her...go back to your own countries, for God's sake...I am sent from God, the King of Heaven, to chase you out of all of France, every last one of you. And if you wish

to obey, I shall have mercy on them...If you do not wish to believe this message from God through the Maid, then wherever we find you we will strike you there, and make such a great uproar as has not been heard in France for a thousand years...You Duke of Bedford, the Maid prays you and requests that you cause no more destruction...if indeed you do not, be mindful soon of your great damages.

Written on Tuesday of Holy Week (i.e. March 22, 1429)[7]

d) An illiterate, seventeen-year-old peasant girl from the sticks with no military training would seem to be an unlikely candidate as an expert in artillery. Especially as gunpowder-propelled artillery was one of the army's newest technological weapons. However... *"In everything that she did, apart from the conduct of the war, Joan was young and simple; but in the conduct of war she was most skillful, both in carrying a lance herself, in drawing up the army in battle order, and in placing the artillery. And everyone was astonished that she acted with such prudence and clear-sightedness in military matters, as cleverly as some great captain with twenty or thirty years' experience; and especially in the placing of artillery, for in that she acquitted herself magnificently."*[8]

B. Battlefield Conduct and Perspectives
"She was the bravest of the brave." Andrew Lang [9]

What characteristics did Joan display on the field of battle? Great courage, compassion, steadfastness, consistency and clinging to do God's will are a few of the words that come to mind.

a. A follower of God involved in warfare? Is this possible? During Joan's time, this was not even a question that came to mind. The question was rather, "Is this warrior indeed sent to us from God?" *"All the soldiers held her as sacred. So well did she bear herself in warfare, in words and in deeds, as a follower of God, that no evil could be said of her."* Maitre Jean Barbin, Trial of Nullification[10]

b. The English commander at Orleans (a certain Glasdale), like his soldiers, detested the French's choice of a girl to lead them. He felt this was an insult. At one point, as the battle raged all around them, Joan and Glasdale saw each other. Glasdale immediately aimed some insults directly at her. Joan replied as follows: *"Glasdale, Glasdale, yield, yield to the King of Heaven. You have called me 'whore', but I pity your soul and the souls of your men."*[11]

Glasdale would not yield. According to the <u>Journal of the Siege of Orleans</u> (the official city journal of Orleans at this time) Glasdale was *"armed from head to toe, and he fell into the Loire River and was drowned. Joan, moved by pity, wept for the soul of this Glasdale and of the many others who drowned there…"* [12]

c. The battle of Orleans was her first taste of the ugly realities of war. After the battle, she immediately made her confession and gave thanks to God for the victory, and strongly invited the whole French army to do the same: *"…the English died there in great numbers. Jeanne was much afflicted when she heard that they had died without confession, and pitied them much. On the spot she made her confession. She ordered me to invite the whole army to do likewise, and to give thanks to God for the victory just gained. Otherwise, she said, she would help them no more, but would abandon them."* [13]

d. She showed kindness, respect, and even love to the wounded and the dying of both the French <u>and</u> the English. Here are two relevant testimonies: *"Jeanne, who was very humane, had great compassion …(she) got down from her horse, had him (a dying English soldier) confessed, supporting his head herself, comforting him to the best of her power."* [14] *"She was good not only to the French, but also to the enemy. All this I know of a surety, for I was for a long time with her, and many times assisted in arming her."* [15]

e. She was not bloodthirsty. As the English forces began to depart from Orleans, she told her soldiers: *"In God's name! They are going. Let them go. And we shall go and give thanks to God. We shall not follow them farther, for it is Sunday. Seek not to harm them. It is enough for me that they go."* [16]

f. She knew where her power came from, and never forgot it. After this great victory at Orleans, the <u>Journal of the Siege</u> tells us: *"The Maid and the other lords and men-at-arms re-entered Orleans to the great rejoicing of the clergy and the people, who together rendered humble thanks to Our Lord along with the well-deserved praise for the very great aid and victories that He had given and sent them against the English, ancient enemies of the kingdom…"* [17]

g. Joan kept her priorities straight. She routinely imposed a truce on Sundays and religious feast days. Fr. Pasquerel tells us that on Ascension Thursday of 1429, Joan told him the following: *"She would not make war and would not even put on her armor out of respect for the feast day, and on that day she wished to confess herself and receive the sacrament of the Eucharist, which she did."* [18]

h. It's interesting to note, that although Joan was always in the very thick of battle with her men, she herself never killed anyone. *"I carried my standard in my own hand when we went to the assault, to avoid having to kill anyone. I have never killed anyone."*[19]

> *"...Jeanne was as expert as possible in the art of ordering an army in battle, and that even a captain bred and instructed in war could not have shown more skill; at this the captains marveled exceedingly."*
> Maitre Aignan Viole, Trial of Nullification [20]

Her well documented battlefield exploits are well known[21], and I encourage those of you interested to read up on them.[22] But for the subject of this book, what is especially striking about her military approach is how she always kept God at the forefront. Although many of the great military leaders of history were religious and strong believers in the God of the Bible, very few if any, outside of those spoken of in the Bible itself, have spoken or acted with such focused and consistent spiritual authority on the field of battle (not to mention off the field as well) as Joan of Arc. This is one of the things that sets her apart, and caused such great faith and devotion in her from the French, and fear and trepidation from the English.

C. "Thus Saith the Lord…"

As soon as I walked in the door, Steven looked up and urgently whispered, "God told me to tell you something! This is what He said, and I quote, '_____!'"

Most of us wouldn't speak in this way. Indeed it would be presumptuous to say such a thing. Unless God <u>did</u> speak to us directly and clearly.

A believer might say something like the following:

    a. "I believe the Lord is calling me to…"
    b. "I feel led by the Lord to…"
    c. "I believe it is God's will that…"
    d. "I am praying for guidance and some kind of a sign to know what He wants me to do."

But most of us would not dare say, "God told me to tell you something, and I quote, '_____!'"

However, the prophets of the Bible spoke in just such a manner. When they added, *"Thus saith the Lord…"* to their message, it carried the meaning of, "God told me to tell you this, and I quote..." Sometimes God would even tell the prophet to preface His words with that phrase, so that there would be no doubt where the message came from. For example: *"Then the Lord said unto Moses, 'Go in unto Pharaoh, and tell him, Thus saith the Lord God of the Hebrews, Let my people go, that they may serve me.'"* Exodus 9: 1

When dealing with military affairs, Joan often followed this pattern. She spoke with authority and no ambiguity. On Ascension Day (i.e. May 5, 1429), shortly before the battle of Orleans, she gave her *"...third and final message"* to the English: *"You, O English, who have no right to this kingdom of France, the King of Heaven orders and commands you through me, Joan the Maid, to leave your fortresses and return to your country, and if you do not I will make such a uproar that it will be remembered forever. Pay attention to this my third and final message; I shall write you no further."*[23]

Here's an excerpt from a letter Joan wrote on July 17, 1429 to the Duke of Burgundy: *"Jesus Maria. High and dread prince, duke of Burgundy, the Maid calls upon you by the King of Heaven, my rightful and sovereign Lord, to make a firm and lasting peace with the king of France...And I must make known to you from the King of Heaven, my rightful and sovereign Lord, for your good and for your honor and upon your life, that you will win no more battles against loyal Frenchmen and treat all those who wage war against the aforesaid holy kingdom of France are warring against King Jesus, King of Heaven and of all the earth, my rightful and sovereign Lord. And I pray you and call upon you with hands joined not to seek any battle nor war against us, neither you nor your men nor subjects, and believe firmly that no number of men that you bring against us will win and that there will be great pity for the battle and the bloodshed there of those who come against us...I commend you to God; may He guard you, if it pleases Him; and I pray God that He will establish a good peace. Written in the aforesaid place of Reims, on the aforesaid seventeenth day of July."*[24]

As you see, this teenager spoke with great authority. She follows the pattern seen with the Old Testament prophets (800-500 B.C.). They too spoke boldly and with authority. We see the epitome of this with Jesus. *"When Jesus had finished saying these things, the crowds were amazed at his teaching, because he taught as one who had authority, and not as their teachers of the law."* Matthew 7: 28-29

Before the prophets, God's revelations were much less frequent. *"In those days the word of the LORD was rare; there were not many visions."* 1 Samuel 3: 1 (Written around 1000 B.C.) It seems that God's revelations were progressive, pointing to and finally leading up to His son Jesus. It's interesting to note that this phrase, *"Thus saith the Lord"*, is found in the Old Testament (KJV) 433 times. However, once we get to the New Testament, it is heard no more. This is fitting, as the Lord Himself was then present to deliver the message personally.

After Jesus, it appears that God, according to His own good purpose, has continued to call some to a specific mission. Many come to mind, including the apostles, Paul, Augustine, Constantine, Irenaeus, Justin Martyr, St Francis, John Wycliff, Martin Luther, Mother Teresa, Brother Roger of Taize, and so many others. I believe this is also the case with Joan of Arc.

II. Isn't war always bad and evil?

Indeed, in a perfect world, one of perpetual love, peace and harmony for all, war would always be bad and evil. In a perfect world, war would not exist, because sin would not exist. Unfortunately, that world does not yet exist. Here's an object lesson: the state of twentieth century...

Nazi Germany
"Rebellion to Tyrants is Obedience to God." [25]
Thomas Jefferson, Ben Franklin and John Adams, First Great Seal Committee notes, Journals of Continental Congress, July 4, 1776

Those persecuted and killed because of race, religion, nationality, sexual orientation, etc. by the Nazi war machine would probably not have felt that all war would be bad and evil. For example, a war waged in their defense and liberation. For most of them, that would have been an answered prayer. One of Hitler's main goals was extermination of all the Jews in the world. With no resistance to his plans, he would have at least come close to achieving this goal. In this case, not fighting back, and thus facilitating the extermination of millions of people, would have been manifestly immoral, and more evil than standing up and fighting the Nazis to their end. Indeed, fighting against evil appears to be foundational in Scripture:

"Who will rise up for me against the wicked? Who will take a stand for me against evildoers? Unless the LORD had given me help, I would soon have dwelt in the silence of death..." Psalm 94: 16-17

However for some, it appears that the nature of evil is so terrible that they simply prefer to close their eyes to the many examples surrounding them. It's just too painful and scary to confront. Many hope that somehow the world is evolving beyond this "antiquated" concept of evil. However, in order to hold such a viewpoint, one must disregard history, current events, and Scripture.

Scripture is insistent regarding the existence of evil.[26] Indeed, according to the Bible, a cosmic battle between good and evil has been going on from almost the very beginning (see Genesis 3-4).

It's interesting to note the great interest in "scary" films and books. Stephen King has made millions off of his novels. <u>The Lord of the Rings</u>, <u>Harry Potter</u> and <u>Star Wars</u> movies have all broken records for attendance and worldwide sales. Many people I know love these action films and books. Why? Well, they <u>are</u> well-made adventure stories. But I believe there may be another element involved as well. In all of these a battle between good and evil is portrayed. It is a make-belief battle though, and often one without God. However, this classic battle between good and evil speaks to the heart of all. Young and old, rich and poor, believer and non-believer. Perhaps, deep in our hearts, we all somehow sense this age-old battle raging all around and within us. Many seem only willing to acknowledge it on the big screen or a novel page. Perhaps anything closer, and the horror becomes just too close to handle. Unlike previous generations, such as that of World War II, we in the West seem able to isolate ourselves from the reality of evil. Even after 9/11, a thick curtain of illusion still surrounds many. Evidently for some, we haven't yet been assaulted with such obvious evil, in doses strong or long enough, to destroy this self-imposed curtain of illusion. But this is dangerous. As Rev. Dr. Martin Luther King Jr. (1929-1968) reminds us: *"To ignore evil is to become an accomplice to it."*[27]

You can't appease evil. Nor negotiate with it. You can only fight it. There was no negotiating with Hitler. Appeasement didn't work either, as Neville Chamberlain found out.[28] Hitler was so obsessed with total Jewish genocide, that he was even willing to destroy Germany itself before giving up on his dream. Towards the end of the war, Hitler's priorities for his much needed military trains were often strangely non-military. Such as transporting Jews to death camps![29] Eventually evil had to be acknowledged, confronted with total war, and destroyed. Hitler was responsible for the deaths of 6,000,000 people in concentration camps alone. Without the total war that was waged against him, millions more would have been slaughtered, and German could have easily been the dominant language spoken throughout Europe today, or perhaps even the world.

"If we desire to avoid insult, we must be able to repel it; if we desire to secure peace…it must be known, that we are at all times ready for war." George Washington [31]

III. What does Scripture have to say about war?

"The LORD is a warrior; the LORD is his name." Exodus 15: 3

Actually, quite a lot. Judging from the last four thousand years, man does not seem to have made much progress in dealing with war, with the exception of becoming more efficient at killing each other.

A. Twelve Points

1. First of all, what the Bible records is not necessarily what the Bible approves. For example in Judges 19 there is a story of a woman being raped, cut into twelve pieces and then one piece sent to each of the twelve tribes of Israel. But the Bible certainly doesn't approve of that. In fact, there are no cruel executions commanded by God found in Scripture.

2. In the Bible we never find war or violence praised as an end in itself. Instead we see a God who in certain violent acts overturns a situation of injustice, and in so doing, offers a new beginning to an oppressed people.

3. Holy War and the Warrior God are theological images especially prominent in the books of Deuteronomy and Joshua. There God is presented as the Divine Warrior, fighting for a holy cause.

4. In Scripture, war itself is never glorified.

5. Instructions for war are specifically discussed in Deuteronomy 20.

6. The military weakness of the Israelites compared to the military strength of the Canaanites is shown to be part of God's plan (see the book of Joshua). God is the warrior on the side of the weak who makes possible their victory over the strong. And it is God who goes to war, not Joshua or the people. The people make up the armies, but they do only what they're told by God. And its God who gives them power and victory.[32] Here's an example: *" Moses said to Joshua, 'Chose some of*

our men and go out to fight the Amalekites. Tomorrow I will stand on top of the hill with the staff of God in my hands.' As long as Moses held up his hands, the Israelites were winning, but whenever he lowered his hands, the Amalekites were winning. When Moses' hands grew tired, they took a stone and put it under him and he sat on it. Aaron and Hur held his hands up-one on one side, one on the other- so that his hands remained steady til sunset. So Joshua overcame the Amalekite army with the sword." Exodus 17: 8-9, 11-13 We'll see the Amalekites again a little later.

7. A permanent, well-armed military is not part of the theology presented in Deuteronomy. For example, kings must *"not acquire many horses"* for their armies (Deuteronomy 17: 16). For kings and emperors, horses were of the greatest military importance. They provided quick and lethal mobility against enemies. Not having many horses would mean a greatly reduced military capability. There is a lesson here. Military victory is possible because God makes it so. Trust is not to be placed in arms, but in God. *"A horse is a vain hope for deliverance; despite all its great strength it cannot save."* Psalm 33: 17

And Joan? *"She often told my mother, in whose house she lodged, that she must put her trust in God and that God would aid the town of Orleans and drive away the enemy."*[33]

8. From the book of Joshua through 2 Kings, Israel's kings and their armies are nearly always corrupt and unfaithful to God, and they repeatedly pay the price for it. This lesson of trusting in God for deliverance above all else, is apparently not an easy one to learn. Maybe that's why the Bible speaks so often about it.

"No king is saved by the size of his army; no warrior escapes by his great strength. May your unfailing love rest upon us, O LORD, even as we put our hope in you." Psalm 33: 16, 22

9. Was Jesus a pacifist? Although Jesus never speaks directly about war in the Bible, He did say some interesting and relevant things in this regard. Here are two well-known examples:

   a. *"Do not resist an evil person. If someone strikes you on the right cheek, turn to him the other also."* Matthew 5: 39
   b. *"Love your enemies and pray for those who persecute you, that you may be sons of our Father in heaven."* Matthew 5: 44

These quotes are sometimes used to support the viewpoint that Jesus would never condone any war or violence whatsoever, no matter what. Is this true? If so, that would appear to contradict not only the argument I made earlier regarding Nazi Germany, but also some of the above Old Testament quotes. But Scripture does not contradict itself. Perhaps the God of the Old Testament is different from the God of the New Testament? No (see more on that below). So what gives here?

Well, for one thing, many believe (including this author) that Jesus' above quotes do not address war per se. Rather, these quotes seem to address <u>personal</u> relationships; i.e. relationships between individuals, not between nations. Not only does a common sense reading seem to confirm this, but also the context makes it clear that He is addressing personal issues throughout this passage (i.e. Mt. 5: 21-48). Not national. Also, His audience here is the common people; His own *"disciples and a great number of people from all over Judea, from Jerusalem, and from the coast of Tyre and Sidon, who had come to hear him and to be healed of their diseases."* Luke 6: 17-18 It is not the military, politicians, ambassadors, etc., coming to hear a political or national discourse. No, this appears to be a straightforward sermon to the common people without national political ramifications.

Also, in the same Gospel Matthew[34] as these above Sermon on the Mount passages, we find eight of Jesus' parables in which God deals violently with evildoers. For example, we have this: *"As the weeds are pulled up and burned in the fire, so it will be at the end of the age. The Son of Man will send out his angels, and they will weed out of his kingdom everything that causes sin and all who do evil. They will throw them into the blazing furnace, where there will be weeping and gnashing of teeth. Then the righteous will shine like the sun in the kingdom of their Father. Whoever has ears, let them hear."* Matthew 13: 40-43 (Other examples in Matthew include Mt. 13: 47-50, 18: 23-35 and 25: 41.) And this type of violent recompense is not limited to Matthew, but can be found in Jesus' parables throughout the gospels. For example in Luke we have this: *"...But as for these enemies of mine, who did not want me to reign over them, bring them here and slaughter them before me."* Luke 19: 27 ESV

Another thing, Jesus once instructed his disciples to sell their outer garments in order to purchase a sword for self-defense: *"Then Jesus asked them, 'When I sent you without purse, bag or sandals, did you lack anything?' 'Nothing', they answered. He said to them, 'But now if you have a purse, take it, and also a bag; and if you don't have a sword, sell your cloak and buy one. It is written: And he was numbered with the transgressors; and I tell you that this must be fulfilled in me. Yes, what is written about me is reaching its fulfillment.' The disciples said, 'See, Lord, here are two swords.' 'That's enough!' he replied."* Luke: 35-38 Hmm.

And finally, here's a description of Jesus during the last great cosmic battle yet to come: *"I saw heaven standing open and there before me was a white horse, whose rider is called Faithful and True. With justice he judges and wages war. His eyes are like blazing fire, and on his head are many crowns. He has a name written on him that no one knows but he himself. He is dressed in a robe dipped in blood, and his name is the Word of God. The armies of heaven were following him, riding on white horses and dressed in fine linen, white and clean. Coming out of his mouth is a sharp sword with which to strike down the nations. 'He will rule them with an iron scepter.' He treads the winepress of the fury of the wrath of God Almighty. On his robe and on his thigh he has this name written: KING OF KINGS AND LORD OF LORDS."* Revelation 19: 11-16

So, was Jesus a pacifist? According to Merriam-Webster's dictionary, a pacifist is someone who is *"strongly and actively opposed to conflict and especially war."*[35] So while Jesus is the *"Prince of peace"* Isaiah 9:6, He is not a pacifist.[36] At least not according to Merriam-Webster's definition. No doubt, this worthy debate will continue on, just as it has for centuries.

10. Here's a relevant quote from John the Baptist. *"When some soldiers asked him, 'what should we do?' He replied, 'Don't extort money and don't accuse people falsely-be content with your pay."* Luke 3: 14 Notice that John does not tell them to abandon their work as soldiers and become pacifists, but rather to do their work honestly.

11. Paul too says something interesting in this regard: *"For rulers are not a terror to good conduct, but to bad. Would you have no fear of the one who is in authority? Then do what is good, and you will receive his approval, for he is God's servant for your good. But if you do wrong, be afraid, for he does not bear the sword in vain. For he is the servant of God, an avenger who carries out God's wrath on the wrongdoer."* Romans 13: 3-4

12. And one last word from Scripture...

"There is a time for everything, and a season for every activity under heaven...

> *a time to love and a time to hate,*
> *a time for war and a time for peace…"*
> Ecclesiastes 3: 1, 8

B. God is on Our Side?

> *"Sir, my concern is not whether God is on our side; my greatest concern is to be on God's side, for God is always right."*
> Abraham Lincoln [37]

Some believe that God would not involve Himself in man's "trivial land disputes", or take sides in a war. Joan, however, stated that God had sent her to save <u>France</u>. Not the world or another country, but France alone. She claimed that God was in fact on the side of the French, and He wanted the occupying English out of France. Note the following interaction taken from her Trial of Condemnation on March 17, 1431:

Question: *"Do you know if Saint Catherine and Saint Margaret hate the English?"*
Joan of Arc: *"They love what God loves, and hate what God hates."*
Question: *"Does God hate the English?"*
Joan of Arc: *"Of the love or hate God may have for the English, or of what He will do for their souls, I know nothing; but I know quite well that they will be put out of France, except those who shall die there, and that God will send victory to the French against the English."* [38]

During a time of war, everyone seems to claim that God is on their side. Some even believe He takes sides during a football game. In any case, there can be no doubt that Joan believed that God did take a side in the Hundred Years War: the side of the French. Here she is speaking to her generals just before the important Battle of Patay:

"In God's name! We must fight them. Even if they hung from the clouds we would have them. For God is sending them to us to punish. And today our noble king will have the greatest victory he has ever had. And my counsel has told me they will all be ours. Ride bravely, and we shall be well led!" [39]

Although outnumbered five to one, Patay would nonetheless be the greatest victory the French would have up to that point. We'll look at the Battle of Patay in more detail in <u>Chapter 11-Prophecy and Miracles?</u>

Do we see God taking sides in any conflicts in the Bible? Yes, more than once we see God involving Himself in "trivial land disputes". A good example is found in Genesis: *"On that day the LORD made a covenant with Abram and said, 'To your descendants I give this land, from the river of Egypt to the great river, the Euphrates-the land of the Kenites, Kenissites, Kadmonites, Hittites, Perizzites, Rephaites, Amorites, Canaanites, Girgashites and Jebusites.'"* Genesis 15: 18-19

Have you ever had lunch with a Canaanite? Maybe been to the movies with a Kenite? Surely you've at least met an Amorite or a Hittite? The fact is that all these nations listed in the above Genesis verses no longer exist today. Meanwhile God's chosen people, after two thousand years of worldwide dispersion, are now back in their God-given land of Israel, in spite of the largest, longest, most obsessive and vicious persecution recorded in history. And they are thriving and prosperous.

The Jewish people were not chosen because they were a great people. In fact, they were a small and insignificant people. But they <u>were</u> chosen. *"The Lord did not set his affection of you and choose you because you were more numerous than other peoples, for you were the fewest of all people. But it was because the Lord loved you and kept the oath he swore to your forefathers that he brought you out with a mighty hand and redeemed you from the land of slavery, from the power of Pharaoh king of Egypt. Know therefore that the Lord your God is God; he is the faithful God, keeping his covenant of love to a thousand generations of those who love him and keep his commands."* Deuteronomy 7: 7-9; see also Ezekiel 36: 22-23

From the very beginning, God's plan was to establish a people from which the Messiah would come, and thus provide a way for all mankind to be saved and spend eternity with Him. The people God chose were the Hebrews (i.e. the Jews), and the land He gave them was Israel. Although controversial today, the Bible is clear and consistent about this in several places (e.g. Gen 12: 1-3).

Against ALL odds, the Jews continue to survive. Meanwhile, all of their ancient foes have disappeared from the world's stage. This list of ancient foes is a long one, including: *"...the Kenites, Kenissites, Kadmonites, Hittites, Perizzites, Rephaites, Amorites, Canaanites, Girgashites and Jebusites..."* Genesis 15: 18-19 And of course there have been others since these including the Babylonians, Assyrians, Romans and Nazis.

Israel's enemies today are just as rabid as the Nazis were. In fact the vast majority of the Muslim world sympathized with the Nazis during World War II, and supported their genocidal plans.[40] For many of them, this obsessive, ancient hatred of the Jewish people is apparently even greater than the love they have for their own children. We sometimes see some of these proud parents on TV, whose children "successfully" blew themselves up, in order to kill a few Israeli civilians. Ultimately, such hatred against God's people will not stand.

> *"The strong, active power given in the language of the Warrior Lord means that there is a force in the universe set against the forces of evil and perversity. Life, then, is a battleground, but the Divine Warrior will not be defeated."* George Ernest Wright [41]

IV. Jesus: meek and mild?
"Gentle Jesus, 'meek and mild' is a sniveling modern invention, with no warrant in the gospels."
George Bernard Shaw [42]

A loving, compassionate and humble servant of the Lord? Yes. But meek and mild? Uh, not really. He was the Son of God. Here are two relevant excerpts:

Excerpt A: At one point, Jesus told the religious authorities of his day: *"Woe to you, teachers of the law and Pharisees, you hypocrites!...blind guides...You blind fools...You are like whitewashed tombs, which look beautiful on the outside but on the inside are full of dead men's bones and everything unclean...you are the descendants of those who murdered the prophets...You snakes! You brood of vipers! How will you escape being condemned to hell? ...upon you will come all the righteous blood that has been shed on earth..."* Matthew 24: 13-36

Is this any way to speak to your elders? And these were the leaders of the faith at that time! A contemporary analogy could be confronting the Pope and his closest advisers with the above words in front of crowds of people at St Peter's Cathedral in Rome. Is Jesus' approach to these people politically correct? Not so much. And obviously not meek and mild.

Excerpt B: *"In the temple courts he found men selling cattle, sheep and doves, and others sitting at tables exchanging money. So he made a whip out of cords, and drove all from the temple area, both sheep and cattle; he scattered the coins of the moneychangers and overturned their tables. To those who sold doves he said, 'Get these out of here! How dare you turn my Father's house into a market!'"* John 2: 14-16

Is this any way to act in public?! What <u>would</u> people think?! Not so meek, and not so mild.

It is of course true that through Jesus we often see a God full of love and compassion. Grace and eternal life in God's presence is the reward for all those who choose to repent of their sin and turn to Him. But grace and love can be rejected, and there are consequences for our choices in life. Sodom and Gomorrah is a case in point. There they rejected their heavenly Father with their centuries of unrepentant sin (Genesis 19), and eventually paid the consequences with their destruction.

With Jesus we sometimes tend to focus only on His love, but neglect His justice. However Jesus talks more about judgment than anyone else in the NT (e.g. Matthew 25: 31-46). For those who refuse His free gift of grace, Jesus is quiet clear what awaits them: eternal separation from God in an unappealing destination (e.g. Mt. 25: 31-46; Luke 16: 19-31). And ultimately, this will be their own choice.

V. Two Gods in the Bible?

Still, some see a big difference between the God of the Old Testament (one of justice) and the God of the New Testament (one of love). But in fact it is the same God. He is a God of <u>both</u> genuine love and true justice. You can't have one without the other, and God has not changed from the Old to the New Testament. *"I the LORD do not change."* Malachi 3: 6

On the other hand, perhaps man's perceptions of God have grown some. Over the course of time, God has gradually revealed more and more of Himself. We can see this as we read through the Bible, beginning with Adam and Eve, then Noah, the Patriarchs, the prophets... As time goes on, we slowly begin to get a better understanding of who this mysterious God really is. When Jesus finally arrives on the world stage, our picture of God becomes clearer still. This is not to say that we of the 21st century have finally figured out all the great mysteries of God. No, of course not. Rather I am suggesting that God's identity is not as cloudy to us today as it was three-four thousand years ago.

A. Love <u>and</u> Justice
"Yet the LORD longs to be gracious to you; he rises to show you compassion. For the LORD is a God of justice. Blessed are all who wait for him!" Isaiah 30:18

In the OT, God actually presents Himself first and foremost as a

God of love. Here's one of many examples: *"The LORD, the LORD, the compassionate and gracious God, slow to anger, abounding in love and faithfulness, maintaining love to thousands, and forgiving wickedness, rebellion and sin."* Exodus 34: 6

Yet, to have a more complete picture of who He is, we need to continue reading. The very next sentence says, *"Yet he does not leave the guilty unpunished..."* Exodus 34: 7 Mankind's evil ways demand justice from a Holy God, and justice is part of who He is. He often speaks about justice, sometimes directly: *"For I, the LORD, love justice..."* Isaiah 61: 8 And justice often demands judgment. God is a loving father, but not an indulgent parent. He will bring justice. He is not in the judgment business, but rather in the love, compassion and forgiveness business. However He cannot forgive those who do not seek His forgiveness.

B. The Amalekites

Nonetheless, at first glance, some of the judgments we see in the OT are shocking. The case of the Amalekites is a good example. In 1 Samuel God, through Samuel the prophet, tells King Saul the following: *"This is what the LORD Almighty says: 'I will punish the Amalekites for what they did to Israel when they waylaid them as they came up from Egypt. Now go, attack the Amalekites and totally destroy everything that belongs to them. Do not spare them; put to death men and women, children and infants, cattle and sheep, camels and donkeys."*
1 Samuel 15: 2-3

Is this the merciful God we hear so much about in the New Testament? Let's take a little closer look. First of all, the Amalekites were far from innocent. They were a persistent, vicious and warring people. Their mission in life seems to have been total Jewish genocide. Psalm 83 speaks of the Amalekites, as well as other tribes equally focused on Israel's destruction:

"O God, do not keep silent; be not quiet, O God, be not still. See how your enemies are astir, how your foes rear their heads. With cunning they conspire against your people; they plot against those you cherish. 'Come', they say, 'let us destroy them as a nation, that the name of Israel be remembered no more.' With one mind they plot together; they form an alliance against you-the tents of Edom and the Ishmaelites, of Moab and the Hagrites, Gebal, Ammon and Amalek, Philistia, with the people of Tyre. Even Assyria has joined them..." Psalm 83: 1-7

Unfortunately things have not changed that much for the Jews.

Their complete destruction still appears to be the primary goal for some nations/peoples. Iranian president Mahmoud Ahmadinejad made international headlines on October 27, 2005, when he declared in Persian that *"Israel must be wiped off the map."*[43] And the *"regime reiterated its English translation on billboards and murals."*[44] This is not an isolated case. Iran's supreme leader, Ayatollah Ali Khamenei has repeatedly made similar statements and threats.[45]

Although it's fashionable today to accuse Israel of being imperialistic, warmongering, etc., the facts speak for themselves. The Jewish people have <u>never</u> persecuted another people. During a span of more than 4,000 years, they have never gone over their God-given borders to conquer a neighbor.

Back to the Amalekites. During Moses' time (around 1500 B.C.), the Amalekites had been targeting, following, and systematically slaughtering the most vulnerable of the Israelites (i.e. the weak, elderly, and disabled who were lagging behind). Moses warned the Israelites, *"Remember what the Amalekites did to you along the way when you came out of Egypt. When you were weary and worn out, they met you on your journey and cut off all who were lagging behind; they had no fear of God."* Deut. 25: 17-18 Today, the killing of the most vulnerable and innocent for "political reasons" is called terrorism.

The following essay explains some of the things involved with God's ultimate judgment on them: *"God dedicated...*(the Amalekites)*...to destruction because they violently and steadfastly impeded or opposed his work over a long period of time...God waited for centuries while the Amalekites and those other Canaanite groups slowly filled up their own cups of condemnation by their sinful behavior. God never acted precipitously against them; his grace and mercy waited to see if they would repent and turn from their headlong plummet into self-destruction. Not that the conquering Israelites were without sin. Deuteronomy 9:5 makes that clear to the Israelites: 'It is not because of your righteousness or your integrity that you are going into take possession of their land; but on account of the wickedness of these nations.' These nations were cut off to prevent the corruption of Israel and the rest of the world (Deut. 20: 16-18). When a nation starts burning children as a gift to the gods (Lev 18: 21) and practices sodomy, bestiality and all sorts of loathsome vices, the day of God's grace and mercy has begun to run out. Just as surgeons do not hesitate to amputate a gangrenous limb, even if they cannot help cutting off some healthy flesh, so God must do the same. This is not doing evil that good may come; it is removing the cancer that could infect all of society and eventually destroy the remaining good..."*[46]

The Amalekites follow a pattern seen in Scripture. In every case where God commanded that a people be wiped out, they had been warned for centuries, refused to repent, and were becoming increasingly depraved with the passage of time. They were given plenty of opportunity to change their ways and avoid a final judgment. Indeed, one could ask, "If these people were so evil, then what took God so long to judge them?" Peter the apostle, gives us the answer: *"But do not forget this one thing, dear friends: With the Lord, a day is like a thousand years, and a thousand years are like a day. The Lord is not slow in keeping his promise, as some understand slowness. He is patient with you, not wanting anyone to perish, but everyone to come to repentance."* 2 Peter 3: 8-9 Even with such a people as the Amalekites, God was not seeking vengeance. Indeed, in Ezekiel He says, *"As surely as I live, declares the Sovereign LORD, I take no pleasure in the death of the wicked, but rather that they turn from their ways and live."* Ezekiel 33: 11 And Paul tells us that God *"...wants all people to be saved and to come to a knowledge of the truth."* 1 Timothy 2: 4

But, we might ask, what about their children? Surely they are innocent. Well in a sense God's action was an act of mercy. The ways of the Amalekites were so thoroughly corrupted, that their children had no chance to escape this deeply embedded evil. If the children had continued to live in that society past the age of accountability, they undoubtedly would have become corrupted and thereby lost forever. Unfortunately, many of the children of Israel's enemies today may also end up falling into this same category.

There is also something else to keep in mind. We sometimes tend to take for granted that God is the one who gave us life in the first place. He has the right to take it back whenever He wishes. The only question is when and how, which we have to leave up to Him. *"The LORD giveth, and the LORD taketh away; Blessed be the name of the Lord."* Job 1: 21

And finally, let us not forget what was hanging in the balance: the Israelites were the chosen people through whom God would bring salvation to the entire world through Jesus the Messiah. Had some hardcore Amalekite remnant survived, they likely would have resumed their aggression against the Israelites and God's plan. God took action not only for the sake of the Israelites, but ultimately for the sake of every soul throughout history, whose salvation would come from the coming Messiah of Israel. God's purpose in these instances was to destroy the corrupt nation because <u>the national structure</u> was inherently evil, not destroy people willing to repent.

C. Nineveh
Repentance and Belief [47]

And some were willing to repent. In the Old Testament book of Jonah, 800 years before the birth of Jesus, we see just such a people: the people of *"the great city Nineveh."* Jonah 3: 2 God was going to judge them because *"their wickedness has come before me."* Jonah 1: 1 But they believed Jonah's warning about God's impending destruction, repented and God saved them all. *"When God saw what they did and how they turned from their evil ways, he had compassion and did not bring upon them the destruction he had threatened."* Jonah 3: 10

Here's the point: if anyone wants to escape judgment, God will let them. Whoever turns to Him, God is willing to save. When the Ninevites repented, *"he had compassion and did not bring upon them the destruction he had threatened."*

This same pattern, i.e. repent and believe, is the same one Jesus presented 800 years later: *"'The time has come,' he said. 'The kingdom of God is near. Repent and believe the good news!'"* Mark 1: 15

As you see, repentance <u>and</u> belief are asked for in both the Old and the New Testaments. We can't have one without the other. Love <u>and</u> justice are displayed in both the Old and the New Testaments. We can't have one without the other. And why not? Because the God of both the Old and the New Testament is one and the same.

D. But isn't the God of the Bible
a God of love and peace, not war?

Yes, the God of the Bible is a God of peace. However, lasting peace is inextricably linked to justice. You can't have one without the other. This is seen throughout Scripture. An example: *"The LORD works righteousness and justice for all the oppressed...The LORD is compassionate and gracious, slow to anger, abounding in love."* Psalm 103: 6, 8

God does display His great love for us. He's the One who came down from Heaven to rescue us. He unlocks the doors of our captivity that human strength is unable to unlock. He is the rescuer and deliverer:

"For he is the living God
And he endures forever;
His kingdom will not be destroyed,
His dominion will never end.
He <u>rescues</u> and he <u>saves</u>;

He performs signs and wonders in the heavens and on the earth.
He has rescued Daniel
From the power of the lions."
Daniel 6: 26-27 (Underlining by author)

    King Darius of Babylon was so impressed with God's rescue of Daniel from the lion's den, that he issued the above decree for his entire kingdom. There are many other examples of God as the rescuer/deliverer (e.g. see Ex 6: 6-8, 18:10). For Israel, God was first and foremost their Liberator. From the beginning the Israelites knew that their very existence depended completely on God's merciful acts. It was from these very acts that God gave them an identity and a history (see Exodus chapters 7-14). Violent images and tales of war and victory often accompany their story. There is no getting around this. A couple of examples...

    a. *"But the LORD is with me like a mighty warrior; so my persecutors will stumble and not prevail."* Jeremiah 20: 11
    b. *"The LORD will march out like a mighty man, like a warrior he will stir up his zeal; with a shout he will raise the battle cry and will triumph over his enemies."* Isaiah 42: 11-13

    As we see, the LORD is often spoken of as a warrior in Scripture, and this not always symbolically. An often used ancient name for God is Sabaoth, i.e. "Lord God of Hosts". This refers either to the warriors of Israel or the armies of heaven. In fact, *"Lord God of Hosts"* is used ninety-seven times in the Old Testament (e.g. see 2 Samuel 5:10 KJV, 1 Kings 19:10 KJV, 1 Kings 19:14 KJV , Psalm 59:5 KJV, Psalm 69:6 KJV , Psalm 80:4 KJV, Isaiah 10:23 KJV, Jeremiah 5:14 KJV, Amos 9:5 KJV ...).

    Two of the oldest literary compositions in the Bible are both songs of victory:

    a. From the Song of Deborah: *"So may all your enemies perish, O Lord!"* Judges 5: 31
    b. From the Song of Moses: *"I will sing to the Lord, for he is highly exalted. The horse and its rider he has hurled into the sea!"* Exodus 15: 1

    Compared to these war cries, the stories of the Old Testament "Patriarchs" (Abraham, Isaac, and Jacob-found in Genesis) seem rather tame. Is it really the same God? The easy answer to this would be to simply reject any consideration of a God who makes use of acts of war and violence, like our friend Michelle at the beginning of this chapter. Although tried many times, I believe that such an approach leads only to an incomplete and inaccurate picture of the Biblical message. The story of Moses (i.e. Exodus-Deuteronomy) includes, as one of its essential aspects, the activities of a God who destroys oppression and battles for His people. Far from splitting God into a god of peace and a god of war, the Bible shows us from beginning to end a fullness of life and peace, and this necessarily involves a struggle against everything that contradicts such a vision.

VI. Are there any examples of "holy warriors" in the Bible?

"If ever there was a holy war, it was that which saved our liberties and gave us independence."
Thomas Jefferson [48]

Yes, there are many. Among others, Joshua, Deborah, Gideon, Samson, Saul, and David are good examples. We can learn much from them all, but here we'll take a quick look at Deborah (Judges 4-5) and Gideon (Judges 6-7).

A) Deborah

Deborah's case is especially interesting. Like Joan, she was a woman leading her people at a time and place where women were not normally accorded rights or respect equal to those of men. For a woman to be a leader of her people in such circumstances, she must have truly been exceptional and/or chosen by God.

Deborah lived in the 12th century B.C. She led a successful Israelite revolt against Canaanite domination in the northern part of the country. She was a "Judge" of Israel. That is, a person whose moral authority was regarded as inspired by the Lord. She too spoke with great authority, sometimes as if quoting God. Either she truly was quoting Him, or she was a false prophet. Here she is speaking to Barak (the commander of northern Israel): *"The LORD, the God of Israel, commands you: 'Go, take with you ten thousand men...and lead the way...and I will lure the commander...with his chariots and troops...and give him into your hands.'"* Judges 4: 6-7

Deborah's perspective on battle is consistent with the rest of Scripture: yes, the soldiers must fight, but God gives the victory. *"Then Deborah said to Barak, 'Go! This is the day the LORD has given Sisera into your hands. Has not the LORD gone ahead of you?' At Barak's advance, the LORD routed Sisera and all his chariots and army by the sword...not a man was left."* Judges 4: 14-16 And Joan? *"In the name of God! The soldiers will fight and God will give the victory!"*[49] Everything happened just as Deborah prophesied. After their great victory, she follows the Scriptural pattern of always giving credit and praise to God for His victory. *"Hear this, you kings! Listen, you rulers! I will sing to the LORD, I will sing; I will make music for the LORD, the God of Israel."* Judges 5: 3 All through Joan's story we see this same pattern. *"All that I have done is by our Lord's bidding."*[50] *"Whatever I have done that was good, I have done at the bidding of my voices."*[51] *"As to whether victory was my banner's or mine, it was all our Lord's."*[52]

And finally, what was the outcome of God's intervention through Deborah? The Canaanite's power over the Israelites was broken and, *"The land had peace for forty years."* Judges 5: 31

B. Gideon

Another example of the "holy warrior" is found with Gideon, the Judge who follows Deborah. An angel of the Lord appears to Gideon and greets him with these words, *"The LORD is with you, O valiant warrior."* Judges 6: 12 He will be directed by the Lord to defeat the Midianites, and so save Israel. Here we see the same patterns as before:

    1) Gideon's people are weak, and are being sorely oppressed by the many and powerful Midianites. Like Pharaoh oppressing Moses' people, the Hebrews. Or the English oppressing Joan's people, the French.

    2) As seen with Joan and Moses, the Lord again chooses the lowly (Gideon), to confront the mighty. *"Jeanne... said: 'No, do not fear their numbers; do not hesitate to make the attack; God will conduct your enterprise; if I were not sure that it is God Who guides us, I would rather take care of the sheep than expose myself to such great perils!'"* The Duke d'Alencon, Trial of Nullification

    3) And like Moses and Joan of Arc, the chosen one doesn't really want the job (see Chapter 6). *"'But Lord', Gideon asked, 'how can I save Israel? My clan is the weakest in Manasseh, and I am the least in my family.'"* Judges 6: 15

4) Again like Joan and Moses, God shows Gideon the way the powerful will be defeated: *"The Lord answered, 'I will be with you, and you will strike down all the Midianites together.'"* Judges 6: 16 They must trust the Lord, and they must fight. Then God will give the victory.

A Holy Warrior in France

"All the soldiers held her as sacred. So well did she bear herself in warfare, in words and in deeds, as a follower of God, that no evil could be said of her. I heard Maitre Pierre de Versailles say that he was once in the town of Loches in company with Jeanne, when the people, throwing themselves before the feet of her horse, kissed her hands and feet; and he said to Jeanne that she did wrong to allow what was not due to her, and that she ought to protect herself from it lest men should become idolatrous; to which she answered: 'In truth, I know not how to protect myself, if God does not protect me.'"
Maitre Jean Barbin, Doctor of Laws, King's Advocate, Trial of Nullification

VII. Other Scriptural Examples of God's Involvement with Nations

"God reigns over the nations..." Psalm 47: 8

Here are a few more examples:

"Blessed is the nation whose God is the LORD..." Psalm 33: 12

"I will drive out nations before you and enlarge your territory..." Exodus 34: 24

"But I said to you, 'You will possess their land; I will give it to you as an inheritance...I am the LORD your God, who has set you apart from the nations.'" Leviticus 20: 23-25

"Like the nations the LORD destroyed before you, so you will be destroyed for not obeying the LORD your God." Deuteronomy 8: 20

"This is what the LORD Almighty, the God of Israel, says: 'I will put an iron yoke on the necks of all these nations to make them serve Nebuchadnezzar King of Babylon, and they will serve him...'" Jeremiah 28: 14

For those interested, here are still more examples: Genesis 35: 11; Deuteronomy 9: 5; 12: 29; 15: 6; 19: 1; 20: 16; 26: 19; 28: 1; 30: 3; 31:

3; Joshua 24: 18; 2 Samuel 7: 23; Ezekiel 39: 28 and Revelation 19: 15.

VIII. Wrap Up

*"Sir we are not weak, if we make a proper use of these means
which the God of nature hath placed in our power...
Besides sir, we shall not fight our battles alone. There is
a just God who presides over the destinies of nations..."*
Patrick Henry [53]

That God would be intricately involved in the affairs of nations, including war, is a troubling concept for some. Nonetheless, as we have seen in this chapter, Scripture does consistently affirm this. It presents a God who has at various times throughout history been an active participant in His creation. A God who defends the weak, and jealously looks out for those who are His.

We've seen that the God presented in the Old and New Testament is the same God: a God of love and justice. Genuine love and true justice are inextricably bound together, and we can't have one without the other. In Genesis we read, *"God created man in his own image."* Gen. 1: 27 Perhaps this might help to explain man's innate and deep thirst for both authentic love and true justice.

We looked at the idea of a "holy warrior", and found that this concept is based in Scripture. We glanced at a couple of Biblical examples of "holy warriors" (Deborah and Gideon), and see that this "holy warrior" pattern is closely followed by Joan of Arc.

And finally, I tried to show, citing several Biblical verses, that in Scripture God's involvement with nations is something that is often, rather than seldom, seen.

I am indebted to Brother John of Taize for his book, <u>The Pilgrim God</u>, which provided insightful help for part of this chapter.

[1] From Doyle's translation of Leon Denis' <u>Jeanne D'Arc Medium</u>, Librairie des Sciences Psychiques, Paris, 1910; Doyle was author of Sherlock Holmes,1924.
[2] Joan of Arc, said to the French Captains on June 11, 1429; Joan of Arc translated by Willard Trask, <u>Joan of Arc: In Her Own Words</u>, Turtle Point Press, New York, 1996, p. 45
[3] Joan said this to her soldiers on April 28, 1429; Joan of Arc translated by Willard Trask, <u>Joan of Arc: In Her Own Words</u>, Turtle Point Press, New York, 1996, p. 34
[4] Said to her chaplain on May 4, 1429; Joan of Arc translated by Willard Trask, <u>Joan of Arc: In Her Own Words</u>, Turtle Point Press, New York, 1996, p. 35
[5] See Régine Pernoud et Marie-Véronique Clin, <u>Joan of Arc-Her Story</u>, St Martin's Press, New York, 1998, p. 38
[6] Joan of Arc translated by Willard Trask, <u>Joan of Arc: In Her Own Words</u>, Turtle Point

Press, New York, 1996, p. 36
[7]Régine Pernoud et Marie-Véronique Clin, Jeanne d'Arc, Editions Fayard, Mesnil-sur-l'Estrée, 2001, p. 55-56
[8]Spoken by Jean, Duke of Alencon, one of Joan's two co-commanders of the French army. Stephen Richey, Joan of Arc A Military Appreciation, 2000, p. 9. Mr. Richey is author of: Joan of Arc: The Warrior Saint, Greenwood Publishing Group, Westport, CN, 2003.
[9]Mr. Lang (1844-1912) was a Scottish poet, novelist, literary critic, and contributor to the field of anthropology. Here he was comparing Joan to William Wallace (also known from the film "Braveheart"), and other brave leaders.
[10]Maitre Jean Barbin, a Doctor of Laws, was the King's Advocate.
[11]Régine Pernoud, Jeanne d'Arc par elle-meme et ses témoins, Editions du Seuil, Paris, 1996, p. 105
[12]Régine Pernoud, Jeanne d'Arc par elle-meme et ses témoins, Editions du Seuil, Paris, 1996, p.105
[13]Fr. Pasquerel, Trial of Nullification
[14]Trial of Nullification, Louis de Contes.
[15]Simon Baucroix, Squire, Trial of Nullification
[16]Joan of Arc translated by Willard Trask, Joan of Arc: In Her Own Words, Turtle Point Press, New York, 1996, p. 37
[17]Régine Pernoud, Jeanne d'Arc par elle-meme et ses témoins, Editions du Seuil, Paris, 1996, p. 107
[18]Régine Pernoud et Marie-Véronique Clin, Jeanne d'Arc, Editions Fayard, Mesnil-sur-l'Estrée, 2001, p. 72-73
[19]Régine Pernoud et Marie-Véronique Clin, Jeanne d'Arc, Editions Fayard, Mesnil-sur-l'Estrée, 2001, p. 115
[20]Maitre Viole was Licentiate in Law and Advocate of the Court of Parliament.
[21]Here's one short example: *"I knew nothing of Jeanne until she came to Orleans to raise the siege...I afterwards saw her at the assault of the Forts of Saint Loup, the Augustins, Saint-Jean-le-Blanc, and at the Bridge. In all these assaults she was so valorous and comported herself in such manner as would not have been possible to any man, however well versed in war; and all the captains marveled at her valor and activity and at her endurance...I believe that she was good and worthy, and that the things she did were divine rather than human...Apart from affairs of war, she was simple and innocent; but in the conduct and disposition of troops and in actual warfare, in the ordering of battle and in animating the soldiers, she behaved as the most skilled captain in the world who all his life had been trained in the art of war."* Thibauld d'Armagnac, Knight, Seigneur de Termes, Bailiff of Charires, Trial of Nullification
[22]See for example Joan of Arc-A Military Leader by Kelly DeVries; or the essay Joan of Arc A Military Appreciation by Stephen W. Richey
[23]Régine Pernoud et Marie-Véronique Clin, Jeanne d'Arc, Editions Fayard, Mesnil-sur-l'Estrée, 2001, p. 73
[24]Régine Pernoud et Marie-Véronique Clin, Jeanne d'Arc, Editions Fayard, Mesnil-sur-l'Estrée, 2001, p. 383
[25]On July 4, 1776, the Continental Congress named Thomas Jefferson, Ben Franklin and John Adams to the first committee to design a Great Seal, or national emblem, for the country. They suggested *Rebellion to Tyrants is Obedience to God*, for the motto, but it was never used. Thomas Jefferson liked it so much, he later used it on his own personal seal.
[26]An example: *"Then the LORD saw that the wickedness of man was great in the earth, and that every intent of the thoughts of his heart was only evil continually. And the LORD was sorry that He had made man on the earth, and He was grieved in His heart."*

Genesis 6: 5–6. For other examples, see Genesis 8:21; Deuteronomy 30:15; 1 John 3:8...
[27]Alex Ayers (Editor), The Wisdom of Martin Luther King, Jr., Plume Publishing, New York, 1993
[28]See http://en.wikipedia.org/wiki/Neville_Chamberlain, August, 2011
[29] *"The movement of trains to the death camps was a high priority, and large numbers of transports of Jews were scheduled even as the Wehrmacht (German army) launched its final offensive in the Moscow area in order to avoid the Russian winter. Raul Hilberg*[30] *put it best when he wrote, 'Apparently, military considerations also were not to be considered in the 'Final Solution' of the Jewish problem.'"*
http://organizedhell.devhub.com/blog/641704-reichsbahn-railway-administration. Accessed October 2011
[30] *"Raul Hilberg (1926-2007) was an Austrian-born American political scientist and historian. He was widely considered to be the world's preeminent scholar of the Holocaust, and his three-volume, 1,273-page magnum opus,* The Destruction of the European Jews, *is regarded as a seminal study of the Nazi Final Solution."* See http://en.wikipedia.org/wiki/Raul_Hilberg
[31]George Washington, December 3, 1793, from his annual address to Congress. Washington (1731-1799) was the first President of the United States of America, serving from 1789 to 1797, and the dominant military and political leader of the United States from 1775 to 1799. He led the American victory over Great Britain in the American Revolutionary War as commander-in-chief of the Continental Army from 1775 to 1783, and presided over the writing of the Constitution in 1787. Washington became the first president by unanimous choice, and is universally regarded as the "Father of his country".
[32]Here again we see a parallel with Joan of Arc. Asked by the priests at Poitiers why God would need soldiers if He desired victory for the French, she answered, *"In the name of God! The soldiers will fight and God will give the victory!"* Régine Pernoud et Marie-Véronique Clin, Jeanne d'Arc, Editions Fayard, Mesnil-sur-l'Estrée, 2001, p. 49
[33]Charlotte Boucher, daughter of Jacques Boucher of Orleans, Trial of Nullification
[34]Gospel is a term used for any of the first four New Testament books (i.e. Matthew, Mark, Luke and John), that tell of the life, death, and resurrection of Jesus Christ. Christians may additionally use the term in reference to the general message of the New Testament, otherwise known as the "Good News".
[35]http://www.merriam-webster.com/dictionary/pacifistic, accessed Dec. 2011
[36]Also, see below for **III-Jesus: meek and mild?**
[37]1858 Lincoln-Douglas Debates, Lincoln's Senatorial Speech, July 10, 1858. Abraham Lincoln (1809-1865) was the 16th President of the United States, until his assassination in April 1865. He successfully led his country through a great constitutional, military and moral crisis – the American Civil War – preserving the Union, while ending slavery, and promoting economic and financial modernization.
[38]Joan of Arc translated by Willard Trask, Joan of Arc: In Her Own Words, Turtle Point Press, New York, 1996, p. 122
[39]Ibid, p. 46
[40]An example: *"The Grand Mufti of Jerusalem, Haj al-Husseini (the leader of the Arabs in Palestine and the person responsible for interpreting Muslim law since the 1930s), made no secret of his close affinity for the Nazis and their final solution for the Jews. He kept a copy of Hitler's Mein Kampf next to his Koran ...In November, 1941 he fled to Germany and met with Adolf Hitler, Heirnich Himmler, Joachim Von Ribbentrop and other Nazi leaders. He wanted to persuade them to extend the Nazis' anti-Jewish program to the Arab world. The Mufti sent Hitler a declaration that 'they accord to Palestine and to other Arab countries the right to solve the problem of the Jewish elements in Palestine and other countries in accordance with the interest of the Arabs and, by the same method, that the question is now being settled in the Axis countries'...he*

told them, 'The Arabs were Germany's natural friends because they had the same enemy, namely...the Jews...'" Mitchell G. Bard, Myths and Facts-A Guide to the Arab-Israeli Conflict, AICE, Chevy Chase, MD, 2001, p. 48-49; Hal Lindsey, The Everlasting Hatred, Oracle House Publishing, Corona, CA, 2002, p.206-207

[41]George Ernest Wright, Old Testament Theology: Flowering and Future, edited by Ben C. Ollenburger, 2004, p. 87. Mr. Wright (1909-1974) was a leading American Old Testament scholar and Biblical archeologist.

[42]George Bernard Shaw, Preface to Androcles and the Lion: On the Prospects of Christianity, Public Domain,1912, Preface. Mr. Shaw (1856-1950) was a well-known Irish playwright who wrote more than 60 plays.

[43]Islamic Republic of Iran Broadcasting (Tehran), Oct. 27, 2005. Ahmadinejad has since made several other statements threatening the complete destruction of Israel.

[44]Agence France-Presse, Mar. 9, 2008; Reuters, Mar. 9, 2008

[45]Here is a recent example. In Feb. 2012, Iran's supreme leader, Ayatollah Ali Khamenei, said the opportunity must not be lost to remove *"this corrupting material. It is a jurisprudential justification to kill all the Jews and annihilate Israel, and in that, the Islamic government of Iran must take the helm"...The doctrine includes wiping out Israeli assets and Jewish people worldwide...the Quran is quoted (Albaghara 2:191-193): 'And slay them wherever ye find them, and drive them out of the places whence they drove you out, for persecution [of Muslims] is worse than slaughter [of non-believers]...and fight them until persecution is no more, and religion is for Allah'...Khamenei, as utmost authority, the Velayete Faghih (Islamic Jurist), also believes that Israel and America not only must be defeated but annihilated."* WND.com, http://www.wnd.com/2012/02/ayatollah-kill-all-jews-annihilate-israel, February 06, 2012

[46]Kaiser, Davids, Bruce, and Brauch; Hard Sayings of the Bible, Inter Varsity Press, Downers Grove, Illinois, 1996, p. 206

[47]"Is repentance necessary for salvation? Emotions run high and opinions vary widely on this issue...The word "repent" has to be understood within the context in which it is being used. Repent in the Greek...basically means a change of mind and the context must determine what is involved in that change of mind. In passages where salvation is in view it is equivalent to *believe* or *trust in* and involves a change of mind about any form of self-trust in human works, good deeds, religious tradition, etc. followed by a trust in the finished work of Christ which alone has the power to save us. It means a turning from self-trust to trust in Christ. Believe and repent are never used together as if teaching two different requirements for salvation. When salvation from eternal condemnation is in view, repent (a change of mind) and believe are in essence used as synonyms...In Luke's rendering of the Great Commission he uses repentance as a single requirement in the same sense as believing in Christ (Luke 24:46-47). As Dr. Ryrie says of this verse, *'Clearly, repentance for the forgiveness of sins is connected to the death and resurrection of Christ.'* The repentance comes out of the recognition of one's sin, but the object of repentance is the person and work of Christ, or faith in Christ. Interestingly, in Luke 8:12 he uses believe alone, *'Those along the path are the ones who hear, and then the devil comes and takes away the word from their hearts, so that they may not believe and be saved.'* A comparison of other passages clearly supports the fact that repentance often stands for faith in the person and work of Christ. Compare Acts 10:43 with 11:17-18; 13:38-39 with 2:38. Also, note Acts 16:31 which uses "believe" alone. The stated purpose of the Gospel of John is to bring men to faith in Christ (20:31), yet John never once uses the word repent, not once. Speaking of the absence of John's use of repent in His gospel, Ryrie writes: *'And yet John surely had many opportunities to use it in the events of our Lord's life which he recorded.'* To the Samaritan harlot, Christ did not say repent. He told her to ask (John 4:10), and when her testimony and the Lord's spread to other Samaritans, John recorded not that they repented but that they believed (vss. 39, 41-

42). There are about fifty more occurrences of 'believe' or 'faith' in the Gospel of John, but not one use of "repent." The climax is John 20:31: *'These have been written that you may believe . . . and that believing you may have life in His name.'* (Charles C. Ryrie, *So Great Salvation*, Victor Books, p. 98)... Of course, there is also a repentance needed in the Christian life in relation to specific sins (2 Cor. 7:9; Rev. 2:5) but this repentance has nothing to do with salvation (Matt. 21:28-30)." https://bible.org/question/repentance-necessary-salvation, accessed Feb. 2014.

[48]Thomas Jefferson's letter To John W. Eppes (son-in-law, at the time Chairman of the Committee of Ways and Means of the House of Representatives) Monticello, November 6, 1813. Jefferson (1743-1826) was an American Founding Father who was the principal author of the United States Declaration of Independence (1776) and the third President of the United States (1801–1809).

[49]Joan of Arc at Poitiers-Régine Pernoud, Jeanne d'Arc par elle-meme et ses témoins, Editions du Seuil, Paris, 1996, p. 60

[50]Trial of Condemnation, February 27, 1431; Joan of Arc-Self Portrait, Willard Trask, The Telegraph Press, Harrisburg, Pa, 1936, p. 135

[51]Trial of Condemnation, March 12, 1431; Joan of Arc-Self Portrait, Willard Trask, The Telegraph Press, Harrisburg, Pa, 1936, p. 148

[52]Trial of Condemnation, March 14, 1431; Joan of Arc-Self Portrait, Willard Trask, The Telegraph Press, Harrisburg, Pa, 1936, p. 160

[53]From Patrick Henry's speech to the Virginia Revolutionary Committee on March 23, 1775, at Richmond--in what is now called St. John's Church. Henry was an attorney, planter and politician who became known as an orator during the movement for independence in Virginia in the 1770s. A Founding Father, he served as the first and sixth post-colonial Governor of Virginia, from 1776 to 1779 and from 1784 to 1786.

Chapter 11
Prophecy and Miracles?
"It lies with the Lord to make revelations to whom He pleases."
Joan of Arc, Trial of Condemnation, March 28, 1431

~~~~~~~~~~~~~~

"Sir, *Madam. Good afternoon to you. Here's my card. You can reach me day or night at my cell phone number. Or text me if you prefer. I get all my messages."*

Trying to reach out and touch someone? A business card usually gives us all the essential information needed. It can serve as a calling card, an identification card, a Public Relations tool, an advertisement notice... It might even include a mini-resume.

For His many roles, God has several business cards. Prophecy is one of them. And with this card, there's an added bonus: we can see if His actions are consistent with His claims.

When we think of prophecy, we often connect it with predicting the future. However, it is not always used this way in the Bible. Rather, prophecy in Scripture often simply means bringing a message from God to the people. Nonetheless, it is sometimes used to predict the future. In Joan's case, we see it used both ways.

Predictive prophecy is a key standard that the Bible tells us to use to test whether something is truly from God. Only the Bible, among all the purported holy books, instructs its readers to *"test everything"*. Here are two examples:

1) *"...do not treat prophecies with contempt. Test everything. Hold on to the good. Avoid every kind of evil..."* 1 Thessalonians 5: 20-22

2) *"Dear friends, do not believe every spirit, but test the spirits to see whether they are from God, because many false prophets have gone out into the world."* 1 John 4: 1 See also Isaiah 41: 21-24; Is 42: 9; Is 44: 6-8...

Fulfilled prophecy is one of the defining differences between Christianity/Judaism and all other religions, both past and present. No other sacred book has the prophetic accuracy of the Bible. Most of them, including those of the other major world religions, are noticeably void of <u>any</u> prophecy. There are a few that contain limited attempts at prophecy, but their results fall far short of God's requirement of perfect accuracy (see Deuteronomy 18: 19-22; page 149). In fact, one would expect works not from God to avoid prophecy, or their prophecies to contain errors. Only the Bible is 100% accurate in hundreds of specific prophecies. They speak about people, places, things and unexpected events. Only in the Bible is the future foretold with precision and total accuracy. *"There are over 1000 specific prophecies recorded in the Bible. Of the 667 historical prophecies to date, all but three can be verified as being fulfilled. That does not mean that the other three weren't fulfilled; only that up to this point we have no record."*[1]

Almost every one of the sixty-six books of the Bible contains some prophecy. Sixteen Old Testament books have specific prophecies regarding the expected Messiah (i.e. the "Anointed One"), Jesus of Nazareth. Still today, Jesus' own prophecies remain so specific, accurate, and historically documented, that they are hard to explain away by His many critics. Here are two examples:

1) *"Heaven and earth will pass away, but my words will never pass away."* Luke 21: 33

2) *"Jesus left the temple and was walking away when his disciples came up to him to call his attention to its buildings. 'Do you see all these things?' he asked. 'I tell you the truth, not one stone here will be left on another, every one will be thrown down.'"* Matthew 24: 2

This was literally fulfilled some 35 years after Jesus said it, when the Romans destroyed the temple down to its foundation in 70AD.[2] According to first century Jewish historian Josephus, this was far from the goal of General Titus, the Roman commanding officer. He wanted to spare the temple. However the Roman soldiers, in their fury, ignited a firestorm there. This fascinating prophecy deserves a closer look.

In the eighteenth year of his reign (20-19 BC), King Herod rebuilt Solomon's Temple (circa 960 B.C.) in the same place, but on a more magnificent scale. It was an amazing architectural feat, and at that time was the epitome of extravagance. The Roman historian Tacitus describes the Temple as *"possessing enormous riches"*.[3] It was taller than a fifteen story building, and the temple buildings were made of gleaming white marble. The whole eastern wall of the large main structure was covered with gold plates[4], and was designed to be the most elevated part of the temple so that the gold would be visible from far away. It was especially brilliant when the rays of the morning sun fell upon it. There were even golden spikes affixed to the roof to keep birds from landing on it.[5] Two of the impressive doors that separated the portico from the

Holy Place measured eighty-four feet high and twenty-four feet wide. They too were covered with gold. Above these were "golden vines".[6] The temple mount (the large plaza at the entrance of the temple) was enormous. It was more than twice the size of the Acropolis in Athens, or put another way, it was the size of 20 football fields. One of the surviving stones of the temple complex measures 45 x 11.5 x 12 feet, and is estimated to weigh 570 tons. The mount was surrounded by nearly one thousand columns, each 30 feet high, six feet in diameter, and each topped by a Corinthian sculpture called a "capital". The beauty and size of the Temple Mount exceeded that of most of the seven wonders of the world.[7]

Josephus[8] was an eyewitness to the destruction of the temple, and the events preceding and following it. He tells us, *"...Titus then gave the command that no matter what happened, the temple should be spared, because it would always be a great tribute to the empire...*(however, during the battle) *...a soldier recklessly grabbed a torch. He hurled the fire-stick through the doors made of gold... A messenger rushed to the tent of Titus to inform him of the fire. Immediately, Titus ran to the temple to put out the flames...Pretending not to hear the commands of their general* (Titus)*, and filled with hatred, the soldiers rushed on, hurling their torches into the temple...Ordering a centurion to club anyone if they disobeyed his commands, he rushed forward and pleaded with his soldiers to put out the flames. But because of their hatred of the Jews and their desire for riches, the soldiers disregarded the orders of their general. Seeing that all the surroundings were made of gold, they assumed that inside there would be great treasures... A mighty fire shot up inside. Caesar* [9] (i.e. Titus) *and his generals fled for safety, and thus, against his wishes, the sanctuary was burned...The city and the temple were then leveled to the ground by the command of Caesar* (i.e. Titus)*."*[10] During the 'firestorm', most of the gold that had covered the walls had melted, and seeped in between the remaining stones still standing. So in order to get to this gold, Titus ordered these last stones be dismantled, so that *"not one stone here will be left on another, every one will be thrown down."*[11] Thus against Caesar's wishes, but by his command, Jesus' prophecy of Matthew 24: 2 was fulfilled to the letter.

~~~~~~~~~~~~~~~~~~~~

God speaks often about prophecy in the Bible. Here are some examples:

"'Present your case,' says the LORD. 'Set forth your arguments,' says Jacob's King. 'Bring in your idols, to tell us what is going to happen. Tell

us what the former things were, so that we may consider them and know their final outcome. Or declare to us the things to come, tell us what the future holds so we may know that you are gods. Do something, whether good or bad, so that we will be dismayed and filled with fear. But you are less than nothing and your works are utterly worthless; he who chooses you is detestable.'" Isaiah 41: 21-24

"See, the former things have taken place, and new things I declare; before they spring into being I announce them to you." Is. 42: 9

"I am the first and I am the last; apart from me there is no other God. Who then is like me? Let him proclaim it. Let him declare and lay out before me what has happened since I established my ancient people, and what is yet to come---yes, let him foretell what will come. Do not tremble, do not be afraid. Did I not proclaim this and foretell it long ago?"
Is. 44: 6-8

"Ignorant are those who carry about idols of wood, who pray to gods that cannot save. Declare what is to be, present it—let them take counsel together. Who foretold this long ago, who declared it from the distant past? Was it not I, the LORD? And there is no God apart from me, a righteous God and a Savior; there is none but me. Turn to me and be saved, all you ends of the earth; for I am God, and there is no other."
Is. 45: 20-21

"Remember this, fix it in mind, take it to heart, you rebels. Remember the former things, those of long ago; I am God, and there is no other; I am God, and there is none like me. I make known the end from the beginning, from ancient times, what is still to come. I say: My purpose will stand, and I will do all that I please...What I have said, that will I bring about; what I have planned, that will I do." Is. 46: 8-11

"I foretold the things of long ago, my mouth announced them and I made them known; then suddenly I acted, and they came to pass. For I knew how stubborn you were...Therefore I told you these things long ago; before they happened I announced them to you so that you could not say, 'My idols did them; my wooden image and metal god ordained them.' You have heard these things; look at them all. Will you not admit them?"
Is 48: 3, 5-6

"But the prophet who prophesies peace will be recognized as one truly sent by the LORD only if his predictions come true." Jeremiah 28: 9

And this last one is foundational: *"If anyone does not listen to my words that the prophet speaks in my name, I myself will call him to account. But a prophet who presumes to speak in my name anything I have not commanded him to say, or a prophet who speaks in the name of other gods, must be put to death. You may say to yourselves, 'How can we know when a message has not been spoken by the LORD?' If what a prophet proclaims in the name of the LORD does not take place or come true, that is a message the LORD has not spoken. That prophet has spoken presumptuously. Do not be afraid of him."* Deuteronomy 18: 19-22

Yikes! One hundred percent accuracy is required, or death is the punishment!? Whoa-a-a. Look out Jeane Dixon![12] Nonetheless, this was the law during Biblical times in the land of Israel.

Ralph Muncaster, a contemporary Christian author, says this: *"One hundred-percent accurate historical prophecy provides irrefutable 'proof' that a God from beyond time and space inspired the Bible. Why? Because there are well over 600 historical (thus verifiable) prophecies contained in the Bible–with none ever shown to be wrong. The odds of this happening without the involvement of God are inconceivable-considered 'absurd' by statisticians. For example, just 48 of the prophecies about Jesus* [13] *coming true in any one person by coincidence is like winning 22 state lotteries in a row with the purchase of one ticket for each. Put another way, the odds are similar to those of one person being struck by lightning 31 times. Since these prophecies were written hundreds of years before Jesus' birth (which has been confirmed by archeology)* [14]*, we know they were not contrived after the events. The prophecies were extremely specific, giving names of people, places, timing, and specific descriptions of unusual events. No other purported holy book contains even a few miraculous prophecies, let alone the hundreds found in the Bible."* [15]

Through prophecy we see:
   -The words of God.
   -The character of God.
   -The hand of God.
   -The role of prophecy.
   -And of course, the prophecies themselves.

Short and Long-Term Prophecy in Scripture

The prophets of the Bible often gave both short-term and long-term prophecies. Short-term prophecy is prophecy that was recorded and then fulfilled a short time thereafter. These were important to the Jews because they were one of the means by which prophets were validated. If significant short-term prophecy was made and then consistently fulfilled, it would confirm that that prophet was truly speaking from God, and would give confidence in his long-term prophecies.

A good example of short-term prophecy is found in 2 Samuel 12. King David of Israel[16] had taken to bed the wife (Bathsheba) of one of his military officers (Uriah). David wanted to keep her for himself, and so made sure that Uriah would be killed in combat. So...

"The Lord sent Nathan (David's personal prophet) *to David..."* to confront David, which he does: *"This is what the LORD, the God of Israel, says: 'I anointed you king over Israel, and I delivered you from the hand of Saul. I gave your master's house to you, and your master's wives into your arms. I gave you the house of Israel and Judah. And if all this had been too little, I would have given you even more. Why did you despise the word of the LORD by doing what is evil in his eyes? You struck down Uriah the Hittite with the sword and took his wife to be your own. You killed him with the sword of the Ammonites. Now, therefore, the word will never depart from your house, because you despised me and took the wife of Uriah the Hittite to be your own. This is what the LORD says: Out of your own household I am going to bring calamity upon you. Before your very eyes I will take your wives and give them to one who is close to you, and he will lie with your wives in broad daylight. You did it in secret, but I will do this thing in broad daylight before all Israel.' Then David said to Nathan, 'I have sinned against the Lord.' Nathan replied, 'The Lord has taken away your sin. You are not going to die. But because by doing this you have made the enemies of the Lord show utter contempt, the son born to you will die.'"* 2 Samuel 12: 7-14

In this short-term prophecy, all of what Nathan tells David comes true during David's lifetime. Calamity falls upon him through his *"own household"*. First, the child conceived by Bathsheba dies seven days after its birth. Then one of David's own sons, Amnon, rapes his sister Tamar, i.e. David's daughter (2 Samuel 13). This leads to one of his other sons, Absalom, killing Amnon. Absalom then is forced to flee for his life, and is gone for three years. David forgives him and he returns home. Instead of being grateful for David's forgiveness, he begins plotting to take over the kingdom from him. Now it is David who has to flee for his life. In order to humiliate David and show everyone that he has taken his place, Absalom has a tent pitched *"...on the roof, and he lay with his father's concubines in the sight of all Israel."* 2 Samuel 16: 21-22

Long-term prophecies are those made and then fulfilled at a much later time, sometimes hundreds of years later. These prophecies provide additional assurance of the prophet being God-inspired. Today, their fulfillment can often be supported by objective history and/or archaeology.

Here's an example of long-term prophecy: *"But you, Bethlehem Ephrathah, though you are small among the clans of Judah, out of you will come for me one who will be ruler over Israel, whose origins are from old, from ancient times."* Micah 4: 5 Here the prophet Micah prophesizes the birth of the Messiah in Bethlehem, a very small village, some 700 years before the birth of Jesus.

Prophecy in Joan's Life

"I told them things that have happened, and things that shall happen yet."
Joan of Arc, Trial of Condemnation, March 3, 1431 [17]

"...a great fear came over me and I was amazed at Joan's words, and all these events that came about."
Duke of Alencon, Trial of Nullification [18]

Joan's prophecies were famous even in her own time. Mark Twain provides us an interesting introduction to this: *"Her* (i.e. Joan of Arc's) *history has still another feature which sets her apart and leaves her without fellow or competitor: there have been many uninspired prophets, but she was the only one who ever ventured the daring detail of naming, along with a foretold event, the event's precise nature, the special time-limit within which it would occur, and the place—and scored fulfillment. At Vaucouleurs she said she must go to the King and be made his general, and break the English power, and crown him sovereign—'at Reims'. It all happened. It was all to happen 'next year'—and it did. She foretold her first wound and its character and date a month in advance, and the prophecy was recorded in a public record-book three weeks in advance. She repeated it the morning of the date named, and it was fulfilled before night. At Tours she foretold the limit of her military career—saying it would end in one year from the time of its utterance—and she was right. She foretold her martyrdom—using that word, and naming a time three months away—and again she was right. At a time when France seemed hopelessly and permanently in the hands of the English she twice asserted in her prison before her judges that within seven years the English would meet with a mightier disaster than had been the fall of Orleans: it happened within five-the fall of Paris. Other prophecies of hers came true, both as to the event named and the time-limit prescribed."* Mark Twain, Joan of Arc-An Essay, 1896

It's important to note just how specific her prophecies are. She didn't make vague predictions like so many others. Nostradamus (1503-1566) for example. He was another well-known French prophet that came on the world stage shortly after Joan. His prophecies were very general, and only very loose interpretations could prove him right. For example, according to many Nostradamus' admirers, the following is a prediction about Adolf Hitler:

"Beasts wild with hunger shall cross the rivers: Most of the fighting shall be close by the Hister, it shall result in the great one being dragged in an iron cage, While the German shall be watching over the infant Rhine."[19]

"This is often interpreted to be a prediction of the war against Adolf Hitler's Nazi state in the twentieth century. However, none of the reputable sources…support this view. In fact all of them point out that the name 'Hister' (as Nostradamus himself explains in his Almanac for 1554) in fact refers in his writings to the Danube…"[20] By the way, the "River Hister", as far as can be reliably established, does not exist and never has.

In contrast Joan gave specific events, dates and names, and she was never wrong. Did Joan of Arc give both short-term and long-term prophecies? Yes, as you'll see. The following list is not all of Joan's prophetic statements, but will give you an idea of the role prophecy played in her life. I will go into more detail with some of them, hoping to better reveal just how remarkable they really are.

1. In order to meet Charles VII, Joan looked for help from Sir Robert Beaudricourt, the Governor of Vaucouleurs. She testified that although she had never seen Sir Robert, her messengers told her that they would point him out to her, and that this is indeed what happened.[21] But the first time she spoke with him, Sir Robert didn't believe her. God-sent to save France? Impossible! He dismissed her brusquely and sent her home.[22] Joan however persevered, and went back to see him two more times. On the morning of Feb 12, 1429, trying to impress on him the importance of her mission and that time was of the essence, she told him that France was, that very morning, engaged in losing an important battle near Orleans.[23] Now Orleans was a full eight-day journey away, and needless to say, telephone, telegraph, TV, and Internet communications didn't exist at that time. One week later, word arrived to the Governor that on the morning of February 12, 1429, the French had indeed lost an important battle near Orleans: the 'Battle of Herrings'. This loss was a crushing blow to both morale and strategy for the French. Upon hearing

this news, Sir Robert gave Joan *"...a sword and his blessing"*[24], and sent her on her way to Chinon to see Charles VII.[25] She would now be in position to present her case to Charles.

2. Once in Chinon, Joan was summoned to see the King. As she *"...was going into the royal lodgings that day, a man sitting on his horse near the entrance said, 'Is not that the Maid there?,' swearing to God that if he had her for a night she would be no maid next morning. Then Joan said to the man, 'In God's name, do you take His name in vain when you are so near your death?' And an hour later that man fell into the river and was drowned. And I tell you this as I heard it from Joan and from several others who said they had been present."*[26]

3. Joan had sent word to the King that she would recognize him when she saw him. The king decided to put this prophetess to the test. Without her knowledge he put someone else (that he had dressed in royal apparel and the crown) on the throne, and hid himself (dressed in ordinary clothes) among the court crowd of three hundred. Joan instantly perceived the ruse and picked him out from the crowd. During her trial, she stated that her voices told her at that moment who the real King was.[27]

4. In Chapter 1 I touched on the first meeting between Joan and Charles, that was held on March 6, 1429. Here we'll take a look at the prophetic implications. *"... (the King) asked Joan her name and she replied: 'Kind Dauphin, Joan the maid is my name, and to you is sent word by me from the King of Heaven that you will be anointed and crowned in the town of Reims and you will be Lieutenant to the King of Heaven who is King of France'".*[28] As unlikely as it seemed at the time[29], Charles was indeed *'anointed and crowned in the town of Reims'*. Later on during this same conversation, Joan told Charles: *"I tell you, on behalf of Our Lord, you are the true heir of France and King's son, and He has sent me to you to lead you to Reims, so that you may receive your coronation and your consecration, if you are willing."*[30]

5. During this first meeting, Joan asked to see the King alone for a few moments, and this was granted. Charles later said that she had told him things only God could have known.[30] Now convinced of her divine mission, he immediately provided royal quarters for her in his castle[31]. Next he sent her to Poitiers to be examined by religious authorities and professors. This examination lasted three weeks. One of these scholars was Brother Seguin Seguin of the Order of Preaching Friars, a professor

of theology. He states: *"We were told that we had been summoned by the King to interrogate Joan, and to report to him what we made of her. Then she told me, me and the others present, four things which were then to come and which thereafter happened. First, she said that the English would be defeated and that the siege which was laid to the town of Orleans would be raised and that the town of Orleans would be liberated of the English, but that first she would send them summonses* (i.e. to leave Orleans). *She said next that the King would be crowned at Reims. Thirdly, that the town of Paris would return to its obedience to the King; and that the Duke of Orleans would return from England. All that I have seen accomplished. As for me, I believed she was sent from God, because, at the time when she appeared, the King and all the French people with him had lost hope: no one thought of nothing but to save himself."* [32]

During her Trial of Condemnation, Joan once again revisited some of her fulfilled prophecies, including the four above. Let's break them down a little more:

(A) The English would be defeated.
(B) The siege of Orleans would be lifted.
(C) The town of Orleans would be liberated from the English.
(D) Before attacking, she would send the English *"summonses"*. (See Chapter 10).
(E) Next, the King would be crowned at Reims.
(F) Paris *"...would return to its obedience to the King."* For eleven years, since May 29, 1418, Paris had been occupied by the English. Under the circumstances, this was certainly a bold prediction to make. Note here that Joan did not associate herself with this. Paris was recaptured on April 13, 1436, a few years after her death (May 30, 1431).
(G) The Duke of Orleans *"...would return from England."* The Duke, since being captured during the French defeat of Agincourt (1415), had been an English prisoner for thirteen long years. A huge ransom would be required for his release. However, at the time Joan predicted this, the French were completely bankrupt. Nevertheless, the Duke was returned to France in 1440, nine years after Joan's death.

6. On March 24, 1429, after having convinced France's leading scholars and religious authorities of her divine mission, Joan left Poitiers to speak with Charles at Chinon. She again focused on the main goals of her mission, but first she tells him, *"I shall last a year, and but little longer."* (Indeed. On May 23, 1430, she was captured and taken prisoner at

Compiègne.) Then she reiterates, *"We must think to do good work in that year. Four things are laid upon me: to drive out the English; to bring you to be crowned and anointed at Reims; to rescue the Duke of Orleans from the hands of the English; and to raise the siege of Orleans."* [33]

7. The following incident happened shortly before the Battle of Orleans: *"I remember that two heralds were sent on the part of the Maid to Saint-Laurent, one named Ambeville, and the other Guienne, to Talbot, the Earl of Suffolk, and Lord Scales, telling the English in God's name to return to England, or evil would come to them. The English detained one of these heralds, named Guienne, and sent back the other Ambeville to the Maid, who told her that the English were keeping back his companion Guienne to burn him. Then Jeanne answered Ambeville and assured him in God's Name that no harm should happen to Guienne, and told him to return boldly to the English, that no evil should happen to him, but that he should bring back his comrade safe and sound. And so it was."* [34]

8. Another event happened shortly before the Battle of Orleans, and falls under not only a prophetic category, but a miraculous one as well. It is therefore listed below, under **Miracles? Get Real!**

9. On May 4, 1429, Joan told Fr Paquerel, *"... that within five days the siege of Orleans would be raised and that there would linger no more English before the city..."* [35] (Underlining by author) This prediction also seemed most unlikely. The French were running very low on weapons, supplies and food. The English held all eleven forts that surrounded Orleans. Under normal circumstances, they now controlled all French re-supply routes (again, see Miracles section below for some abnormal circumstances). Also, another English army was already on the way to Orleans to reinforce the English soldiers currently present. Things looked grim.[36] Joan's predictions not only claimed that the siege of seven months would be lifted in five days (!), but also implied that all the English would be completely gone. Not likely!

Out of the eleven English occupied fortresses encircling Orleans, *les Tourelles* was the largest, strongest and most well defended. It was located directly in front of the city of Orleans. When Joan arrived on the scene, the French military officers in charge wanted to attack from another side of the town, in fact from any side except a direct assault on *les Tourelles*. Joan insisted on attacking them at their strongest point. There was not another officer present who was in agreement with her. Nonetheless, she would not be swayed, and eventually the others went along with her wishes.

On May 7, Joan was wounded, but returned to the battle to lead her troops to victory, as the English lost their strong fort, *les Tourelles*. On May 8, the English assembled in battle formation outside the city walls. The French responded and also assembled in battle formation outside the city walls, up close to the English soldiers. As usual, Joan was on the battlefield with her troops. As it was a Sunday, she ordered her troops not to be the first to start fighting. They could however defend themselves if necessary. She turned her back to the English, and waited to see how it would all play out. For one hour the French and English were face to face with each other, in some places so close together they could almost touch. Then, the English just turned around and marched away. The fighting was over. The siege of Orleans was lifted, and <u>no more English lingered before the city</u>. Joan had said that this would be accomplished *"within 5 days"*. From the time she made this claim, to the time of its fulfillment, four and a half days had passed.[37] It is interesting to note that it was the English who initiated many of the events of this day, not Joan.

10. Joan had predicted that she would be wounded during the battle of Orleans, but survive. On May 7, 1429, she was struck by an arrow from a crossbow above her breast. Later that same day, she returned to the battle and rallied the French to victory. A Flemish diplomat (Sire De Rotslaer) was visiting the area at this time, and wrote a letter to his home country dated April 22, 1429. In it he mentioned Joan's prophecy of being wounded, and quotes her as saying: *"...that she would save Orleans and would compel the English to raise the siege, and that she herself in a battle <u>in front</u> of Orleans would be wounded by <u>a shaft</u> but would not die of it."*[38] (Underlining by author) This letter was documented as being received in Brussels before the event and still exists. It can be found in the Library of Brussels. It should also be noted that she was wounded <u>in front</u> of Orleans, and by an arrow (not a sword, ax, knife or one of the many other possible weapons), as she had prophesied.

At the Trial of Nullification, Fr Jean Pasquerel testified that on May 6, 1429, Joan told him: *"...and tomorrow blood shall flow from my body above my breast."*[39]

11. During her trial, Joan stated that she had been divinely informed of the whereabouts of a special sword:

Question: *"Have you been to St Catherine Fierbois?"*

Joan of Arc: *"Yes, and I heard there three masses in one day...I sent to seek for a sword which was in the Church of Saint Catherine de Fierbois, behind the altar; it was found there at once; the sword was buried in the ground, and rusty; upon it were five crosses; I knew by my Voice where it was. I had never seen the man who went to seek for it. I wrote to the Priests of the place, that it might please them to let me have this sword, and they sent it to me. It was under the earth, not very deeply buried...As soon as it was found, the Priest of the church rubbed it, and the rust fell off at once, without effort..."* [40]

The story of Joan's sword is well known. Legends abound as to who might have left this sword. One of the more plausible stories is that it belonged to Charles Martel, grandfather of Charlemagne, who halted the Muslim invasion of Europe on October 10, 732 AD, at the Battle of Tours (a.k.a. the Battle of Poitiers).

12. Now I'd like to return to the Battle of Patay, which I touched on in the previous chapter. On June 17, 1429, after the Battle of Orleans and during the Loire campaign, Joan received news that the English were rapidly approaching. The English sent heralds to the French to challenge them. Joan answered them, *"Go and make camp today, because it is quite late. But tomorrow, at the pleasure of God and our Lady, we will take a closer look at you."* [41]

Knowing that still more English reinforcements were already on the way, the French grew increasingly nervous. During an officer's meeting, Joan proclaimed to all in attendance, *"Be sure that you all have spurs."* This confused them. They asked her if the spurs would be needed for a quick retreat. She replied, *"No, it is the English who will not defend themselves and who will be conquered. You will have need of good spurs as you chase after them."* [42]

In the first place, the French were normally reluctant to engage the English head-on in open field combat because the well-trained English soldiers were masters of this type of warfare, and almost always won. At this time, the French numbered around 1,500 men, principally cavalry. They knew the English had far superior forces (5,500 men present, not counting the other English army already on the way). The next day, June 18, 1429, Joan told her captains, *"In God's name! We must fight them. Even if they hung from the clouds we would have them! For God is sending them to us for us to punish. And today our noble king will have the greatest victory he has ever had. And my counsel has told me that they will all be ours. Ride bravely, and we shall be well led."* [43] Well led indeed. Her meaning is clear here. Well led by God Himself.

Then something strange happened. A stag suddenly appeared in a field close to the English hidden position. Some of the English soldiers, evidently thinking of dinner, began chasing after it. In so doing, they inadvertently and unknowingly gave away their position to the French. Consequently, the French were able to spring a quick surprise attack on them. The battle quickly turned into a rout. As the English began running, trying to escape, they were ridden down from behind and massacred by the French cavalry.[44] The outcome was catastrophic for the English. Their longbow archers, so accurate and feared, were virtually decimated. According to Jean, Count de Dunois, Bastard of Orleans, *"...as she had predicted: the English took to flight, and of killed and prisoners there were more than 4,000."*[45] The French lost only three men.[46] The English reinforcements that were on the way, never got there in time.

Against a nearly 4:1 English advantage (not counting the other English army on the way), Joan had made five prophetic statements, all of which happened:

A. The English would not defend themselves.
B. They would be beaten.
C. The French would chase after them.
D. King Charles would have *"the greatest victory he has ever had"*.
E. The English *"will all be ours"*.

Did divine intervention come into play here? For example, how did that stag turn up at just the perfect time and place for the French? Coincidence? Well...you make the call. In any case, everything she said that can be verified proves her right on target.

She also made two other statements that can't be verified this side of heaven:
  a. God was sending the English to the French to be punished.
  b. God Himself would lead the French in battle.

13. After clearing the way of the English from the Loire valley, Joan escorted Charles to Reims to be anointed and crowned, just as she said she would. To get there, they had to go through more than two hundred kilometers of dangerous enemy territory. Before setting out on this journey, Joan *"...told the King and the soldiers to go boldly forward, that everything would turn out well, and that they must fear nothing. For they would find no one able to harm them and would not even meet with any resistance. She also said that she had no doubts about their having*

enough men, for many would follow them. And Joan called the soldiers together between the towns of Troyes and Auxerre, and there were many of them, for everyone followed her. And the King and his people reached Reims without hindrance. In fact, the King met with no resistance. The gates of all the cities and towns were opened to him." [47]

14. As they traveled to Reims, they came to Troyes, a city solidly loyal to the English/Burgundian side. Charles became nervous and hesitant to attack. Joan told him, *"Within three days I will take you into the city of Troyes by love or by force or by courage, and false Burgundy* (i.e. the French who supported the English) *will stand amazed."* [48] The next day (July 10, 1429), *"...the inhabitants of Troyes, fearing an assault, sent to the king to negotiate their surrender. The king reached an agreement with the inhabitants and he entered Troyes with great ceremony, and Joan carried her standard near him."* [49]

15. As they approached Reims, Charles again became fearful. In the first place, the French hadn't brought their artillery and war machines with which to attack the city if necessary and Reims was still loyal to the Duke of Burgundy/England. Joan tells him, *"Doubt not; for the citizens of Reims will come out to meet you."* [50] As Charles approached the city, the citizens of Reims did indeed come out to meet him, just as Joan had predicted. Without a fight they switched their allegiance to Charles that very day.

16. The Duke of Alencon, one of the commanding officers of the French, became one of Joan's good friends. He testified to a couple of interesting things:

    a. After a battle during the Loire campaign, Joan tells him, *" 'Ah, gentle Duke, were you afraid? Don't you know that I promised your wife to bring you back safe and sound?' It is true that when I left my wife to go with Joan to the army, my wife said to Joan that she was very afraid for me and that I had formerly been a prisoner and that it had been necessary to pay so much money for my ransom that she would readily have begged me to stay behind. Then Joan answered her: 'Lady, fear not, I will bring him back to you safe and sound and in as good condition as he is now, or even better.'"* [51]
    Joan made good on her promise. The Duke of Alencon returned home to his wife with no wounds and in good shape. His testimony continues:

b. *"During the assault on the town of Jargeau, Joan said to me at a moment when I stood in a certain spot, that I should withdraw from that spot and that if I did not withdraw, 'that machine...' pointing out to me a war machine which was in the town, 'will kill you'. I withdrew and just a little time thereafter, at that very spot where I had been someone was killed. His name was my lord de Lude. Realizing all that, a great fear came over me and I was amazed at Joan's words, and all these events that came about."*[52]

17. On April 22, 1430, at Melun, Joan stated, *"Last Easter week, while I was on the moat of Melun, Saint Catherine and Saint Margaret told me that I would be captured before Saint John's day* (i.e. June 24, 1430) *and that it had to be this way, and to not be dismayed, and take all in good part and that God would help me."*[53] She was captured on May 23, 1430.

18. On March 14, 1431, during her Trial of Condemnation, she testified that her voices had told her that she would be martyred: *"... my voices have told me that I shall be delivered by a great victory; and they add: 'Be resigned; have no worry for your martyrdom; you will come in the end to the Kingdom of Paradise.' They have told me this simply, absolutely, and without fail. What is meant by my martyrdom is the pain and adversity that I suffer in prison; I do not know if I shall have even greater suffering to bear, for that I trust in God."*[54] She was burned at the stake on May 30, 1431.

19. On March 1, 1431, Joan gives two prophecies: first a specific 7-year time element to a prophecy given earlier (see above # 5):

Joan: *"Before seven years are passed, the English will lose a greater wager than they have already done at Orleans. They will lose everything in France. The English will have in France a greater loss than they have ever had, and that by a great victory which God will send to the French."*

Question: *"How do you know this?"*

Joan: *"I know it well by revelation, which has been made to me, and that this will happen within seven years; and I am sorely vexed that it is deferred so long. I know it by revelation, as clearly as I know that you are before me at this very moment."* Trial of Condemnation, March 1, 1431[55]

As mentioned above, the English had occupied Paris for eleven years.

But when the French army, led by General Richemont, finally entered Paris on April 13, 1436 (five years and one month after Joan gave the above prophecy), the key to control of the Seine River and central France was regained. Although conflicts continued for several years, regaining Paris was essentially the end of the Hundred Years' War.

Secondly, Joan reveals England's ultimate destiny in France. *"They will lose everything in France."* This second prophecy was made while England still occupied half of France, and apparently had the upper hand on the outcome of the war.

20. Said to Jean De Luxembourg: *"I know well that these English will put me to death, thinking that after I am dead they will win the kingdom of France. But even if the Goddamns* (what the French called the English, as the English often took the Lord's name in vain) *were a hundred thousand more than they are now they shall not have the Kingdom."*[56] The English did put her to death, and they fervently hoped that once she was dead France would resume its losing ways, leading to total defeat. Unfortunately for them, this was not to be the case. Just as Joan said, her death would not change the outcome of the war. In fact, the French rallied to her martyrdom.

21. On March 14, 1431, she spoke about an earlier escape attempt. She testified that one of the reasons she was trying to escape was to help the people who were under English siege at Compiègne. *"...Saint Catherine...told me...without fail, those at Compiègne would have help before St Martin's Day* (i.e. before November 11)."[57] The French liberated Compiègne on Oct 24, 1430.

22. And here is one last interesting testimony. As it could fall under a short-term prophecy I have placed it here. This event happened during the battle of Jargeau, just after Orleans. Although outnumbered 5,000 to 3,000, the French were nonetheless attacking the walls of the well-defended city of Jargeau! Like Orleans, here was another unlikely scenario for a resounding victory. On the second day of battle, *"Joan was on a ladder, holding her standard in her hand; this standard was torn, and Joan herself was struck on the head by a stone, which broke on her steel cap. She was thrown to the ground, and as she picked herself up she cried to the soldiers, 'Up, friends, up! Our Lord has doomed the English. At this very hour they are ours. Be of good cheer!' And at that moment the town of Jargeau was taken, and the English retired toward the bridges with the French in pursuit. And in the course of the pursuit more than eleven hundred of the English were killed."*[58] The losses of the

French were described as light.

Is Joan of Arc's pattern of prophecy consistent with what we see in Scripture?

As we have seen, fulfilled prophecy without error follows the pattern of Scripture. I have not found anything in Joan of Arc's prophecies that is inconsistent with the pattern displayed by the prophet/servants of the Bible. And nothing in her character, actions or words, that is at odds with the prophet/servants of Scripture.

Miracles? Get Real!
"If anything extraordinary seems to have happened, we can always say we have been the victims of an illusion. If we hold a philosophy which excludes the supernatural, this is what we shall always say." C. S. Lewis [59]

God's choice of prophecy as one way to verify both His existence and involvement in history is significant. Although some believe that miracles are the strongest evidence of God, we need to be careful here. There have been counterfeit miracles used to deceive people (e.g. Exodus 7: 11-12; Acts 8: 9-25; Acts 16: 16-19; 2 Thessalonians 2: 9). Indeed, the Bible tells us that Satan *"masquerades as an angel of light."* 2 Corinthians 11: 14 Jesus also speaks about this. When talking about the end of the age, He says: *"At that time, if anyone says to you, 'Look, here is the Christ!' or 'Look, there he is!' Do not believe it. For false Christs and false prophets will appear and perform signs and miracles to deceive the elect-if that were possible."* Mark 13: 21-22

Instead of miracles, God often called the prophets to "prophesize"; i.e. to speak with divine inspiration (including prophecy). In many of the Biblical prophetic books (e.g. Amos, Hosea, Isaiah, Ezekiel, Micah, Jeremiah, Habakkuk, Haggai, Zephaniah, Zechariah, and Malachi), no miracles are recorded. Instead, these prophets speak of their God-given visions or dreams, or God speaking to them, often accomplished through one of God's messengers. As we have seen, this was also God's method of communication with Joan.

Nonetheless, God did do some miracles through some of His prophets. In the Old Testament, Moses (Exodus 7-17) and Elijah (1 Kings 18, 2 Kings 2) are obvious examples.

However, when it comes to Biblical miracles, Jesus of Nazareth breaks the mold. He has no parallel. If Jesus really was who He claimed, i.e. *"...the Son of God"* [60], then His miracles should come as no great surprise to us. It would only make sense that the One who created the universe would have no problem supernaturally adjusting its laws to His will. His miracles demonstrated his authority over illness, laws of nature, knowledge, the demonic world, creation, and finally life itself. Here again is a partial list:

- healing ten men of leprosy (Luke 17: 11-19)
- healing a man born blind (John 9)
- healing a deaf and mute man (Mark 7: 31-37)
- calming a threatening storm (Matthew 8: 23-27; Luke 8: 22-25)
- walking on water (John 6: 16-24)
- prophesizing in detail without error (e.g. Luke 18: 31- 34)
- exorcising demons (Matthew 8: 28-32; Luke 8: 26-39)
- changing water into wine (John 2:1-11)
- feeding 5,000 people with only 5 loaves of bread and two fish (Mark 6: 32-44)
- raising the dead (three separate examples- Mark 5: 21-43; Luke 7: 11-17; and John 11: 1-44)

His enemies <u>never</u> denied that He did miracles. They could not. They were done in front of many people, and most of the recipients of them were still alive and available for questioning and investigation (e.g. John 9: 13-34). So they were reduced to acknowledging the miracles, but saying that they must come from the devil (see Matthew 12: 22-38). Here we can draw another parallel with Joan. Her enemies couldn't deny her amazing military victories, so they set out to prove that her power must come from the devil, not God.[61] However, both Jesus and Joan claimed steadfastly that it all came from God. And ultimately they would both die for this.

Joan's Miracles?

"All the deeds of the Maid seemed to me to be more divine and miraculous than otherwise, and it was not possible for so young a Maid to do such things without the will and guidance of our Lord."
Jean d'Aulon, Trial of Nullification

Did Joan of Arc do miracles? Well, some say that the liberation of Orleans was a miracle: *"I ...saw the works which had been raised by the English before the town. I was able to study the strength of these works: and I think that, to have made themselves masters of these...the French needed a real miracle. If I had been (there)...with only a few men, I should have ventured to defy the power of a whole army for six or seven days: and they would not have been able, I think, to have mastered it. For the rest, I heard from the captains and soldiers who took part in the siege, that what had happened was a miracle; and that it was beyond man's power…"* Duke d'Alencon, Trial of the Nullification

Some believed that her victory at Patay was a miracle (see #12 above). And still others say that saving France was a miracle. But others would say that, strictly speaking, she did no miracles. If she didn't do any miracles, then that would be consistent with the majority of the Old Testament prophets. However, there are a couple of things that don't fit so neatly in any categorical box:

a. *"…It was necessary to go upstream against the current and the wind was absolutely contrary, then Joan spoke to me the following words, 'Are you the Bastard of Orleans?' I answered her: 'Yes, I am so and I rejoice at your coming.' Then she said to me: 'Did you give the counsel that I should come here to this side of the river and that I go not straight there where Talbot and the English are?' I answered that myself and others wiser had given this counsel, thinking to do what was best and safest. Then Joan said to me: 'In God's name, the counsel of the Lord your God is wiser and safer than yours. You thought to deceive me and it is yourself above all whom you deceive, for I bring you better aid than has reached you from any soldier or any city: it is help from the King of Heaven. It comes not from love of me but from God himself* [62]*, who at the request of Saint Louis*[63] *and Saint Charlemagne*[64]*, has taken pity on the town of Orleans…' Right then, as if in the same moment, the wind which was contrary and absolutely prevented the boats from moving upstream in which were laden the victuals for Orleans, changed and became favorable. Right away I had the sails hoisted, and sent in the rafts and vessels…and we passed beyond the Church of Saint Loup despite the English. From that moment I had good hope in her…All this was much more the work of God than of man: the sudden change of wind immediately when Jeanne had announced it; the bringing in of the convoy of supplies in spite of the English, who were in much greater force than all the King's army; and the statement of Jeanne that she had seen Saint Louis and Saint Charles the Great praying God for the safety of the King and of the City."*[65] Another witness to this event was Sieur de Gaucourt. He was governor of Orleans when Joan arrived there. He was also an officer in the army and participated often in combat. He states, *"On the subject of the sudden change of wind and of the way in which the convoy of supplies was brought into Orleans, I am in agreement with Lord Dunois' testimony. I would only like to add that*

Jeanne had expressly predicted that, before long, the weather and the wind would change; and it happened as she had foretold. She had, in like manner, stated that the convoy would enter freely into the town." [66] Which it did. Father Jean Pasquerel said, *"Jeanne...came to meet us; and together we entered Orleans without difficulty, bringing in the provisions in sight of the English. This was a marvelous thing; for the English were in great number and strength, all prepared for fight. They had opposite them our army, very inferior to theirs: they saw us; they heard our Priests singing; I was in the midst of the Priests bearing the banner. The English remained immovable, never attempting to attack either the Priests or the army which followed them."* [67] Taking advantage of this *"...sudden change of wind..."*, the heavy barges were brought five miles farther up the river to a place where the supplies were safely unloaded. The English knew that these supplies were crucial to Orleans, but for no discernible reasons, they simply observed, and didn't interfere in any way. Was this abrupt and timely change of the wind a miracle? Whatever one wishes to call it, this author agrees with the Count of Dunois, *"All this was much more the work of God than of man."* [68]

b. During her Trial of Condemnation, she was asked about the baptism of a "dead" infant in the town of Lagny in May of 1430:

Question: *"What age was the child that you held at the baptismal font?"*

Joan: *"The child was three days old and it was carried before the image of Our Lady of Lagny; the maidens of the town were before the image and I wanted to go and pray to God and Our Lady that life be given to the child. I went there with the other maidens and I prayed, and at last life appeared in the child who yawned three times and was immediately baptized; it died thereafter and was buried in holy ground. Three days had passed, so they said, during which no life had appeared in this child. It was as black as my coat, but when it yawned color began returning to it..."* [69]

To my knowledge, no similar case exists in medical literature today. Someone in a coma would breath, have a pulse, temperature, reflexes, and obligatory urination. Over three days some knowledgeable people must have examined this infant.

So, how shall we classify these two events? As noted above, doing or not doing miracles is not the deciding factor for judging the validity of a Biblical prophet. However, for the subject of this book, I felt it necessary to present them to the reader. Ultimately, we must all decide for ourselves what meaning they may have.

> *"There are only two ways to live, one is as though nothing is a miracle, the other is as if everything is."* Albert Einstein

> *"Miracles are not a contradiction of nature. They are only in contradiction of what we know of nature."*
> St. Augustine [70]

Wrap Up

-According to the Bible, God chose perfect prophecy, i.e. without error, to be a strong witness for Him and His word.

-How to recognize a true prophet of God is spelled out in Scripture, and there is no room for error (Deut. 18: 19-22).

-No other religion has dared rely on prophecy as a proof to validate its claims.

-The case for Joan of Arc being a true prophet of God is supported by her many detailed prophecies without apparent error.

[1]John Walvoord, The Prophecy Knowledge Handbook, Victor Books, Wheaton, 1990, p. 77. Dr. Walvoord (1910-2002), an expert on prophecy, was president of Dallas Theological Seminary beginning in 1953 for thirty-four years, then chancellor from 1986-2001.
[2]This occurred in 70 AD, during the Siege of Jerusalem.
[3]Histories 5.8.1
[4]"B. J." v. 5, § 4
[5]Josephus, War of the Jews, 5.5.6; 223-24; m. Middot. 4.6
[6]Josephus, War of the Jews, 5.5.4; 210; Ant. 15.9.2; 394; m. Middot. 3.8; see also Tacitus, Histories 5.5
[7]www.livius.org/se-sg/7wonders/seven_wonders.html; en.wikipedia.org/wiki/Solomon's_Temple; www.therivercrc.com/library/study/temple.htm---all three websites accessed February, 2012; also see Crossway Bibles, ESV Study Bible-English Standard Version, Good News Publishers, Wheaton IL, 2007, p. 2002
[8]Josephus (37-100 AD) was a 1st-century Romano-Jewish historian of priestly and royal ancestry who recorded Jewish history. Through his father, Josephus was a descendant of the High Priest Jonathon. He fought the Romans in the First Jewish-Roman War of 66–73 as a Jewish military leader in Galilee. According to his account, he acted as a negotiator with the defenders during the Siege of Jerusalem in 70, in which his parents and first wife died. In 71, he went to Rome in the entourage of Titus, becoming a Roman citizen. The works of Josephus provide important information about the First Jewish-Roman War and are also important literary source material for understanding the context

of the Dead Sea Scrolls, post-Temple Judaism and early Christianity.
[9]"Caesar" was a title of imperial character, often used for the Roman Emperors. It derives from the Roman dictator Julius Caesar (100-44 BC). After his death, it became regularized into that of a title given to the Emperor-designate, the heir-apparent. Titus became the tenth Roman Emperor, reigning from 79 AD until his death in 81.
[10]*Flavius* Josephus, The War of the Jews, Book 6, chapter 4
[11]Matthew 24: 2
[12]Jeane L. Dixon (January 5, 1904 – January 25, 1997) was one of the best-known American astrologers and psychics of the 20th century. Dixon reportedly predicted the assassination of President John F. Kennedy. In the May 13, 1956, issue of *Parade Magazine* she wrote that the 1960 presidential election would be "dominated by labor and won by a Democrat" who would then go on to "[B]e assassinated or die in office though not necessarily in his first term." She later admitted, "During the 1960 election, I saw Richard Nixon as the winner", and at the time made unequivocal predictions that JFK would fail to win the election. In the 1956 pronouncement, she merely stated that a President would "be assassinated or die in office", not necessarily that one would be assassinated. By emphasizing a few coincidentally correct predictions and ignoring those that were wrong, and supported by an uncritical following among the media, she acquired both fame and notoriety. The ability to persuade the public in this matter came to be known as the "Jeane Dixon effect," a term coined by John Allen Paulos, a mathematician at Temple University. It refers to a tendency to promote a few correct predictions while ignoring a larger number of incorrect predictions. Many of Dixon's predictions proved false, such as her claims that a dispute over the offshore Chinese islands of Quemoy and Matsu would trigger the start of World War III in 1958, that American labor leader Walter Reuther would run for President of the United States in the 1964 presidential election, that the second child of Canadian Prime Minister Pierre Trudeau and his young wife Margaret would be a girl (it was a boy), and that the Russians would be the first to put men on the moon. http://en.wikipedia.org/wiki/Jeane_Dixon; accessed Jan. 2014.
[13]The book of Isaiah is especially rich in prophecies regarding the coming Messiah. The amount of detail in these Messianic prophecies that conform to the life, death and resurrection of Jesus is striking. For example, take a look at those found, one after another, from Isaiah 52: 13 through Isaiah 53: 12.
[14]Indeed, the archeological evidence that the prophecies pre-date the events is compelling. The Dead Sea Scrolls (ancient Biblical manuscripts-see Chapter 13) were discovered in 1947 in caves near Qumran, close to the Dead Sea. They have provided powerful evidence for the credibility of Biblical scripture. All of the Old Testament books (except Esther) are represented. Many of these scrolls were written as far back as 250 BC. All the Biblical prophecies relating to Jesus Christ are found in the scrolls. The nearly intact **Great Isaiah Scroll** is almost identical to the most recent manuscript version of the Bible (i.e. the Masoretic text) from the 900's AD. Scholars have discovered a handful of spelling, grammatical and tense-oriented scribal errors, but nothing of significance. This provides assurance that the documents were accurately duplicated over many centuries. As far as dating, the Great Isaiah Scroll (1Qls-a) has been carbon-14 dated at least four times, including a study at the University of Arizona in 1995 and a study at ETH-zurich in 1990-91. The four studies produced calibrated date ranges between 335-324 BC and 202-107 BC. That is, 100 to 335 years before the birth of Jesus! See Price, Secrets of the Dead Sea Scrolls, 1996; Eisenman & Wise, The Dead Sea Scrolls Uncovered, 1994; Golb, Who Wrote the Dead Sea Scrolls?, 1995; Wise, Abegg & Cook, The Dead Sea Scrolls, A New Translation, 1999.

    Other evidence also exists, including the Septuagint (a translation from the original Hebrew into Greek completed at least 200 years before the time of Jesus). A few copies of this ancient document are also still in existence. The Septuagint, Masoretic Text and

Dead Sea Scrolls have disproved unfounded theories that the Biblical text has been corrupted by time or conspiracy

[15] Ralph Muncaster, Why Does God Allow Suffering?, Harvest House, Eugene, 2000, p. 8

[16] King David is considered Israel's greatest king and "the apple of God's eye" (Psalms 17: 8).

[17] Joan of Arc-Self Portrait, Willard Trask, The Telegraph Press, Harrisburg, Pa, 1936, p. 143

[18] Régine Pernoud et Marie-Véronique Clin, Jeanne d'Arc, Editions Fayard, Mesnil-sur-l'Estrée, 2001, p. 95

[19] Almanachs, Presages and Pronostications, 1550–1567; Les Propheties, Lyon, 1555, 1557, 1568

[20] http://en.wikipedia.org/wiki/Hister; accessed December 2011

[21] Trial of Condemnation, Feb 22, 1431-Willard Trask, Joan of Arc-Self Portrait, The Telegraph Press, New York, New York, 1936, p. 37

[22] Albert Bigelow Paine, The Girl in White Armor-The Story of Joan of Arc, The Macmillan Company, New York, 1967 p. 23

[23] NEW ADVENT CATHOLIC ENCYCLOPEDIA, http://www.newadvent.org/cathen/08409c.htm, Dec. 2011-originally from the 'Journal of the Siege of Orleans' of 1467.

[24] Albert Bigelow Paine, The Girl in White Armor-The Story of Joan of Arc, The Macmillan Company, New York, 1967 p. 28

[25] Albert Bigelow Paine, Joan of Arc: Maid of France Vol. 1, Macmillan Company, 1925, p. 44-45

[26] Testimony from her priest and confessor, Fr Jean Pasquerel, Trial of Rehabilitation; Régine Pernoud, The Retrial of Joan of Arc, Ignatius Press, San Francisco, 2007, p. 182; Frances Gies, Joan of Arc-The Legend and the Reality, Harper & Row Publishers, New York, 1981, p. 46

[27] Trial of Condemnation, February 22, 1431

[28] Régine Pernoud, Jeanne d'Arc par elle-meme et ses témoins, Editions du Seuil, Paris, 1996, p. 57

[29] Fr. Pasquerel, Trial of Rehabilitation; Régine Pernoud, Jeanne d'Arc par elle-meme et ses témoins, Editions du Seuil, Paris, 1996, p. 57. Reims was located more than 350 kilometers within enemy territory, and all the surrounding cities, including Reims, were loyal to the enemy (i.e. the English/Burgundian side).

[30] www.saintjoanofarc.com, accessed Feb. 2012; www.stjoan-center.com/topics/Arnold.html, accessed Feb. 2012

[31] She was lodged in the tower of Couldray, *"a superb keep built two centuries earlier."* Régine Pernoud et Marie-Véronique Clin, Joan of Arc-Her Story, St Martin's Press, New York, New York, 1998, p. 24-25

[32] Br Seguin Seguin, Trial of Nullification; Régine Pernoud et Marie-Véronique Clin, Jeanne d'Arc, Editions Fayard, Mesnil-sur-l'Estrée, 2001, p. 50. At the time of his testimony he was Dean of the Faculty at Poitiers University.

[33] Joan of Arc translated by Willard Trask, Joan of Arc: In Her Own Words, Turtle Point Press, New York, 1996, p. 27

[34] Jacques l'Esbahy, Trial of Nullification

[35] Albert Bigelow Paine, The Girl in White Armor-The Story of Joan of Arc, The Macmillan Company, New York, 1967, p. 74

[36] *"I believed, like all in the town, that, had the Maid not come in God's Name to our help, we should soon have been, both town and people, in the hands of the enemy: we did not believe it possible for the army then in the town to resist the power of the enemy who were in such force against us."* Jean Luillier, Burgher of Orleans, Trial of Nullification

[37] Albert Bigelow Paine, The Girl in White Armor-The Story of Joan of Arc, The Macmillan Company, New York, 1967, p. 74
[38] Albert Bigelow Paine, The Girl in White Armor-The Story of Joan of Arc, The Macmillan Company, New York, 1967, p. 78
[39] Régine Pernoud, Jeanne d'Arc par elle-meme et ses témoins, Editions du Seuil, Paris, 1996, p. 103
[40] Joan of Arc, Trial of Condemnation, February, 27, 1431
[41] Régine Pernoud, Jeanne d'Arc par elle-meme et ses témoins, Editions du Seuil, Paris, 1996, p. 136-137
[42] Ibid.
[43] Joan of Arc translated by Willard Trask, Joan of Arc-In Her Own Words, New Your, Turtle Point Press, 1996, p. 46 (Underlining by author)
[44] Régine Pernoud et Marie-Véronique Clin, Joan of Arc-Her Story, St Martin's Press, New York, New York, 1998, p. 61
[45] Jean, 'Bastard of Orleans', Trial of Nullification
[46] In fact in one eye witness account, only one French soldier was killed: *"Joan had promised the French that none-or very few-of their men would be killed or wounded. Which proved correct. For only one of our men was killed: a nobleman of my company..."* Thibault d'Armagnac or de Termes, a companion at arms of Joan, and a knight and captain of Chartres: Régine Pernoud, The Retrial of Joan of Arc, Ignatius Press, San Francisco, 2007, p. 121
[47] Gobert Thibault, one of the King's squires, Trial of Nullification; 119
[48] Joan of Arc translated by Willard Trask, Joan of Arc: In Her Own Words, Turtle Point Press, New York, 1996, p. 53; Albert Bigelow Paine, The Girl in White Armor-The Story of Joan of Arc, The Macmillan Company, New York, 1967, p. 106
[49] Testimony of Simon Charles, an eyewitness to these events; Régine Pernoud and Marie-Véronique Clin, Joan of Arc-Her Story, St Martin's Griffin, New York, New York, 1998, p 63
[50] Simon Charles, President of the Council, Trial of Nullification; Kelly DeVries, Joan of Arc-A Military Leader, Sutton Publishing, Midsommer Norton, Bathe, 1999, p. 133
[51] Duke of Alencon, Trial of Nullification; Régine Pernoud, Jeanne d'Arc par elle-meme et ses témoins, Editions du Seuil, Paris, 1996, p. 133
[52] Duke of Alencon, Trial of Nullification; Régine Pernoud et Marie-Véronique Clin, Jeanne d'Arc, Editions Fayard, Mesnil-sur-l'Estrée, 2001, p. 95
[53] Joan of Arc translated by Willard Trask, Joan of Arc: In Her Own Words, Turtle Point Press, New York, 1996, p. 79
[54] Joan of Arc, Trial of Condemnation, March 14, 1431; Régine Pernoud et Marie-Véronique Clin, Jeanne d'Arc, Editions Fayard, Mesnil-sur-l'Estrée, 2001, p. 190
[55] Régine Pernoud, Jeanne d'Arc par elle-meme et ses témoins, Editions du Seuil, Paris, 1996, p. 220-221
[56] Régine Pernoud et Marie-Véronique Clin, Jeanne d'Arc, Editions Fayard, Mesnil-sur-l'Estrée, 2001, p. 204
[57] Trial of Condemnation, March 14, 1431
[58] Jean, the Duke of Alencon, Trial of Nullification - Régine Pernoud, The Retrial of Joan of Arc, Ignatius Press, San Francisco, 2007, p. 158
[59] C. S. Lewis, Miracles, Touchstone, New York, 1947, p. 9; Mr. Lewis (1898-1963) was a novelist, poet and Christian apologist, known for The Screwtape Letters, The Chronicles of Narnia, Mere Christianity, Miracles and many others.
[60] See John 10: 36
[61] Régine Pernoud and Marie-Véronique Clin, Joan of Arc-Her Story, St Martin's Griffin, New York, New York, 1998, p. 115-117
[62] Regarding any miracle that a prophet may have played a part in, he is always to give

credit and honor to God, not themselves. Here, Joan is quite careful to give credit where credit is due. It is God Himself who *"has taken pity on the town of Orleans."* She is only His servant. Numbers 20: 1-13 provides an example where Moses did not give God credit for a miracle that He performed through Moses, and the high price he had to pay for this (see verse 12).

[63] At his coronation as king of France, Louis IX (1226-1270, a.k.a Saint Louis) bound himself by oath to behave as God's anointed, as the father of his people and feudal lord of the King of Peace. Other kings had done the same, but Louis was different in that he actually interpreted his kingly duties in the light of faith. After the violence of two previous reigns, he brought peace and justice. Louis was devoted to his people, founding hospitals, visiting the sick and, like his patron St. Francis, caring even for people with leprosy. Louis united France—lords and townsfolk, peasants and priests and knights—by the force of his personality and holiness. For many years the nation was at peace. Every day Louis had 13 special guests from among the poor to eat with him, and a large number of poor were served meals near his palace. During Advent and Lent, all who presented themselves were given a meal, and Louis often served them in person. He kept lists of needy people, whom he regularly relieved, in every province of his dominion. He was canonized (i.e. made a saint) in 1297 by Pope Boniface VIII.

[64] Saint Charlemagne (742-814, a.k.a Saint Charles the Great) was first sovereign of the Christian Empire of the West. He was King of the Franks from 768 and Emperor of the Romans from 800 to his death in 814. He expanded the Frankish kingdom into an empire that incorporated much of Western and Central Europe. His rule is also associated with the Carolingian Renaissance, a revival of art, religion, and culture through the medium of the Catholic Church. Through his foreign conquests and internal reforms, Charlemagne helped define both Western Europe and the European Middle Ages.

[65] Jean, Count of Dunois (the "Bastard of Orleans"), Trial of Nullification; Régine Pernoud et Marie-Véronique Clin, Jeanne d'Arc, Editions Fayard, Mesnil-sur-l'Estrée, 2001, p. 65-66

[66] Lord Raoul de Gaucourt, Trial of Nullification

[67] Father Jean Pasquerel, Trial of Nullification

[68] Jean, Count de Dunois (the "Bastard of Orleans"), Trial of Nullification

[69] Régine Pernoud et Marie-Véronique Clin, Jeanne d'Arc, Editions Fayard, Mesnil-sur-l'Estrée, 2001, p. 137

[70] Augustine of Hippo, 354-430AD, also known as Saint Augustine, was an early Christian theologian whose writings were very influential in the development of Western Christianity and Western philosophy. He was bishop of Hippo Regius (present-day Annaba, Algeria) located in the Roman province of Africa. Writing during the Patristic Era, he is viewed as one of the most important Church Fathers. Among his most important works are *City of God* and *Confessions*, which continue to be read widely today.

Chapter 12
"If you love me..."

"Though our feelings come and go, God's love for us does not."
C.S. Lewis [1]

Dubious De De wondered out loud, *"Does God really love us?"*

Bad Boy Billy knew he didn't know everything. But for a question as stupid as this one, he didn't hesitate, *"Well, He may love you De De, but He doesn't love me!"*

Dubious De De: *"Oh, Billy! Why would you say such a thing?"*

Bad Boy Billy: *"Well, He couldn't possibly love me! And if you knew who I <u>really</u> am inside, you wouldn't love me either. So how could God? Anyway, I don't have a lot of time to get into all this right now. I'm already late for my support group, and I still have to do my 'Receding Hairline Is Good' affirmations."*

DDDe: *"Still working on your self-esteem, huh."*

BBBilly: *"Well after all, you have to first love yourself before you can love others. Right?"*

~~~~~~~~~~~~~~~~~~~~~

Hmm. This conversation may be a reflection of contemporary society, but is it what Jesus taught?

"If anyone would come after me he must deny himself and take up his cross and follow me. For whoever wants to save his life will lose it, but whoever loses his life for me will find it. What good will it be for a man if he gains the whole world, yet forfeits his soul? Or what can a man give in exchange for his soul?" Matthew 16: 24-26

I wonder if Joan recited self-help affirmations. Or maybe she did other "self-esteem exercises"? From what we've seen up to this point, trying to build up her own self-esteem doesn't seem to have been a top priority.

Is our self-esteem really found in "self"? According to the Bible, real and lasting self-esteem can only be found in God. If God loves us enough to give us the gift of life, surely we have worth. And God gave us much more than the gift of life. He gave His only Son, that we might be saved and spend eternity in heaven with Him. *"But God demonstrates His own love toward us, in that while we were yet sinners, Christ died for us."* Romans 5:8

This fact that the Creator of the universe loves us gives us a solid foundation to build on. Did Joan feel loved by God? Here's a prayer from her, taken down during her trial:

"Most gentle God,
In honor of your holy passion,
I'm asking you, if you love me,
That you reveal to me how I should
answer to these people of the church.
I know very well that it was because of your
Commandment that I took on the dress of a man,
But I don't know at all, in what way
I should stop wearing them.
So for this, please teach me." Joan of Arc [2]

"If you love me"? Her question here is not, "Does God love me?" She already knows that He does. Rather it is part of a prayer request. It's like saying, "I know you love me, so please reveal to me..." With this prayer Joan shows a deep love and implicit trust in her Creator. As she said a little later in her trial: *"I rely upon God, my Creator, for everything. I love Him with all my heart."* [3]

This is the only recorded prayer we have from her, and it comes during a really difficult time. She's in prison, and on trial for her life. Yet, she doesn't appear focused on this. She's simply asking God what He would have her do at this point. Her "self-esteem", indeed her entire life, appears to be built around a simple foundation: the love of God. *"And so we know and rely on the love God has for us. God is love. Whoever lives in love lives in God, and God in him."* 1 John 4: 16

Do we carry such certitude of God's love for us? If we do, we have a solid base to build on. If not, then running towards God, not away from Him, would seem to be the best direction to go.

It may be hard to believe that the Creator of all actually knows and loves each of us individually. I can just hear Bad Boy Billy now: *"Loves me!? In spite of all the stuff I've done!!??"* Yes. *"But does He know who I <u>really</u> am...deep inside?"* Yes. *"For God so loved the world, that He gave His only Son, that whosoever believed in Him might have eternal* *life and not perish."* John 3: 16

Without such a firm foundation of God's love, I don't think Joan could have done all that she did, nor persevered to the end. In life, everything depends on the foundation we lay. Jesus spoke about this:

"Therefore everyone who hears these words of mine and puts them into practice is like a wise man who built his house on the rock. The rain came down, the streams rose, and the winds blew and beat against that house, yet it did not fall, because it had its foundation on the rock. But everyone who hears these words of mine and does not put them into practice is like a foolish man who built his house on sand. The rain came down, the streams rose, and the winds blew and beat against that house, and it fell with a great crash." Matthew 7: 24-27

Can "working on our self-esteem" save us? There are many helpful things we can learn from 21st century psychology, and I believe that God wishes us to use the tools given to us, including our minds, appropriate medications, etc. However, ultimately, we can't save ourselves. Only God can. May we aim for a firm foundation based on God's love, just as Joan of Arc did.

"For I am convinced that neither death nor life, neither angels nor demons, neither the present not the future, nor any powers, neither height nor depth, nor anything else in all creation will be able to separate us from the love of God that is in Christ Jesus our Lord." Romans 8: 38-39

---

[1]C. S. Lewis, Mere Christianity, Book III, chapter 9
[2]Trial of Condemnation, March 28, 1431; Régine Pernoud, Jeanne d'Arc par elle-meme et ses témoins, Editions du Seuil, Paris, 1996, p. 229
[3]Trial of Condemnation, May 2, 1431

Chapter 13
The Ultimate Game Changer

*"It's unbelievable how much you don't know about
the game you've been playing all your life."*
Mickey Mantle (1931-1995)
New York Yankees Hall of Fame baseball player 1951-1968.

*"...I am the God of your father Abraham.
Do not be afraid, for I am with you..."* Genesis 26: 24

There's a lot of talk here about this 'God of the Bible'. But just who is He? Well, for one thing, He is the ultimate Game Changer! He changes people, nations and situations. It's time to take a closer look at this God that Joan believed in, prayed to, followed, and ultimately gave her life for.

When the subject of God comes up, many questions come to mind. We'll take a look at three of them here, as they have direct bearing on our subject.

(1) Are there many paths to God, or many gods?
*"I have a good master-that is, our Lord-
to whom only I look, and to none other."*
Joan of Arc, Trial of Condemnation, May 2, 1431

What's important in our culture? Our language gives us some clues. Here are some popular and revealing contemporary expressions:
1. "Evil does not exist."
2. "It's all good!" (Although popular today, these first two were not frequently heard among the genocide victims of Rwanda[1], the killing fields of Cambodia[2], Nazi concentration camps[3], Gilles de Rais' castle of horrors (see below), etc.
3. "I'm spiritual, not religious."
4. "Everything is relative."
5. "All paths lead to God."

Are these statements true? Our belief system determines how we evaluate what's true, but not necessarily what is true. And although all the major world religions today (i.e. Judaism, Islam, Christianity, Buddhism, Hinduism, Secularism, New Ageism...) claim to have the truth, there are large foundational differences that appear to be irreconcilable. They could all be false, but they can't all be true. I have included Secularism and the New Age movement here, as definitions from Webster's dictionary seem to fit them quite well:

Religion: *Any specific system of belief, worship, conduct, etc., often involving a code of ethics and a philosophy...or...Any system of beliefs, practices, ethical values, etc. resembling, suggestive of, or likened to such a system; as 'humanism is his religion'.*[4]

What are some of these irreconcilable foundational differences?

    1) God is impersonal vs. God is intimately involved in our lives.
    2) We live many lives vs. we only have this one: *"...man is destined to die once, and after that to face judgment..."* Heb. 9: 27
    3) God will judge us after death, and some will go to heaven and some to hell for eternity vs. there is no heaven, no hell, no judgment.
    4) All paths lead to God vs. the way to God is narrow.

Let's take a closer look at this last one. There have always been many paths or "gods" to choose from. Joan's time, the Middle Ages, was no exception. Gilles de Rais was born in France in 1404. He was brought up in the lap of luxury, and in 1420 found himself at the court of the Charles VII. From 1427-1435 he served as a commander in Charles' Royal Army, including service with Joan of Arc during her 1429 Loire campaign. He was present with her when the Siege of Orléans ended. On Sunday July 17, 1429, Gilles was chosen as one of only four lords for the great honor of bringing the holy ampulla[5] to Notre-Dame de Reims for the consecration[6] of Charles VII. On that same day, de Rais was officially made a Marshal of France[7]. Although he knew, rode with and admired Joan of Arc, shortly after her death he chose another path and a different "god".

In 1431 de Rais began experimenting with the occult under the direction of a man named Francesco Prelati. Prelati told him that through a demon called "Barron", he could regain his squandered wealth, simply by utilizing the "art" of alchemy (i.e. turning iron or lead into gold). Following close behind this unsuccessful venture, de Rais turned to overt devil worship. He quickly "graduated" to the serial killing of children from the age of six to sixteen. Eventually he was caught, and went to trial. These trial transcripts, like Joan of Arc's, still exist to this day. They reveal unimaginable evil and depravity[8], providing vivid description of the devil worship, torture, rape and murder that he perpetrated on these poor innocent children. Through the testimony of numerous parents of the missing children, graphic descriptions provided by his two accomplices (his servants), and his own testimony, the truth slowly came out: de Rais was directly responsible for the torture, rape, mutilation and murder of between 100-200 children. His servants had lured mostly young boys to his castle, but would settle for young girls if they were all that they could find. After quickly being found guilty, he was hanged at Nantes on October 26, 1440. He is believed to be the inspiration for the 1697 fairy tale <u>Bluebeard</u> by Charles Perrault.

Still today, Satan remains very active on Planet Earth. Although sometimes worshipped as a "god", Satan is in fact, according to Jesus, only a fallen angel (see Luke 10: 18). And his path leads to destruction. However Scripture tells us that the earth is his Kingdom until Jesus' return[9], and we see no letup of his activity at this time in history. If anything, there is an increase of evil in the world today (see <u>Chapter 8-Persecution</u>, your local newspaper, etc.). We follow his path at our own risk.

> *"I do not fear Satan half so much as I fear those who fear him."*
> Saint Teresa of Avila [10]

I wonder what this God of the Bible would say about this idea of many paths and gods? Well, we don't have to guess. Fortunately, He speaks for Himself:

"Before me no god was formed, nor will there be one after me. I, even I, am the LORD, and apart from me there is no savior. I have revealed and saved and proclaimed---I, and not some foreign god among you. You are my witnesses," declares the LORD, "that I am God. Yes, and from ancient days I am he." Is. 43: 13-14

"This is what the LORD says---Israel's King and Redeemer, the LORD Almighty: I am the first and the last; apart from me there is no God. Who then is like me? Let him proclaim it..." Is 44: 6-7

"I am the LORD, and there is no other; apart from me there is no God. I will strengthen you, though you have not acknowledged me, so that ...men may know there is none besides me. I am the LORD, and there is no other. I form the light and create darkness..." Is. 45: 5-7

"...I am the LORD, and there is no other. I have not spoken in secret, from somewhere in a land of darkness; I have not said to Jacob's descendants, 'Seek me in vain.' I the LORD, speak the truth; I declare what is right. Gather together and come, assemble you fugitives from the nations. Ignorant are they who carry about idols of wood, who pray to

gods that cannot save...and there is no God apart from me, a righteous God and a Savior; there is none but me. Turn to me and be saved, all you ends of the earth; for I am God, and there is no other." Is. 45: 18-22

If He is the only God, and assuming God doesn't change (see Malachi 3: 6; Psalm 102: 25-27 and Hebrews 1: 10-12; 13: 8), then we would expect to see His prophet/servants speak and act in a consistent way throughout Scripture and time. And Joan of Arc again fits this pattern.

"Do not be misled by what you see around you, or be influenced by what you see. You live in a world which is a playground of illusion, full of false paths, false values and false ideals." Sai Baba [11]

"Enter through the narrow gate. For wide is the gate and broad is the road that leads to destruction, and many enter through it. But small is the gate and narrow the road that leads to life, and only a few find it."
Jesus, Matthew 7: 13-14

(2) How Powerful is this God?
BANG!!
Creator of the Universe.

"All I have seen teaches me to trust the Creator for all I have not seen." Ralph Waldo Emerson (1803-1882)

Like the ancient Roman or Greek deities, many of the gods of history were said to be powerful, but only under limited circumstances. For example, the 'gods of the river'[12] were only able to use their power within the vicinity of their river. On the other hand, the God followed by Joan of Arc is described in Scripture as all-powerful and not limited by anything.[13] If He wishes to be involved in the affairs of men, He is more than able to do so. But just how powerful? Here's one example. Scientists used to believe that the universe was 'eternal'. That is, unchanging, static, no beginning, no end...always 'just there'. Then a strange thing happened on the way to nowhere. With the invention of the Hubble telescope in 1990, strong, consistent, measureable and convincing evidence about the 'Big Bang' theory came to light, and continues to mount. **BANG!!** According to the vast majority of scientists who study these things (i.e. astronomy, cosmology, astrophysics, theoretical physics...) a definite beginning of the universe and time has been found. Like ripples from a rock thrown in a pond, the universe is still expanding outward from that first immense 'explosion'.

"It is I who made the earth and created mankind upon it. My own hands stretched out the heavens; I marshaled their starry hosts..."
Is. 45: 12

"I am he; I am the first and I am the last. My own hand laid the foundations of the earth. And my right had spread out the heavens..."
Is. 48: 12-13 [14]

This concept of 'stretching out' or 'spreading out the heavens' is unique among the ancient writings, and an accurate description of this expanding universe that got its start with a bang. Edwin Hubble verified the expanding universe as early as 1916.[15] Does Scripture give us any other possible indications for such a beginning? Well, there are some intriguing possibilities, including the following:

"In the beginning God created the heavens and the earth... God said (BANG?), *'Let there be light,' and there was light."* Gen. 1: 1, 3

"For He spoke (BANG?), *and it came to be; he commanded* (BANG?) *and it stood firm."* Psalm 33: 9

"In the beginning was the word (BANG?)... *"* John 1: 1

As Joan of Arc often said, God is the King of Heaven, supreme ruler of the entire universe.[16] And God says that it was He who put the whole thing 'in motion'. For life as we know it to exist, this immense explosion had to be just PERFECT. It had to be exactly the right size, the right velocity, the right duration, the right intensity, have the exact percentage of gases and/or materials, use the just-right combinations of chemicals at just the right times... All these conditions and many more, had to be just PERFECT, in order for stars, solar systems, and planets to be created. And finally, under all these perfect conditions, a life sustaining planet was created for man with just the right atmosphere, trajectory, density, orbit, axis tilt, size, planetary system, earthy environment, sun type (a yellow dwarf star), distance from the sun, land to water ration, one moon satellite with the perfect size, orbit distance-to-earth etc., location in the Milky Way, and many other factors.

When scientists began to study the order of the creation events, as found in Genesis 1, some were surprised to find themselves in total agreement with it. There were many other cultures surrounding Israel at the time Genesis was written, but only the Bible gives an accurate representation of the order of these events that is consistent with what scientists believe today. Although this may have come as a shock to some of them, those familiar with the Bible were not surprised.

For many studying these things, the fact that life and/or the universe just somehow came about randomly is considered 'mathematically impossible.'[17] Sir Fred Hoyle (1915-2001), British mathematician and astrophysicist and an atheist for much of his life, tells us that, *"...the probability of life origination at random is so utterly minuscule as to make it absurd, it becomes sensible to think that the favorable properties of physics, on which life depends, are in every respect deliberate. It is, therefore almost inevitable that our own measure of intelligence must reflect higher intelligence...even to the limit of God."*

The entire natural world bears witness to God.[18] In fact, we are surrounded with such beauty, design, complexity, order, usefulness and creativity in such consistent and awe-inspiring ways, that we have become dulled by it.[19] God's amazing creative wonders are obvious to anyone simply watching a magnificent sunset. They extend even to the smallest part of His design.[20] We seem to just take it all for granted. However for many, evidence of some great master plan, and therefore a master planner, are found in abundance throughout nature, biology, the heavens, etc...

What's the point? The 'river gods' never claimed to have created the entire universe. They claimed only power over their river area. This God of the Bible is something altogether different. He is truly all-powerful and able to do what He wills. Including interacting with His creation, if He so desires.

(3) God's Book?
"It ain't those parts of the Bible that I can't understand that bother me, it is the parts that I do understand." Mark Twain

The Bible has been the most ardently loved and bitterly hated book in all history. Skeptics have regarded it as mythological, but archeology has confirmed it as historical time and again (see below). Opponents have attacked its teaching as primitive and outdated, but its moral and legal concepts and teachings remain the bedrock for uncounted millions. It continues to be attacked today by atheism, pseudo-science, psychology, political and secular movements, etc... but it has transformed countless lives and cultures for centuries.

The Bible reveals a reasonable faith, based on evidence. It goes beyond reason, but not against it. It is made up of sixty-six books, written over a 1500 year period, by more than forty different authors from many different walks of life. These include prophets, peasants, kings, shepherds, fishermen, tax collectors, poets, musicians, soldiers, statesmen, scholars, and doctors. It was written in three different languages (Aramaic, Greek and Hebrew), on three different continents (Asia, Europe and Africa), using several different forms (poetry, history, civil and criminal law, ethics, didactic, parable, biography, prophecy, personal correspondence...), during times of both war and peace. It addresses hundreds of controversial subjects, and with no contradictions. At the time of their writing, the authors had no idea that their message was eventually to be made into such a book. Nonetheless, each part fits perfectly into place and serves its own unique purpose as a part of the whole. Anyone who studies the Bible will find remarkable structural and mathematical patterns throughout, and an intricacy and symmetry that is unexplainable by chance or collusion. Even though written from such diverse circumstances, the message remains consistent throughout: God reaching out to His wayward child, Man, and doing so out of love, compassion and justice. Yes, the Bible is God's book. Here are eight interesting aspects supporting such a statement ...

I. God's Supernatural Protection
"The grass withers, the flower fades, but the word of our God will stand forever." Isaiah 40: 8

How is it possible that the Bible even exists today? How has it survived all the elements of the weather and the ravages of time? The books of the Bible were originally recorded on a variety of fragile materials such as papyrus (sheep and goats skins), parchment, leather, clay, stone and vellum (antelope skin). None of these medium are known for surviving thousands of years. Yet the Bible has survived intact. And this protection was accomplished for the most part without any modern storage mechanisms, such as climate control, etc.

And how has it survived the focused persecution and numerous wars of 3500 years? Attempts to destroy it have always been a part of this book's history. And the attacks have been many, determined and vicious. Case in point: the Roman Emperors of the first three centuries AD. Diocletian was Emperor from 284 to 305AD. He was obsessed with the destruction of Christianity, and for a while, believed that he had succeeded. His name is associated with the last and most terrible of the ten persecutions of the early Church.

In 303 AD he issued an edict to destroy all Christians and their Bible. The persecution that followed was one of the most brutal in Roman history. He had so many Christians put to death, and so many Bibles destroyed, that he was sure he had destroyed the Christian religion forever. Over a burned Bible, he built a monument on which he wrote,

"Extineto nomine Christianorum" (meaning "The name Christian is extinguished").[21] He was so pleased with his victory, that for posterity's sake, he ordered a medal to be struck inscribed with the words, *"The Christian religion is destroyed and the worship of the gods restored."*[22] Well... not so much. Twenty-five years later Diocletian was dead, and his successor Constantine had legalized Christianity and ordered Bibles prepared at government expense.

The French philosopher Voltaire (1694-1778) provides another example. In 1776 he announced that, *"One hundred years from my day, there will not be a Bible on earth except one that is looked upon by an antique curiosity-seeker."*[23] With no perceived limits to his own self-importance and brilliance, he said, *"While it took 12 men to write Christianity up, I will show that it takes but one man to write it down!"*[24] One hundred years later, his very own house and printing press were being used to print and store Bibles by the Geneva Bible Society. Ironically, at a public auction held one hundred years to the day of Voltaire's prediction, the first edition of his work sold for $11, while a Bible manuscript was purchased for over half a million dollars.[25]

II. Archaeological Evidence

"In every instance where the findings of archaeology pertain to the Biblical record, the archaeological evidence confirms, sometimes in detailed fashion, the historical accuracy of Scripture."
Dr. Bryant C. Wood [26]

For the last 100-150 years, the Bible has been under attack from liberal scholars as an unreliable historical record. However, the past 75-100 years, it has consistently been corroborated by archaeological discoveries. The amount of archaeological evidence is vast and continually growing.

Theologian and author Bernard Ramm (1916–1992) stated that with, *"...the discovery of the Dead Sea Scrolls*[27] *and the comparison of the text with later copies...*(it has been) *verified beyond a shadow of a doubt that the Old Testament has accurately been handed down for centuries"*.[28] Mr. Ramm continues, *"Jews preserved it as no other manuscript has ever been preserved...they kept tabs on every letter, syllable, word and paragraph. They had special classes of men within their culture whose sole duty was to preserve and transmit these documents with practically perfect fidelity..."*[29]

Nelson Glueck (1900–1971), probably the greatest authority of his time on Israeli archeology, said: *"It may be stated categorically that no archeological discovery has ever controverted a Biblical reference.*

Scores of archeological findings have been made which confirm in clear outline or in exact detail historical statements in the Bible."[30]

William F. Albright (1891-1971), one of the world's most renowned archaeologists, stated: *"The excessive skepticism shown toward the Bible by important historical schools of the eighteenth and nineteenth centuries... has been progressively discredited. Discovery after discovery has established the accuracy of innumerable details, and has brought increased recognition to the value of the Bible as a source of history."*[31]

Millar Burrows (1889-1980), Professor of Archaeology at Yale University, and one of the world's leading authorities on the Dead Sea Scrolls, said: *"The excessive skepticism of many liberal theologians stems not from a careful evaluation of the available data, but from an enormous predisposition against the supernatural."*[32]

Jesus said, *"Heaven and earth will pass away, but my words will never pass away."* Mark 13: 31

III. Science vs. Scripture?

"Religion and science are opposed...but only in the same sense as that in which my thumb and forefinger are opposed - and between the two, one can grasp anything." Sir William Bragg [33]

"We have too many men of science, too few men of God...Ours is a world of nuclear giants and ethical infants...We owe a great debt to people of science for much good that has been achieved by their discoveries, but without a Christian base, where it largely began, our problems will be multiplied." General Omar Bradley [34]

In striking contrast to all other religions, many principles of modern science were recorded in the Bible as facts of nature long before scientists confirmed them through scientific methods. This is another piece of evidence of the Bible's divine inspiration. Of course, the Bible is not a science book, and was not written to describe the workings of the physical world. It was written to explain spiritual principles, the nature of mankind and God, and how we can have a relationship with Him. However, when the Bible describes the physical world, it is scientifically accurate. Many of the statements below were listed in the Bible hundreds or even thousands of years before being recorded elsewhere. Of course, they are not stated in the technical jargon of modern science, but in terms of man's everyday experience. Nonetheless, they are completely in agreement with the most modern scientific facts.

The Bible ...

   a. describes the suspension of the Earth in space. *"He spreads out the northern skies over empty space; he suspends the earth over nothing."* Job 26: 7 Science did not discover this until Copernicus (1473-1543). His major theories were published in 1543.[35]

   b. describes the importance of circumcision on the eighth day. *"For the generations to come every male among you who is eight days old must be circumcised, including...those who are not your offspring."* Genesis 17: 12 Why the eighth day? Vitamin K, mixed with prothrombin, causes blood coagulation, which is important in any surgical procedure. If vitamin K is deficient, hemorrhaging may occur. A newborn infant has *"...peculiar susceptibility to bleeding between the second and fifth days of life...Hemorrhages at this time...may produce serious damage...and cause death..."* [36] Vitamin K is not produced in sufficient quantities until days five through seven. So why did God specify day eight? On the eighth day, the amount of prothrombin present actually is elevated above one-hundred percent of normal—and is the **only day** in the male's life in which this will be the case. If surgery is to be performed, day eight is the perfect day to do it, as Vitamin K and prothrombin levels are at their peak. Genesis 17: 12 was not only scientifically accurate, but was centuries ahead of its time.

   c. describes the importance of blood in life processes. *"For the life of a creature is in the blood..."* Leviticus 17: 11, 14

   d. says that the universe had a beginning. *"In the beginning God created the heavens and the earth."* Genesis 1: 1 The well-known physicist and cosmologist, Stephen Hawking, said: *"... the universe has not existed forever. Rather, the universe, and time itself, had a beginning in the Big Bang*[37]*, about 15 billion years ago."* Stephen Hawking CH, CBE, FRS, FRSA[38]

   e. says that time had a beginning . *"He has saved us and called us to a holy life—not because of anything we have done but because of his own purpose and grace. This grace was given us in Christ Jesus before the beginning of time..."* 2 Timothy 1: 9. Also see d. above. Also Titus 1: 2; 1 Corinthians 2: 7; Genesis 1: 1 Albert Einstein's equations of general relativity (1916) proposed a beginning of time, matter and space. Later these equations were confirmed by repeated experiments.[39]

   f. says that the universe is winding down; that it is "wearing out". *"In the beginning you laid the foundations of the earth, and the heavens are the work of your hands. They will perish, but you remain; they will all wear out like a garment. Like clothing you will change them and they will be discarded. But you remain the same, and your years will never end."* Psalm 102: 25-27 This accurately describes science's Second Law of Thermodynamics, which basically says that everything in the universe falls apart and disintegrates over time; that all things progress from a state of order to a state of disorder. It *"...is a universal law of decay... Nothing stays as fresh as the day one buys it; clothing becomes faded, threadbare, and ultimately returns to dust. Everything ages and wears out. Even death is a manifestation of this law. The effects of this Law are all around, touching everything in the universe. Decaying plants, bodies, buildings, stars...Ultimately, everything in nature is obedient to its unchanging laws...One person described this condition in terms of a wind-up clock. Once wound tightly, it begins to slowly wind down until it reaches the end...All experimental and physical observation appears to confirm that the Law is indeed universal, affecting all natural processes in the long run... The question is... Who wound the clock? ...if the universe was some sort of cosmic egg in the beginning and then hatched, it logically required a cosmic chicken."*[40]

    g. speaks about the currents in the ocean. *"This is what the LORD says—he who made a way through the sea, a path through the mighty waters..."* Isaiah 43: 16; see also Psalm 8: 8 One person who used the Bible as a trusted 'scientific document' was Matthew Maury (1806-1873), the father of oceanography. He took this verse literally, and then searched the oceans of the world to see if there were such 'paths'. In 1855 he discovered and mapped the major currents that have been used ever since for sea travel.[41]

    h. describes the nature of infectious diseases. *"As long as they have the disease they remain unclean. They must live alone; they must live outside the camp."* Leviticus 13: 46 Shortly before Joan's time, when the Black Plague was killing much of Europe, desperate nations turned to the Church for guidance. Germs and infections were not understood at the time. The clergy went back to the books of Moses for guidance and instituted the laws of Moses as taught to the Israelites, including those for dealing with infectious diseases like leprosy. This, combined with the other laws of Moses, helped bring the Black Plague under control.[42]

    There are many more examples, and it is significant to note that no real mistake in science has ever been demonstrated in the Bible. Nor in history. Nor, for that matter, in any other subject. Of course, many have been claimed, but Bible scholars have always been able to work out reasonable solutions to all such problems.

"When I began my career as a cosmologist some twenty years ago, I was a convinced atheist. I never in my wildest dreams imagined that one day I would be writing a book purporting to show that the central claims of Judeo-Christian theology are in fact true, that these claims are straightforward deductions of the laws of physics as we now understand them. I have been forced into these conclusions by the inexorable logic of my own special branch of physics."
Frank Tipler, Mathematical Physicist and Cosmologist [43]

IV. The Apostles Testimony

"For we did not follow cleverly devised stories when we told you about the coming of our Lord Jesus Christ in power, but we were eyewitnesses of his majesty." 2 Peter 1: 16

"Many have undertaken to draw up an account of the things that have been fulfilled among us, just as they were handed down to us by those who from the first were eyewitnesses... I myself have carefully investigated everything from the beginning, I too decided to write an orderly account for you, most excellent Theophilus, so that you may know the certainty of the things you have been taught." Luke 1: 1-4

What happened to the apostles after Jesus' death and resurrection? Well, they followed Jesus as before (e.g. Mark 1: 17). To the very end. Most sources state that all eleven of the first apostles, with the exception of John, were martyred for their witness to Jesus. *"Why would the apostles lie?...If they lied, what was their motive, what did they get out of it? What they got out of it was misunderstanding, rejection, persecution, torture, and martyrdom. Hardly a list of perks!"* Peter Kreeft[44] All these men needed to do to escape a cruel execution was simply to denounce their faith in Jesus:

"Meanwhile, in the case of those who were denounced to me as Christians, I have observed the following procedure: I interrogated these as to whether they were Christians; those who confessed I interrogated a second and a third time, threatening them with punishment; those who persisted I ordered executed. For I had no doubt that, whatever the nature of their creed, stubbornness and inflexible obstinacy surely deserve to be punished." Josephus[45]

When Jesus was taken away for trial and crucifixion, the disciples were scared to death.[46] They fled and went into hiding. Then, just 50 days later, Peter was found in Jerusalem, boldly preaching in public about Jesus.[47] What happened? They saw Jesus alive again! Several times.[48]

V. Believer's Testimony
"I Jesus have sent my angel to testify to you these things in the churches." Revelation 22: 16

Another example that the Bible is the word of God is found in the testimony of those who have experienced it. Its life-changing effect on individuals, and on the history of nations, is undeniable. Multitudes, past and present, have found from personal experience that its promises are true, its counsel is sound, its commands and restrictions are wise, and its message of salvation is our greatest blessing and ultimate destiny.

VI. The Politically Correct Bible?
Not So Much.
"In this era of political correctness, some people seem unaware that being squeamish about words can mean being blind to realities."
Thomas Sowell [49]

The Bible is not politically correct. It does not *"seek to minimize social and institutional offense in occupational, gender, racial, cultural, sexual orientation, disability and age-related contexts."*[50] Rather people, nations and situations are all portrayed honestly and realistically throughout. Warts and all. No one is exempt from this approach. Not even the Bible's 'heroes'. They are like us: imperfect, flawed, full of strengths and weaknesses, successes and failures. And just as their strengths and successes are on display for all to see, so too we see their weaknesses and failures. This is reassuring. It gives us hope. All through the pages of the Bible we see a God that loves and uses flawed and imperfect people. Scripture is full of such examples. As we saw in Chapter 11, King David had an affair with the wife (Bathsheba) of one of his loyal soldiers (Uriah the Hittite), and in order to keep her, engineered Uriah's murder (2 Sam. 12). This is neither omitted nor whitewashed. Not the behavior you'd want or expect from God's poster child for Israel. Definitely not politically correct.

VII. Just the Facts, Ma'am...
"Get your facts first, then you can distort them as you please."
Mark Twain [51]

The Bible does not change the facts to match its viewpoint or agenda. Embarrassing or not, what you see is what you get. For example, after Jesus' crucifixion, the women who had followed Him from the beginning were the first to see and hear the good news of His resurrection (Mt. 28:1-10; Mark 16: 1-7; Luke 23: 55-24: 5; John 20: 1-18). If you were trying to persuade people of a most unlikely event, such as the resurrection of a dead man, the last thing you'd want in biblical Israel would be women as your first eyewitnesses. After all, women faced several limitations in accordance to Jewish law, including restrictions on any authoritative roles. They were not even permitted to testify in court trials. They were placed under the authority of men, and were largely confined to the homes of their husbands or fathers. Many considered them simply second class Jews. So if you wanted to invent the resurrection story, wouldn't it have made more sense to offer 'credible male witnesses'?

"Perhaps the strongest reason of taking the stories of the empty tomb absolutely seriously lies in the fact that it is women who play the leading role. It would have been very unlikely for anyone in the ancient world who was concocting a story to assign the principal part to women since, in those times, they were not considered capable of being reliable witnesses in a court of law. It is surely much more probable that they appear in the gospel accounts precisely because they actually fulfilled the role that the stories assign to them..." John Polkinghorne [52] Indeed. The unvarnished mark of authenticity.

VIII. Prophecy Without Error
"History is the unrolled scroll of prophecy."
James Garfield [53]

And finally, as we saw in some detail in Chapter 11, prophecy without error is another strong evidence of the validity of God's word.

Among all the religions of today, only the Bible's picture of God is consistent with historical, archeological, and scientific facts. The above examples are just the tip of the iceberg.

There have been hundreds of books written on the evidences of the divine inspiration of the Bible. Unfortunately, most people today have not read any of them. In fact, few have even read the Bible itself. Yet, many will reject this God without even a superficial investigation of His word. Such a rejection is revealing. It is not so much a rejection of the 'mind', but of the will; not so much 'I can't believe', but 'I won't.' As Blaise Pascal said, *"People almost invariably arrive at their beliefs not on the basis of proof but on the basis of what they find attractive."* [54] What a sad state of affairs.

Nonetheless, the Biblical writers claimed repeatedly that they were passing on the very Word of God, infallible and authoritative (stated over 3,000 times, in various ways; e.g. 2 Timothy 3: 16-17; Matthew 5: 18; etc.). If one investigates the Biblical evidences available, they will find these claims to be justified.

Here are some good starting points for going deeper: <u>The New Evidence that Demands a Verdict</u>, Josh McDowell; <u>I Don't Have Enough Faith to Be an Atheist</u>, Norman L. Geisler & Frank Turek; <u>What's So Great About Christianity</u>, Dinesh d'Souza; <u>Examine the Evidence</u>, Ralph Muncaster.

> *"For the word of God is living and active. Sharper than any double-edged sword, it penetrates even to dividing soul and spirit, joints and marrow; it judges the thoughts and attitudes of the heart."* Hebrews 4: 12

An often heard question these days goes something like this: what about those who have never heard of the Bible, or the God it talks about? What happens to them when they die? Well, we know intrinsically what's right and what's wrong. Without even knowing God's word, people in pagan societies generally value and attempt to practice its most basic principles. Cultures instinctively value justice, honesty, compassion, and goodness toward others. Even little children pick up on this quickly. Therefore, according to the Bible, those who never had the opportunity to know God's word will be judged on the basis of their obedience to what they do know. Those with access to God's word will be accountable for the greater knowledge, and also judged on their obedience to what they know. As Paul says: *"the Gentiles do not have the Law* (i.e. the word of God); *but whenever they do by instinct what the Law commands, they are their own law, even though they do not have the Law. Their conduct show that what the Law commands is written in their hearts. Their consciences also show that this is true, since their thoughts sometimes accuse them and sometimes defend them. And so, according to the Good News I preach, this is how it will be on the Day when God through Jesus Christ will judge the secret thoughts of all."* Romans 2: 14-16 GNT Speaking about the conscience, the Navajo Native Americans put it this way: *"In every human heart there's a triangle that spins when we do wrong. And the corners of that triangle cut the heart and prick the conscience and it causes us pain."*[55]

By the way, Paul doesn't imply that the human conscience is always a perfect moral guide. Sometimes we have conflicting thoughts about our immoral behavior, and sometimes we simply excuse ourselves from wrongdoing. Also, our conscience can be distorted by sin (e.g. 1 Cor. 9: 7, 10; 10: 29; 1 Tim. 4: 2; Titus 1: 15). And finally, it's always possible to have the light of conscience, and then refuse it.[56] Nonetheless, through conscience, we are all given some light of the divine, which serves as evidence of our Creator. As Solomon said, God *"...has put eternity into man's heart."*[57]

---

[1]The Rwandan Genocide was the 1994 mass murder of an estimated 800,000 people in the small East African nation of Rwanda. See http://news.change.org/stories/statistics-on-genocide-that-i-wish-didn-t-exist.
[2]The Killing Fields are a number of sites in Cambodia where large numbers of people were killed and buried by the Khmer Rouge regime during its rule of the country from 1975 to 1979. Analysis of 20,000 mass grave sites by the DC-Cam Mapping Program and Yale University indicate the total number of deaths range from 1.7 to 2.5 million out of a population of around 8 million. Ibid.
[3]The approximate total number of people killed in the concentration camps alone is 6,000,000 to 6,500,000. Ibid.
[4]Webster's New World Dictionary of the American Language-College Edition, The World Publishing Company, Cleveland, 1994, p.1228
[5]The Holy Ampulla was a glass vial which, from its first recorded use by Pope Innocent II for the anointing of Louis VII in 1131 to the coronation of Louis XVI in 1774, held the chrism or anointing oil for the coronation of the kings of France. It gained a reputation for holiness and authenticity that brought fame, wealth and great honors to the see of Reims.
[6]Consecration is a solemn, ecclesiastical blessing of the King in the performance of his royal duties.
[7]The Marshal of France is a military distinction in contemporary France, not a military rank. It is granted to generals for exceptional achievements. During the time of Joan of Arc, the marshal received a baton, a blue cylinder with fleurs-de-lis, with the Latin inscription: Terror belli, *decus pacis*, which means "Terror in war, ornament in peace".
[8]His testimony was so lurid that the judge of his trial ordered the worst portions to be stricken from the official record.
[9] *"The devil led him up to a high place and showed him in an instant all the kingdoms of the world. And he said to him, 'I will give you all their authority and splendor; it has been given to me, and I can give it to anyone I want to. If you worship me, it will all be yours.' Jesus answered, 'It is written: Worship the Lord your God and serve him only.'"* Luke 4: 5-8 As you see, Jesus did not dispute that *"the kingdoms of the world"* had been given to him. But the time is coming when Satan will lose his kingdom for good (see Revelation 20: 1-15).
[10]Therese (1515-1582) was a prominent Spanish mystic, Roman Catholic saint, and Carmelite nun of the Middle Ages

[11] Sai Baba (1926-2011) was a controversial Indian guru, frequently accused over the years of sexual abuse and fraud---charges he denied as smear campaigns.
[12] The POTAMOI (8th-7th century BC) is an example. They were the Greek gods of the rivers and streams of the earth, "sons of the great earth-encircling river *Okeanos*". Each river had its own god. They were manlike from the chest upwards, but below were bodied with the serpentine tail of a fish. See http://www.theoi.com, 2011; Theoi Greek Mythology Project, 2011.
[13] E.g. Genesis 18: 14; Job 42: 2; Jeremiah 32: 17, 27; Matthew 19: 26; Luke 1: 37; Luke 18: 27; Revelation 19: 6...
[14] There are many other examples, including: Is. 45: 12; Is. 48: 12-13; Zechariah 12: 1-2.
[15] Ralph Muncaster, Examine the Evidence-Exploring the Case for Christianity, Harvest House Publishers, Eugene, Oregon, 2004, p.163; See also previous chapter.
[16] E.g. Joan of Arc, Joan of Arc-Self Portrait, Willard Trask, The Telegraph Press, Harrisburg, Pa, 1936, p. 51; Régine Pernoud and Marie-Véronique Clin. Joan of Arc-Her Story, St Martin's Griffin, New York, New York, 1998, p. 23
[17] http://www.thefreepressonline.co.uk/news/3/941.htm, Nov. 2011; for a deeper investigation see www.reasons.org or http://creation.com
[18] *"The heavens declare the glory of God; the skies proclaim the work of his hands. Day after day they pour forth speech; night after night they reveal knowledge. They have no speech, they use no words; no sound is heard from them. Yet their voice goes out into all the earth, their words to the ends of the world."* Psalm 19: 1- 4; *"... what may be known about God is plain to them, because God has made it plain to them. For since the creation of the world God's invisible qualities---his eternal power and divine nature---have been clearly seen, being understood from what has been made, so that men are without excuse."* Romans 1: 18-20
[19] *"Hear this, you foolish and senseless people, who have eyes but do not see, who have ears but do not hear... these people have stubborn and rebellious hearts; they have turned aside and gone away. They do not say to themselves, 'Let us fear the LORD our God, who gives autumn and spring rains in season, who assures us of the regular weeks of harvest.' Your wrongdoings have kept these away; your sins have deprived you of good."* Jeremiah 5: 21- 25
[20] *"It is the sheer universality of perfection, the fact that everywhere we look, to whatever depth we look, we find an elegance and ingenuity of an absolutely transcendent quality, which so mitigates against the idea of chance. Is it really credible that random processes could have constructed a reality, the smallest element of which - a functional protein or gene - is complex beyond our own creative capacities, a reality which is the very antithesis of chance, which excel in every sense of anything produced by the intelligence of man? Alongside the level of ingenuity and complexity exhibited by the molecular machinery of life, even our most advanced artifacts appear clumsy."* Michael Denton, PhD in Biochemistry, Evolution-A Theory in Crisis, Burnett Books, London, 1985, p. 342
[21] http://preachersfiles.com/my-words-shall-not-pass-away, Nov. 2011
[22] Arthur Walkington Pink, The Divine Inspiration of the Bible, Bible Truth Depot Publishers and Booksellers, Swengel, PA., 1917, p. 115
[23] http://www.newworldencyclopedia.org/entry/Voltaire, Nov. 2011
[24] http://www.investigatechristianity.com/PAGE6.asp, Nov. 2011
[25] http://www.goarch.org/resources/sermons/sermonettes/sermonettes013, Nov. 2011
[26] Dr. Wood is an archaeologist, a specialist in Canaanite pottery of the Late Bronze Age, and author of The Sociology of Pottery in Ancient Palestine, as well as numerous articles on archaeological subjects.

[27] *"Perhaps the single most important religious archaeological find ever..."* Ralph Muncaster, Examine the Evidence-Exploring the Case for Christianity, Harvest House Publishers, Eugene, Oregon, 2004, p. 187; Also see Dead Sea Scrolls of Appendix D-The God of the Bible.
[28] Bernard Ramm, Can I Trust My Old Testament?, The Kings Business, Feb., 1949, p. 190
[29] Bernard Ramm, Can I Trust My Old Testament?, The Kings Business, Feb., 1949, p. 230, 231
[30] Nelson Glueck, Rivers in the Desert: History of Negev, Jewish Publication Society of America, Philadelphia, 1969, p. 176
[31] William F. Albright, Archaeology and the Religions of Israel, Johns Hopkins University Press, Baltimore, 1956, p. 176
[32] Millar Burrows, What Mean These Stones?, Meridian Books, New York, NY, 1956, p. 176
[33] Sir William Bragg (1862-1942) was a British physicist, chemist and mathematician, who uniquely shared the 1915 Nobel Prize in Physics with his son.
[34] From his 1948 Armistice Day address. Gen. Bradley (1893-1981) was a senior U.S. Army field commander in North Africa and Europe during World War II, a five-star General in the United States Army, and the first general to be selected Chairman of the Joint Chiefs of Staff.
[35] Ralph Muncaster, Examine the Evidence-Exploring the Case for Christianity, Harvest House Publishers, Eugene, Oregon, 2004, p.161; http://en.wikipedia.org/wiki/Nicolaus_Copernicus, accessed Dec. 2011
[36] L. E. Holt and R. McIntosh, Holt Pediatrics, Appleton-Century-Crofts; 12th edition, 1961, pp. 125-126
[37] *"Actually, strictly speaking, the 'big bang' was not an explosion because no material was involved. None existed yet. The 'big bang' was the sudden expansion of space-time. That is not the same as an explosion in any physical sense. That said, in terms of the rules of the English language the closest metaphor for the event is to call it an 'explosion of space'. An explosion however is not the best analogy to describe this expansion. Why? In an explosion, such as a bomb or firecracker, matter blasts out from a central location and fills up space that is already there. An explosion did not fill the universe with matter, rather the universe itself began expanding. Rather than thinking of the big bang as a giant explosion, compare it to rising raisin bread dough or blowing up a balloon."* http://paul-a-heckert.suite101.com/the-universe-and-the-big-bang-a16412, accessed Dec, 2011; http://www.physicsforums.com/showthread.php?t=362925, accessed Dec 2011; http://www.desy.de/user/projects/Physics/Relativity/GR/centre.html, accessed Dec 2011.
[38] From a public lecture (The Beginning of Time) in 1996. http://www.hawking.org.uk/index.php/lectures/publiclectures/62, accessed Dec. 2011. Mr. Hawking (1942-) is an English theoretical physicist and cosmologist, an Honorary Fellow of the Royal Society of Arts, a lifetime member of the Pontifical Academy of Sciences, and in 2009 was awarded the Presidential Medal of Freedom, the highest civilian award in the United States. He was the Lucasian Professor of Mathematics at the University of Cambridge for 30 years (1979-2009). He is now Director of Research at the Centre for Theoretical Cosmology in the Department of Applied Mathematics and Theoretical Physics at the University of Cambridge.
[39] Ralph Muncaster, Examine the Evidence-Exploring the Case for Christianity, Harvest House Publishers, Eugene, Oregon, 2004, p. 162.
[40] http://www.physlink.com/education/askexperts/ae280.cfm, accessed Nov. 23, 2011; http://www.physicsplanet.com/articles/three-laws-of-thermodynamics, accessed Dec 1, 2011
[41] Ibid, p. 164-165

[42] Ralph Muncaster, Examine the Evidence-Exploring the Case for Christianity, Harvest House Publishers, Eugene, Oregon, 2004, p. 160-161

[43] The Physics Of Immortality, New York, Doubleday, 1994, Preface. Mr. Tipler (1947-) currently holds a joint appointment in the Departments of Mathematics and Physics at Tulane University. Since the above quote, Mr. Tipler has converted to Christianity. His latest book, The Physics Of Christianity (published in 2007), was described in the New York Times Book Review as *"A thrilling ride to the far edges of modern physics."*

[44] Peter Kreeft's quote from: Norman L. Geisler, Frank Turek, David Limbaugh; I Don't Have Enough Faith to Be an Atheist, Crossway Books, Wheaton, IL, 2004, p. 275

[45] Translated by William Whiston, The New Complete Works of Josephus, A letter from Pliny to Trajan, Kregel Publications, Grand Rapids, MI, 1999, p.198

[46] Matthew 26: 56; Mark 14: 51-52

[47] Acts 2: 14- 41

[48] Mark 16: 15-18; Luke 24: 36-43; John 20: 19-31; John 21: 1-25; 1 Corinthians 15: 5-6; Matthew 28: 16-20

[49] Mr. Sowell (1930-) is an American economist, social theorist, political philosopher, and author.

[50] Wikipedia, http://en.wikipedia.org/wiki/Political_correctness; accessed Nov. 2010

[51] Rudyard Kipling, An Interview with Mark Twain, p. 180, *From sea to sea: letters of travel*, 1899, Doubleday & McClure Company

[52] Mr. Polkinghorne (1930-) is a physicist, Anglican priest and author. He was Professor of Mathematical Physics at the University of Cambridge from 1968 to 1979.

[53] The Speaker's Electronic Reference Collection, AApex Software, 1994. James Garfield (1831 – 1881), was the 20th President of the United States. He was assassinated on July 2, 1881.

[54] Blaise Pascal, De l'Art de persuader (On the Art of Persuasion), written 1658; published posthumously. Mr. Pascal (1623–1662) was a French mathematician, physicist, inventor, writer and Catholic philosopher.

[55] Charity Distribution, http://charitydistribution.com/?p=1002, July, 2011; The Catholic Difference, http://www.stjameshopewell.org/questions/question_conscience.html, July 2011

[56] From John MacArthur, The MacArthur Bible Commentary, Thomas Nelson, Inc., Nashville, TN, 2005, p. 1510; Walter Kaiser-Peter H. Davids-F.F. Bruce-Manfred Brauch, Hard Sayings of the Bible, InterVarsity Press, Downers Grove, IL, 1996, p. 545-546]

[57] Ecclesiastes 3: 11

Chapter 14
Joan's France?

"How can anyone govern a nation that has 240 different kinds of cheese?" Charles de Gaulle [1]

"In Paris they simply stared when I spoke to them in French; I never did succeed in making those idiots understand their language." Mark Twain [2]

I wonder what Joan of Arc would think of her native land these days? At this point I believe it's fitting to take a quick glance at the 'post-Joan' France.

Nations, like individuals, are built on a foundation. France was created from the strong foundation of Christian faith. For centuries it was widely believed by both royalty and the common man, that the kings of France were chosen by and served under God. Clovis became the first French Christian king in 481 AD. Charlemagne (742-814 AD) introduced Christianity everywhere his kingdom went. King Louis IX (1214-1270) was the only French king actually canonized a saint. All three were deeply involved in their faith, and were typical of their time. Joan of Arc (1412-1431) was also a reflection of her time, and as we have seen, God played a very important part in the French national picture during this time. After Joan, God remained part of the national big picture, as demonstrated by Louis XIV, the "Sun King" (1638-1715 AD). He became a pious and devout king, viewing himself as the protector of the Gallican Church. His reign, from 1643-1715, is the longest documented reign of any European monarch. But this Christian foundation would soon be dramatically changed.

The Eternal Sleep?
*"For death begins with life's first breath.
And life begins at touch of death."*
William Arthur Dunkerley [3]

During the French Revolution (1789-1799), France's foundation was altered drastically. Of course, the history of the French Revolution is complex, and to go into it in any great detail here would take us too far afield. However, it is safe to say that the foundational changes made then still play a strong role in today's France.

What changes? Well for one thing, the French revolutionaries "threw God out of power", and replaced Him with their own god: the "god of Reason". They followed their new god on the sharp blade of the guillotine, all the way to their "New France". This was accomplished by introducing a sweeping program of de-Christianization first against Catholicism, and eventually all forms of Christianity. Several things were involved in this "new and improved" program, including:

1) It was decreed that all cemetery gates should bear only one inscription: "Death is an Eternal Sleep."

2) All statues, plates and other iconography were removed from places of worship throughout France.

3) The destruction of crosses, bells and other external signs of worship was ordered.

4) A law enacted on October 21, 1793 made all nonjuring priests[4] and all persons who harbored them liable to death on sight. In their "righteous" zeal, the revolutionaries burned down many of the churches, and killed hundreds of priests.

They soon became inventive in their approach. *Republican marriage*, for example, was a form of execution that occurred during the Reign of Terror in Revolutionary France, and involved tying a naked man (often priests) and woman (often nuns) together, loading them up on a ship, and then sinking that ship out in the middle of the Loire River.[5] These were called the *noyades massacres* (i.e. the drowning massacres), and were practiced between November 1793 and January 1794 in the city of Nantes. Historians believe that around 5,000 were killed this way. Residents claim these massacres have been downplayed so as not to sully the idealized story of the French Revolution.

5) Revolutionary and civic cults were instituted, including the Cult of Reason (an atheistic belief system, intended to replace Christianity). Its goal was the perfection of mankind through the attainment of truth and liberty, made possible only by the exercise of Reason. Though atheism was at the core of this cult, it defined itself as more than a rejection of God. Like conventional religion, it encouraged acts of congregational worship, with frequent and rigorous displays of devotion to Reason as an ideal. The climax was reached with the celebration of the "Goddess of Reason" in Paris' Notre Dame Cathedral on November 10, 1793. First the cathedral was transformed into a modern "Temple of Reason" (i.e. *Temple de la Raison*). An altar to liberty was installed over the old one, and the inscription "To Philosophy" was carved into the church facade. Then as a special highlight, Madame Momoro, a nun turned prostitute,

THE WITCH THAT WASN'T

was carried into the cathedral by four citizens to represent the 'Goddess of Reason'. She was then paraded all through the cathedral for everyone to see.[6] Clothed in white drapery with a blue cloak over her shoulders and a red cap of liberty crowning her long hair, she sat on an ivy-covered chair while speeches were made, songs were sung, and soldiers paraded about the aisles carrying busts of some of the martyrs of the Revolution.[7] Whoa-a-a...Like Party down! Four months later, this same Goddess of Reason was herself guillotined.[6]

6) In order to get rid of Sundays and the church holidays of the Gregorian calendar, the Revolutionaries simply invented a new calendar without them (called the Republican Calendar), which was adopted on October 24, 1793. And so the year 1793 became Year 1 of the Republic. This calendar would emphasize the Republic's association with Nature and Reason. For example the first month was named *Vendemiaire* (named after the French word *vendange*, meaning 'grape harvest'). The year was divided into twelve months, each containing thirty days, with the five days left at the end of the year to be celebrated as secular "festivals". The months rhyme three by three, according to the "sonority" of the seasons. The weeks were divided up into ten days each (named after plants, domestic animals and tools). The names of saints in the calendar were replaced by those of fruits, plants and flowers.

For some, this de-Christianization campaign was the logical next step of the materialist philosophies of the "Enlightenment".[8] For others, it was simply an opportunity to finally express long-held resentments against the Church and Christianity. The goal of these programs was the destruction of Catholic religious practice and ultimately of the religion itself. However, de-Christianization aroused great anger with the common people, and 'Revolutionary Religion' never caught on. It was abolished on January 1, 1806 by Emperor Napoleon. Nonetheless, great damage to the country's foundation had already been done.

Today France, no longer resting on a foundation of Biblical faith, has become a deeply secular and pragmatic country. Of course, this could be said about many countries these days. Indeed, are there any "God-loving countries" left? America too, without God's help, appears headed towards a similar secular destination. But France got a head start with the French Revolution. And today it is increasingly difficult to see God reflected in the fabric of mainstream French society or institutions.

But perhaps all is not lost. Amidst this ever-expanding spiritual darkness, there remains some exceptionally bright lights of faith in France. For example, every year Taizé (the Christian community of reconciliation in Burgundy-see www.taize.fr) attracts thousands of young people from all over the world to their simple prayerful approach to worship. France is also rich in monasteries. They provide a quiet refuge from the world, where God's presence is celebrated in daily living.

Still, two questions come to mind:

(1) Having apparently turned its back on God for more than two centuries, is France now heading towards oblivion, like so many countries of the past?
(2) Has God's purpose for France already been served?

Of course, we can't know God's plans this side of Heaven, but certainly no French historical figure of faith as large as Joan of Arc has stepped forward since her. And it appears that only God can break this downward spiral France has embarked on.

Has exchanging a foundation of faith for one of secular values been good for the nation's "self-esteem"?

For its future?

Would Joan even recognize this France of today?

In this author's opinion, the answer to all three questions is the same: very doubtful.

[1]De Gaulle (1890-1970) was a French general and statesman who led the Free French Forces during World War II. He later founded the French Fifth Republic in 1958 and served as its first President from 1959 to 1969.
[2]Mark Twain, The Innocents Abroad, Chapter 61, 1869
[3]Mr. Dunkerley (1852-1941), a.k.a John Oxenham, was a prolific English journalist, novelist, hymn composer, and poet.
[4] *"The government required all clergy to swear an oath of loyalty to the Civil Constitution of the Clergy* (i.e. the state). *Only about half the clergy agreed: the rest refused; these became known as 'non-jurors'...The Civil Constitution generated considerable resentment among religious peasants...On 5 February 1791, non-juring priests were banned from preaching in public. However, they continued to perform masses and attract crowds...On 9 June, 1791, the Assembly forbade the publication of Papal Bulls or Decrees, unless they had been approved by the Assembly as well...violence on all sides continued...Anti-Catholic persecution by the State would intensify into de-Christianization ...During this time umpteen non-juring priests were interned in chains on prison-ships in French harbors where most died within a few months from the appalling conditions.This might be seen as an example of an 18th century concentration camp."*
http://en.wikipedia.org/wiki/Civil_Constitution_of_the_Clergy#Jurors_and_non-jurors; accessed August 2011
[5]Ruth Scurr, Fatal Purity: Robespierre And the French Revolution, 2006, p. 305.
[6]Ann Coulter, Demonic, Random House Inc, New York, 2011, p.119; from Michael

Burleigh, Earthly Powers: the Clash of Religion and Politics in Europe, from the French Revolution to the Great War, Harper Collins, 2006, p. 79; Gunn; Kennedy, 177
[7]Christopher Hibbert, The Days of the French Revolution, Peguin Books Ltd, New York, New York, 1999, p. 232
[8] *"The Age of Enlightenment (or simply the Enlightenment or Age of Reason) was a cultural movement of intellectuals in 18th century Europe and the American colonies. Its purpose was to reform society using reason (rather than tradition, faith and revelation) and advance knowledge through science. It promoted science and intellectual interchange and opposed 'superstition', intolerance and some abuses by church and state. Originating about 1650 to 1700, it was sparked by philosophers Baruch Spinoza, John Locke, Pierre Bayle, Isaac Newton, and French philosopher Voltaire. Ruling princes often endorsed and fostered figures and even attempted to apply their ideas of government in what was known as Enlightened Despotism. The Enlightenment flourished until about 1790–1800, after which the emphasis on reason gave way to Romanticism's emphasis on emotion and a Counter-Enlightenment gained force."*
http://en.wikipedia.org/wiki/Age_of_Enlightenment, accessed October, 2012.

Chapter 15
All Aboard!

As we near the end of our journey, let's take a brief look from where we've come:

Chapter 1 - Joan of Arc, "Daughter of God" - The goal of this book, a thumbnail sketch of Joan of Arc and her legacy are presented in this chapter. The more we learn, the more we become aware of how unique and amazing her story really is.

Chapter 2 - The Sign - People have always looked for some kind of a "sign" to substantiate claims of being God-sent. In this chapter, we take a closer look at signs. From the Old Testament, Moses and Elijah are among those who presented signs. The New Testament is also full of signs. Jesus' ministry is especially compelling in this regard. Joan of Arc's signs are also examined here.

Chapter 3 - A Call to Serve - How are God's servants called to action? Here we look at some of the many similarities between Joan of Arc and the prophet/servants of the Bible, such as Abraham, Moses, Ezekiel, Daniel, Paul, and John the apostle. Their call to God's service is quite striking. The similarities that Joan shares with them in this regard are hard to miss, and difficult to explain without looking to the God of the Bible.

Chapter 4 - Her Time Had Come - We take a look at Joan's times, the Middle Ages, and her view of reality. Her concept of time is centered in God, just like the prophets of the Bible. Joan didn't have a Rolex, but her sense of time (i.e. God's Time), was more accurate.

Chapter 5 - God's Time - As with all faithful servants of God, Joan had a close connection with Him, and prayer was the center post of her life. From several Bible verses we see the importance God places on prayer, and from some of Joan's quotes we see her dedication in this regard.

Chapter 6 - A Lifelong Pilgrimage - When taken as a whole, Joan's life seems to be one accompanying God from beginning to end, full of meaning and purpose. She gives her entire being to God, and through Him accomplishes great things. It is a total dedication to do God's will, at great expense to herself. We see the same thing with other servants of the

Bible. In this chapter we look at this concept of Lifelong Pilgrimage, and specifically at some of the similarities between Joan's pilgrimage with that of Moses.

Chapter 7 - Remarkable Obedience - Obedience is often spoken of in Scripture. All of God's great servants, as well as many who came before and after the Bible was completed, demonstrated remarkable obedience to their Creator. But none have shown perfect obedience except Jesus. In this chapter we see the difficulties, failures, and ultimate successes in this regard from such great leaders of the faith as David, Peter, and Paul. Joan of Arc too makes a powerful witness for obedience. Not perfect, like Jesus, but powerful like David, Peter, and Paul. And like those three (and countless others), Joan displays obedience in both the small and great things of life. In the end, she is obedient even unto death for the love of her God.

Chapter 8 - Enduring Persecution - Sometimes, the final mark of a true servant of God will be their enduring persecution to the end. Jesus of Nazareth certainly gave us the example of this. In many ways, Joan of Arc follows His pattern, as we see in detail in this chapter. Of course, Christian persecution continues to this day, and we take a glance at its dramatic increase in the last century.

Chapter 9 - God's Help Ever-Present - God's help is present to all who turn to Him. And in so many ways. As we see in this important chapter, Joan made sure to avail herself to His help in every way possible. May we do likewise.

Chapter 10 - A Warrior of God - Some have been troubled that God could be involved in war, and/or actually take sides in a conflict. If true, would that change our perception of a loving God? If not true, then Joan of Arc's mission must not be directed from the God of the Bible. Joan, for her part, never equivocated on this issue. She stated from beginning to end that God Himself wanted the English out of France, and that He had sent her to show them the door. What does Scripture have to say about this subject, and how does Joan of Arc fit in? This chapter is devoted to these important questions.

Chapter 11 - Prophecy and Miracles - The Bible is consistent about the importance of prophecy. Prophesy without error, that is. Joan's many prophecies were unusually precise. Also, what role do miracles play in Scripture? We look at these fascinating subjects in some detail in this chapter.

Chapter 12 - "If you love me..." - Here we explore a little of Joan's foundation: the love of God. In contemporary society, we are taught the importance of self-esteem, hoping it will provide us a strong enough foundation to withstand the storms of life. But can it? We see how self-esteem is not the foundation taught in the Bible. Nor is it the path followed by the Biblical prophet/saints, or Joan of Arc.

Chapter 13 – The Ultimate Game Changer - There are, and always have been, many gods to choose from. However only the God of the Bible, Joan's God, proves to be an omnipotent, omnipresent, omniscient, loving, faithful, holy, and just deity. He is the Ultimate Game Changer. The evidence for this is abounding for those willing to take a look at it. Here we examine some of this evidence, including a brief look at two of God's attributes (His omnipotence and sovereignty), and His book, the Bible.

Chapter 14 - Joan's France - What would Joan think of her native land today? Has France abandoned its spiritual heritage? Today, this is a worthwhile question for America as well. Although we can't know all the answers this side of heaven, the importance of these questions is addressed in this chapter.

Chapter 15 - All Aboard - A view, chapter by chapter, of this journey up to this point.

Chapter 16
The Witch That Wasn't

Glinda: *"Are you a good witch or a bad witch?"*
Dorothy: *"Oh, I'm not a witch at all. I'm Dorothy from Kansas."* [1]

"There was neither sorcery nor any other evil art in anything that I have done." Joan of Arc, October 31, 1430

~~~~~~~~~~

Finally, Joan of Arc was captured and put on trial by her enemies. They pursued a three-part master plan. First of all, they needed her to be convicted as a witch. Secondly, she must be burned at the stake, the appropriate penalty for a witch during those days. And thirdly, once the 'witch' was dead, they would finally finish their conquest of France once and for all. Although they were able to accomplish the first two parts, the third would prove problematic. In fact, it would never happen at all.

As it turned out, Joan wasn't a witch after all. She was the witch that wasn't. God-sent. And God had His own Master Plan. Throughout these pages, I've tried to make this case: Joan of Arc was simply one in a long line of God's Game Changers, custom made for her particular time, place and circumstances. Her interactions with God's messengers, consistently fulfilled prophesies without apparent error, humble spirit, bold actions, love of God, and prayer-centered life all seem to be a reflection of God's servants found throughout Scripture. It is a story like none other.

So, what are we to make of all of this? Well, it comes down to three questions. The first two address the initial goals of this book. They are:

(1) Does Joan of Arc indeed follow the consistent pattern given by the prophet/servants of the Bible?

(2) If yes, does the evidence then indicate that she was indeed called and sent by the God of the Bible to save France?

The short answer to both questions is yes. And I believe the evidence is powerful. The case presented here is cumulative, and the details are found in the preceding pages. As each chapter adds another piece to the puzzle, we finally come to the best explanation of Joan of Arc's story. The one she herself presented boldly, consistently, and without exception: God sent His messengers to Joan of Arc, giving her a specific mission to fulfill, and the supernatural help necessary to accomplish it.[2] First, she was to lift the siege of Orleans, in order to then escort Charles VII to Reims, where he would be anointed and crowned the legitimate King of France. God accomplished all of this through His good servant Joan, for His own good purposes. The consequences of this have rumbled down through the centuries of history to the present day. Even non-believing historians have little other recourse than to admit that Joan of Arc somehow saved France from becoming just another part of England.

Joan followed God to the best of her ability, with earth-shaking results, at the cost of her life. The church finally came to acknowledge and celebrate this. Yes, the same church that put her on trial for witchcraft and sorcery. The same one that had her burned alive at the stake for her "crimes". The change came neither quickly nor easily, but nearly 500 years after her death, on May 16, 1920, she was canonized a saint by Pope Benedict XV.

This leads us to our third and final question:

(3) So what?

If you believe that Joan of Arc was indeed called and sent by the God of the Bible to 'save France', then I would encourage you to take the logical next step: *"Take up the banner of your Lord."* Joan of Arc[3] No doubt many of you have already done so, and are even now spreading the word. As Peter said: *"Always be prepared to give an answer to everyone who asks you to give the reason for the hope that you have. But do this with gentleness and respect..."* 1 Peter 3: 15 Like one hungry beggar sharing with another where to find something good to eat... Yes, many are already following Him now, just as Joan did then.

But perhaps you are not convinced? If not, then may you continue your spiritual search (as evidenced by your reading this book). As we saw in Chapter 5, it's important that our search be accompanied by prayer. May God open the eyes of our hearts. Paul said: *"I pray...that the eyes of your heart may be enlightened in order that you may know the hope to which he has called you..."* Ephesians 1: 18

Something Extraordinary
"Whatever thing men call great, look for it in Joan of Arc, and there you will find it." Mark Twain [4]

<u>Something</u> extraordinary was at work in the life and times of Joan of Arc. If it was not the supernatural God of the Bible, then we are left with many large question marks. What are the odds that all of her story is pure coincidence? If her story was not true, then once captured and on trial for her life, why would she continue to claim that it was true, knowing that such testimony was leading her straight to the stake? Perhaps you have another explanation? If so, does it stand up to scrutiny? Does it answer more questions than it raises?

During her Trial of Condemnation, Joan spoke about the first time she heard the voice (see Chapters 3 and 5). She said that this messenger identified himself as the Archangel St Michael[5], and went on to say, *"I believed it was an angel speaking to me, and I had the will to believe."*[6]

Believe to Know vs. Know to Believe

"Belief is a wise wager. Granted that faith cannot be proved, what harm will come to you if you gamble on its truth and it proves false? If you gain, you gain all; if you lose, you lose nothing. Wager, then, without hesitation, that He exists." Blaise Pascal [7]

In Biblical times, as well as the times of Joan of Arc, the existence of God was not questioned to the extent it is today. James said: *"You believe that there is one God. Good! Even the demons believe that- and shudder."* James 2: 19

Belief is one of those concepts that seems simple to grasp, but is elusive at the same time. Joan said, *"I had the will to believe."* For her, it seems that the first step towards faith was to make a choice. The choice to believe.

Could choosing to <u>first</u> believe, and <u>then</u> continuing our search from a foundation of faith, help us in a search for God? This approach would not mean that we would have no more honest and worthy questions. Rather it would be like knowing that somewhere, there is a treasure buried. We just have to keep looking for it. Such a search, based on the belief that God's truth exists, will lead us to deeper answers and a stronger foundation for our faith.

Can we "prove" the existence of God? No. No more than we can prove the existence of love. We can neither put God nor love in a test-tube and conduct scientific experiments. Still, the evidence for both is all around us. And within us. And science, in many different arenas, supports the case for the existence of God. An objective, open-minded search may be helpful for those with legitimate scientific questions (See <u>Chapter 13</u>).

But why is belief such a deal-breaking requirement in the first place? The Bible says that even our eternal destiny depends on it! Well, for one thing, it's God's will (see verses below). But I'll speculate further. Belief is the great equalizer. The rich can't buy it. The poor can't sell it. The realtor can't rent it. The thief can't steal it. The policeman can't arrest it. The judge can't lock it up. The banker can't save it...

It's free and available to everyone.

It is the currency for all mankind.

It is the currency most valued by God.

Belief is foundational for Biblical faith. "Blind faith" however, contrary to what many believe, is not what we are asked to have. Let us prayerfully use our God-given brains and reason to examine the evidence. *"Ask and it will be given to you; seek and you shall find; knock and the door will be opened to you. For everyone who asks receives; he who seeks finds; and to him who knocks, the door will be opened."* Matthew 7: 7-8

The importance of belief runs all through scripture. Here are some examples of its pre-eminence:

"Abram believed the Lord, and he credited it to him as righteousness..." Genesis 15: 6

"Then they believed his promises and sang his praises." Psalm 106: 12

"Ignoring what they said, Jesus told the synagogue ruler, 'Don't be afraid; just believe.'" Mark 5: 35-37

"Jesus said, 'Everything is possible for him who believes.'" Mark 9: 23

"He (Jesus) *said to them, 'Go into all the world and preach the good news. Whoever believes and is baptized will be saved, but whoever does not believe will be condemned.'"* Mark 16: 15-16

"...Jesus said to Jarius, 'Don't be afraid; just believe, and she will be healed.'" Luke 8: 50

"Yet to all who received him, to those who believed in his name (i.e. the name of Jesus), *he gave the right to become children of God."* John 1: 12

"For God so loved the world, that he gave his one and only son, that whoever believes in him shall not perish but have eternal life." John 3: 16

"Whoever believes in him is not condemned, but whoever does not believe stands condemned already, because he has not believed in the name of God's one and only son." John 3: 18

Jesus said, *"I tell you the truth, whoever hears my word and believes him who sent me has eternal life and will not be condemned; he has crossed over from death to life."* John 5: 24

Jesus said, *"For my father's will is that everyone who looks to the son and believes in him shall have eternal life, and I will raise him up at the last day."* John 6: 40

Jesus said, *"I tell you the truth, whoever believes has everlasting life."* John 6: 47

"Jesus did many other miraculous signs in the presence of his disciples which are not recorded in this book. But these are written that you may believe that Jesus is the Christ, the Son of God, and that by believing you may have life in His name." John 20: 30-31

"Believe in the Lord Jesus, and you will be saved." Acts 16: 31

"...the word of faith that we are proclaiming: That if you confess with your mouth, 'Jesus is Lord', and believe in your heart that God raised him from the dead, you will be saved.'" Romans 10: 8-9

"Who is it that overcomes the world? Only he that believes that Jesus is the Son of God." 1 John 5: 5

"Jesus said to her, 'I am the resurrection and the life, he who believes in me will live, even though he dies. Do you believe this?'" John 11: 25-26

As you see, I listed a lot of quotes on belief (but not all) to show the consistency and importance of this doctrine. When belief is spoken of in the Bible, it is talking about belief in the God of the Bible, and His only Son, Jesus. Not faith in yourself, another person, a cause, a religion, a nation, an idea, a force or another deity.

Yes, belief is the ultimate gold standard for our final destination.[8]

I'd like to end with this. During Biblical times, the name of a person sometimes prophetically captured something in their character, personality, calling or divinely determined destiny. Here are three examples:

Adam means 'Earth Man'- The first man, he was made literally out of the earth (Genesis 2).

Abraham means 'Father of a Multitude'- Abraham, who left everything at God's instruction, eventually became the father of many nations, just as God told him he would (Genesis 12: 1-3). Jews, Christians and Muslims claim him.

Jesus means 'God Saves', or 'Jehovah is salvation'. Enough said.

What about Joan's name? It means 'God is Gracious' (for Biblical examples, see Exodus 34: 6; Psalm 103: 8; 1 Peter 5: 10).

Merriam-Webster's 2009 OnLine Dictionary provides us with these descriptive words for gracious: *"...having or showing kindness and courtesy; generosity of spirit; merciful, compassionate; used conventionally of royalty and high nobility."* Indeed. And "gracious" captures Joan well. She remains a shining example of faith, courage, and yes, graciousness. There's no doubt that we can learn much from her story. And here's a bonus. If we pray to the God of the Bible, believe and love Him, God will use us! And perhaps in ways we could never even imagine, like Joan of Arc. In any case, one thing is sure: whether our service to God is in large or small ways, it will be our greatest blessing.

All through Scripture we see that those chosen by the Lord for His service lived a life close to their maker; one of fullness and true meaning while here on earth. Then one fine day, like those gone before them, they crossed over into the Kingdom of Heaven, finding eternal life in the presence of the living God. What a deal! Jesus said, *"Truly I tell you...No one who has left home or brothers or sisters or mother or father or children or fields for me and the gospel will fail to receive a hundred times as much (brothers, sisters, mothers, children and fields-and with them, persecutions) and in the age to come, eternal life."* Mark 10: 29-30

And one last thing...

Has the ultimate Game Changer chosen you too for His service? Yes, He has. The Lord has chosen **all** of us to love and serve Him.

Otherwise we wouldn't be here. We wouldn't have been given the gift of life. The real question, as always, comes down to this: Do we choose Him?

There is no more important question.

One day, in the blink of an eye, we too will cross over from this life to the next. On that day, I pray that we **all** find ourselves in the presence of the Risen Lord Jesus the Messiah, His apostles, Paul, the prophets and saints of Scripture, Joan of Arc, Martin Luther, Mother Teresa, Billy Graham, Brother Roger of Taize, and all the many others who make up that *"great cloud of witnesses"*.[9] Until that day, *"I commend you to God. May He watch over you."*[10] Amen.

---

[1] From the 1939 movie *The Wizard of Oz*. Glinda is the Good Witch of the North, a fictional character in the Land of Oz, created by American author L. Frank Baum. She is the most powerful sorceress of Oz, ruler of the Quadling Country south of the Emerald City, and protector of Princess Ozma.

[2] *"Up to the end of her life she maintained and asserted that her Voices came from God, and that what she had done had been by God's command."* Martin Ladvenu (a Dominican at the convent of Rouen), Trial of Nullification, May 3rd, 1452

[3] Joan of Arc, from: Willard Trask, Joan of Arc-Self Portrait, The Telegraph Press, New York, New York, 1936, p. 48-49

[4] Mark Twain, Personal Recollections of Joan of Arc, Google Books, accessed Nov. 24, 2013, p. 329

[5] The Bible mentions St Michael two times: Jude 1: 9 and Revelation 12: 7.

[6] Régine Pernoud, Jeanne d'Arc par elle-meme et ses témoins, Editions du Seuil, Paris, 1996, p. 30-31

[7] Blaise Pascal, Pascal's Wager: Pragmatic Arguments and Belief in God, Oxford University Press, 2007. Blaise Pascal (1623-1662), was a child prodigy, who became a mathematician, physicist, inventor, writer and Catholic philosopher.

[8] *"I believe in God, and I trust myself in His hands."* President James Garfield. Reported in Josiah Hotchkiss Gilbert, Dictionary of Burning Words of Brilliant Writers (1895), p. 595

[9] Hebrews 12: 1

[10] Joan of Arc, her final letter sent to the city of Rheims from Sully, March 28, 1430

ABOUT THE AUTHOR

 Chris Snidow, along with his wife Catherine, has been leading Joan of Arc pilgrimages to France since 2002. He is author of several articles on Joan of Arc and the God of the Bible published by *The Dallas Morning News*, *Esprit*, *The Epistle*, and others. Aided by some of the leading Joan of Arc experts in both France and the United States, studies of the life and times of Joan of Arc still continues.
 A professional musician from his teen years, he founded <u>Biblical Sound Pictures</u> in 1985, and has since released seven musical CDs with Biblical themes. His music is currently available in Holland, France, England, Canada, Australia, the United States and through many websites throughout the world, such as Amazon.com. <u>*Joan of Arc, Prophecy and the God of the Bible*</u>, released in 2008, was specifically composed for the Sound and Light Spectacle performed in the Saint Joan of Arc Basilica of Domremy, France in 2007. A DVD slide show based on this was released in both French and English in 2011.
 He is a Registered Nurse, specializing in Psychiatry for more than two decades. Chris and Catherine currently live in Dallas, Texas and are active members of Prestonwood Baptist church.

Bibliography

Astell, Ann W. *Political Allegory in Late Medieval England*, Cornell University Press, Ithaca, N.Y., 1999

Ayers, Alex (Editor). *The Wisdom of Martin Luther King, Jr.*, Plume Publishing, New York, 1993

Bard, Mitchell G. *Myths and Facts-A Guide to the Arab-Israeli Conflict*, AICE, Chevy Chase, MD, 2001

Bataille, Georges. *The Trial of Gilles de Rais*, Amok Books, Los Angeles, CA, 1991

Bigelow, Albert Paine. *The Girl in White Armor-The Story of Joan of Arc*, The Macmillan Company, New York, 1967

Bigelow, Albert Paine. *Joan of Arc: Maid of France Vol. 1*, Macmillan Company, 1925

Barrett, W. P. *The Trial of Jeanne d'Arc*, First Edition, Gotham House Inc, 1932

Burleigh, Michael. *Earthly Powers: the Clash of Religion and Politics in Europe, from the French Revolution to the Great War*, Harper Collins, 2006

Calvin, John. *Institutes of the Christian Religion Volume 1 by John Allen*, Hezekiah Howe, Philadelphia, 1816

Chambers, Oswald. *My Utmost for His Highest: Traditional Updated Edition*, Discovery House Publishers, Grand Rapids, MI, 1992

Coulter, Ann. *Demonic*, Random House Inc, New York, 2011

Crossway Bibles. *ESV Study Bible-English Standard Version*, Good News Publishers, Wheaton IL, 2007

Denton, Michael. *Evolution-A Theory in Crisis*, Burnett Books, London, 1985

DeVries, Kelly. *Joan of Arc-A Military Leader*, Sutton Publishing, Midsommer Norton, Bather, 1999

Dinesh, d'Souza. *What's So Great About Christianity*, Tyndale House Publishers, Inc., Carol Stream, Il., 2008

Felder, Helder. *Christ and the Critics, Vol. 2*, Burns, Oates, and Washbourne, London, 1924

Frere John of Taize. *The Pilgrim God-A Biblical Journey*, Pastoral Press, Portland, Oregon, 1985

Geisler, Norman. *Baker Encyclopedia of Christian Apologetics*, Baker Books, Grand Rapids, MI, 1999

Geisler, Norman L. & Turek, Frank. *I Don't Have Enough Faith to Be an Atheist*, Crossway Books, Wheaton, Il, 2004

Gies, Frances. *Joan of Arc-The Legend and the Reality*, Harper & Row Publishers, New York, 1981

Graham, Billy. *Angels: God's Secret Agents*, Doubleday & Company, Inc., Garden City, New York, 1975

Grundl, James. *This Child*, Carmel of Port Tobacco, La Plata, 2004

Guitton, Jean. *Le Genie de Jeanne d'Arc*, Editions de l'Emmanuel, Paris, France; 1961

Hibbert, Christopher. *The Days of the French Revolution*, Peguin Books Ltd, New York, New York, 1999

Hobbins, Daniel. *The Trial of Joan of Arc*, Harvard University Press, Cambridge, MA, 2005

Holland Smith, John. *Joan of Arc*, Sidgwick & Jackson, London, 1973

Irwin, James and Emerson, William A. Jr. *To Rule the Night*, A. J. Holman Company, 1973

Josephus, translated by William Whiston. *The New Complete Works of*

Josephus, Kregel Publications, Grand Rapids, MI, 1999

Kaiser, Walter C. and Davids, Peter H. and Bruce, F.F. *Hard Sayings of the Bible*, InterVarsity Press, Downers Grove, IL, 1996

Lonig, George & Ray. *100 Prophecies*, CreateSpace, 2008

Lang, Andrew. *The Maid of France*, Longmans, Green, and CO, London, 1908

Lindsey, Hal. *The Everlasting Hatred*, Oracle House Publishing, Corona, CA, 2002

MacArthur, John. *The MacArthur Bible Commentary*, Thomas Nelson, Inc., Nashville, TN, 2005

McDowell, Josh. *The New Evidence that Demands a Verdict*, Thomas Nelson Publishers, Nashville, 1999

Muncaster, Ralph O. *Examine the Evidence-Exploring the Case for Christianity*, Harvest House Publishers, Eugene, Oregon, 2004

d'Orliac, Jehanne. *Joan of Arc and Her Companions*, J.B. Lippincott Company, London, 1934

Paine, Albert Bigelow. *The Girl in White Armor-The Story of Joan of Arc*, The Macmillan Company, New York, 1967

Pernoud, Régine and Marie-Véronique Clin. *Jeanne d'Arc*, Editions Fayard, Mesnil-sur-l'Estrée, 2001

Pernoud, Régine and Marie-Véronique Clin. *Joan of Arc-Her Story*, St Martin's Griffin, New York, New York, 1998

Pernoud, Régine. *Jeanne d'Arc par elle-meme et par ses temoins*, Editions du Seuil, Lanham, New York, Londres, 1996

Pernoud, Régine (translated from the French by Edward Hyams). *Joan of Arc-By Herself and Her Witnesses*, Scarborough House, Lanham, MD, 1982

Pernoud, Régine. *The Retrial of Joan of Arc*, Ignatius Press, San

Francisco, 2007

Pernoud, Régine. *La Spiritualité de Jeanne d'Arc*, Edition Mame, Saint-Amand-Montrond (Cher), 1992

Pink, Arthur Walkington. *The Divine Inspiration of the Bible*, Bible Truth Depot Publishers and Booksellers, Swengel, PA., 191
Richey, Stephen. *Joan of Arc: The Warrior Saint*, Greenwood Publishing Group, Westport, CN, 2003

Spoto, Donald. *Joan: The Mysterious Life of the Heretic Who Became a Saint*, HarperCollins Publishers, New York, 2007

Talbert, Charles H. *Reading Luke: a literary and theological commentary*, Smyth and Helwys Publishing, Inc., Macon, Georgia, 2002

Tavard, George H. *The Spiritual Way of St. Jeanne d'Arc*, The Order of St. Benedict, Inc, Collegeville, Minnesota, 1998

Trask, Willard. *Joan of Arc-In Her Own Words*, Turtle Point Press B.O.O.K.S & Co, New York, New York, 1996

Trask, Willard. *Joan of Arc-Self Portrait*, The Telegraph Press, New York, New York, 1936

Twain, Mark. *Personal Recollections of Joan of Arc, by the Sieur Louis de Conte*, Ignatius Press/Harper & Brothers, San Francisco, 1895

West, V. Sackville. *Saint Joan of Arc*, Country Life Press, Garden City, N.Y., U.S.A, 1936

Winwar, Francis. *The Saint and the Devil/Joan of Arc and Gilles de Rais*, Harper & Brothers Publishers, New York and London, 1948

CPSIA information can be obtained
at www.ICGtesting.com
Printed in the USA
LVOW04s1708281015

460129LV00027B/1328/P